THE
PRINCE
WHO BEAT
THE EMPIRE

About the Author

Moin Mir is a British Indian writer. Working with history and philosophy he writes stories artfully linking the east and west. He is a member of the Nawab family of Surat and next in line to succeed as the Darbar of Kamandiyah. Mir speaks regularly at leading international literature festivals. He lives in London.

THE
PRINCE
WHO BEAT
THE EMPIRE

HOW AN INDIAN RULER TOOK ON THE
MIGHT OF THE EAST INDIA COMPANY

MOIN MIR

AMBERLEY

First published 2018 by the Lotus Collection
an imprint of Roli Books Pvt. Ltd

This edition published 2024

Amberley Publishing
The Hill, Stroud
Gloucestershire, GL5 4EP

www.amberley-books.com

British Library Cataloguing in Publication Data.
A catalogue record for this book is available from the British Library.

ISBN 978 1 3981 2255 0 (paperback)
ISBN 978 1 4456 8693 6 (ebook)

Typesetting and Origination by Amberley Publishing.
Printed in India

Dedicated to my daughters
Aara and Zohaa

And in memory of Meer Jafar Ali Khan's epic struggle against
The English East India Company to safeguard the birthrights
of his daughters.

Meer Jafar Ali Khan was the last custodian of the House of Surat and the Ruling Darbar Shree of Kamandiyah State in Kathiawar, Gujarat. The English East India Company did not officially bestow the title of Nawab of Surat on him. After 1842 the title was extinguished and never restored to any individual.

Contents

Acknowledgements

The city of London today. Such energy and diversity that if a question is asked of it, you would get varying answers and you can then take your pick. I am grateful to the city for re-igniting in me a love for history. While I have been utterly fascinated by the subject, it was London that gave me the platform and means to pursue this subject and make it a passion. I am thankful to the librarians of the British Library at Kings Cross and in particular the keepers of the India Office Records found there. Not only do the staff maintain research and reading material with obsessive care and vigilance, ensuring the library is a temple of knowledge, but they are also devoted custodians of an environment that is conducive to academic study and writing. The accurate collection of research data is the key when writing history. The vast amount of documents, manuscripts and letters I was able to unearth relating to the English East India Company's dealings in Surat and with the Nawab family at the British Library proved invaluable. The Asiatic Library in Mumbai also proved to be a place of great importance in writing this book.

I thank Jessica Douglas-Home for her belief in the story and continuous urging to 'keep writing'. Her wonderful country home,

'Knights Mill,' in Gloucestershire, where I was able to lock myself away on so many occasions and write uninterrupted proved to be a true haven. Luke Douglas-Home's friendship has come to mean so much. He was the first to read the draft and in his typical style sent an email which had just two letters to it – 'V.G.' Thomas Gibson tirelessly spoke about the publishing world and how I should approach it. His insights were most helpful. His belief in the subject and story were unwavering.

Dave Cazalet, for his energy. His introduction to David Campbell ensured a meeting with Charlie Campbell, a highly reputable literary agent who bravely took up my manuscript, read it front to back and became my agent in London. I am also grateful to Charlie for offering me the opportunity to net at Lords with the 'Authors Cricket Team', of which he is captain. Richard Kelly for painstakingly editing my first draft and guiding me through this effort. His insights on how to keep the narrative tight and impactful have been immensely helpful. I am grateful for the warm friendship of Jojo and Jonathan Hull. Their lovely home in Oxfordshire proved to be a great refuge to wander the fields and think.

I thank my publisher Roli Books and in particular Priya Kapoor. On a visit to London she brought me a wonderful painting of the Surat Castle which an ancestor had once held. On hearing my story Priya immediately agreed to publish my yet to be completed work and she kept her word. I am grateful to Ashlesha Khurana of the *Times of India* Surat edition who organised my visits to the Surat Castle, the Portuguese, Dutch and English cemeteries and to the mausoleum of Meer Jafar Ali Khan, and for the research material she provided.

My gratitude for my parents who have supported me in all endeavours grows constantly. I am thankful to my fiancée Leonie whose love and understanding has been so crucial for the completion of this book. Leonie, who works for Christie's London, followed me with great interest as I chased a portrait of an ancestor.

Without her constant words of encouragement this book would not have emerged from mere thought into printed matter.

I would like to thank Dr. Shashi Tharoor for his endorsement and his brilliant presence at the book launch in India. Dominic West took the time from his busy schedule to read my manuscript and gave a wonderful quote for which I am very grateful. I thank Bruce Wannell for his translation of a Persian document. Amberley Books, my publishers in the UK, have been superb in their execution of the UK edition and for that I thank them wholeheartedly.

Finally, thank you to my daughters who come to London every year and walk down Warwick Avenue with me; the street from where their ancestor launched the greatest legal offensive against the East India Company in the Victorian era.

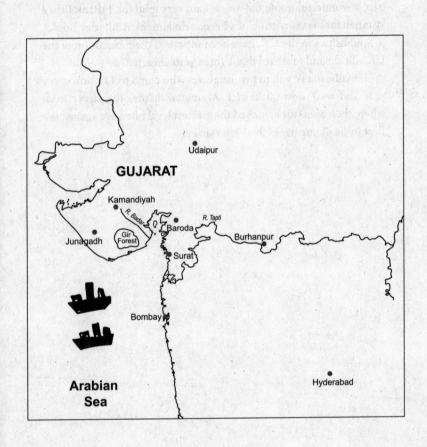

Introduction

In 1856 as Hindustan was about to burst into flames against the
oppression of the English East India Company, one Hindustani
prince was on the verge of creating history in England. He had
fearlessly led the greatest legal counter attack against the corporation
on their home soil and in the House of Commons. In 1800 the East
India Company had annexed Surat and signed a treaty with the
Nawab. Ruthlessly, the treaty was violated by the Company leaving
the Nawab's descendants on the verge of destitution. Meer Jafar Ali
Khan, who was never officially bestowed with the title of Nawab of
Surat (but carried his paternal title of Darbar Shree) had risen above
the petty desire to claim ceremonial titles and devoted his energy to
ensuring his girls had a future – a future that had been devastated at
the hands of the Company.

The East India Company in 1856 was the wealthiest colonising
corporation in the world. It was at the forefront of Empire expansion.
It had the most powerful stakeholders including prominent British
MPs, Lords, Dukes, Earls and businessmen. Its army in Hindustan
stood close to 300,000 making it the most powerful in the
subcontinent. At the peak of its powers it faced the most unlikely
adversary on its home turf in Meer Jafar Ali Khan, who had given

up all that he possessed in Hindustan to take the 'good fight' to Parliament.

Through his years of struggle in London Meer Jafar Ali Khan had come to occupy a unique position in Victorian England. While a steady flow of Hindustani princes came to England, some to enjoy the sights and sounds and others just to complain about the treatment they received at the hands of the Company without any strategic planning, Meer Jafar Ali Khan had over many years in England meticulously planned and mobilized the most powerful alliances in the British political establishment to challenge the injustice of the Company in Surat and particularly against his infant daughters. Voyaging twice to England, first in 1844 and then again in 1853, Meer Jafar Ali Khan went onto become one of the most well-known figures in Victorian England. Backed by the British press which addressed him as 'Nawab' and carried daily reports on him and his case, Meer Jafar Ali Khan strove tirelessly to achieve his goals. What made his character an utterly fascinating one was his tenacity in opposing the English East India Company's injustice and malpractices in Surat, navigating the political divide in Victorian England towards the Company, masterfully crafting his arguments with the help of his allies, retaining his Hindustani identity in all the drama his case generated in England, and then falling in love with an English actress and bringing her back with him to Hindustan at the height of the first war of independence. His spirited charge in England and his legacy faded with time and became confined to the archives of the British Library. This untold story needed to be unearthed.

What was also of vital importance was the story of the fall of Surat—Hindustan's greatest port to the English East India Company. The annexation of Surat and the breach of the treaty of 1800 led to the grim situation Meer Jafar Ali Khan found himself in 1856. And so the detailed historical account of the fall of Surat had to be researched and understood.

Much has been written about the East India Company's rise to power in Hindustan. Accomplished historians have dedicated years of research to writing accounts of the Company's territorial expansion. The victory Robert Clive achieved in Plassey in 1757 over Siraj-ud-daula, the Nawab of Bengal, has come to be viewed quite correctly by historians as the turning point in the Company's fortunes. For it was from then on that the Company was given the right to collect revenue on behalf of a weakening Mughal Empire. However, what many historians have not necessarily devoted time and attention to is that within two years of the victory in Bengal, the Company had attacked the Surat Castle in 1759 and for the first time Hindustan's greatest port had partially fallen into European hands. In 1800, the Company finally annexed Surat in totality by forcing the Nawab to sign away his administrative powers under threat of forceful invasion of the city.

Subsequent to Mysore in 1799 and Surat in 1800, Delhi fell in 1803 and encouraged by what seemed like a freefall of princely Hindustan, the Company annexed Satara, Sindh, Punjab, Awadh and Jhansi. There are many books on all of them and the fate they suffered at the hands of the Company, but in some odd way the tragic fall of Surat had not received its literary due; hence this book.

—

Spellings: In order to keep consistency I have kept 'Meer' as is. Over time and in many documents it has been spelt as 'Mir'. Originally a title bestowed by the Emperor on descendants of the Prophet, it was also used as an honourable title amongst Mughal nobility. 'Jafar' was spelt varyingly by the English. On occasions it has been spelt as 'Jafur'. I have kept it as 'Jafar'. The name 'Ali' too has also been spelt differently by the English. It has appeared in documents as 'Alee' and 'Alyy'. I have kept it as 'Ali'. 'Kamandiyah' has been spelt in documents as Kummundia, Kamandia and Kamadhiya. I have chosen to go with the rustic manner in which it is pronounced – Kamandiyah. The spelling of Gaekwad comes across as Gaikwad in certain records. In order to maintain consistency I have kept it as Gaekwad in the main text.

Prologue

London, 30 May 1844

The city was bathed in brilliant midday sunshine. The shop windows of the Strand sparkled, and shadows were sharply etched all down the great thoroughfare. Two English ladies walked by the lion of Northumberland House, noting how handsomely the stone beast appeared to bask in the sun.

Abruptly, their attention was seized by a splendid light blue carriage dashing by in the road. As it sped past them they were afforded just a fleeting moment to peer into the box. Within sat two swarthy men, one of obvious distinction and handsomeness, wearing crimson robes bedecked with jewels. Observing the ladies in turn, both men raised their hands with a graceful salaam of recognition. The ladies recognised at once the distinguished man of whom they had just caught sight: His Highness Meer Jafar Alee Khan Bahadoor of Surat.[1]

One of them had already encountered Meer Jafar Ali rather intimately in London, and knew him well. Excitedly the ladies fell to conversation of this prince and the world from which he had come: the magical orient, the fabulous palaces of Hindustan, the famed city of Surat and its rulers, the magnificent Nawabs. In common with a great swathe of London society, they were endlessly ready to hear tales of the fading grandeur of the Mughals, of jewels, harems, elephants and howdahs.

Within the carriage, however, the atmosphere was quite different, coloured by anxiety and tension. The driver whipped the black horses to spur them on: there was an appointment to be kept, for which lateness would not be excused.

The destination was East India House on Leadenhall Street. Meer Jafar Ali Khan was 26 years old and about to meet the Chairman of the most powerful business entity in the world – the English East India Company, master of the destinies of close to two hundred million Hindustanis.

The Company had systematically destroyed the floundering Mughal Empire and established itself as the supreme authority in Hindustan. Its astonishing rise was built on the ruins of many a Hindustani prince – including the princes of Surat. But this prince, Meer Jafar Ali Khan, last custodian of the House of Surat, was heading straight to the bastion of Company power to make a bold demonstration to their authority.

The carriage reached the entrance of East India House. The two passengers disembarked and entered the building, Jafar full of anxiety as he contemplated the closed door meetings he was about to attend. The Company's officials in Hindustan had decimated the Surat Nawabship, and the power that came with it was now the Company's. Along with the loss of power, his family's vast private estates, which included magnificent palaces, orchards, gardens, mosques and even stables had been unjustly confiscated by the Company and their incomes ruthlessly stopped. As such, their fate now hung by a thread.

The confrontation with the Company was only the first of the challenging assignations Jafar would face in London. After his meeting at East India House, his next important visit would be to the Lord Chancellor's Court. As a Hindustani, in alien Victorian England, the young Jafar was attempting to create political alliances through resoluteness of purpose, persistence, charm and the power of truth – the better to challenge the might of England's greatest company on its home soil.

Jafar was aware, at least, that at the Lord Chancellor's Court his entrance would be observed with great interest and curiosity. He had come from Hindustan with a great story to tell the British people, and his very presence commanded attention wherever he went in London. Jafar believed that London society needed to be made aware of the fall of Surat, one of the great cities of Hindustan; and of the violations of treaties that the Company had made with his family – violations that had brought the future prospects of his infant daughters perilously close to poverty.

This was the first time the East India Company had been met by an Indian prince pressing them over the legality of their practices, on their own soil. They would be confident of success, no doubt – but Jafar intended to give them the legal battle of their lives, all the way to the Houses of Parliament if need be.

Jafar looked forward, at least, to an engagement in his diary that lay a few days' ahead, when he would leave his temporary residence in Sloane Street to meet His Royal Highness Prince Albert. Jafar had every confidence that a temperament as noble as Albert's would be sympathetic to the story he had to tell, of what had befallen his beloved Surat and of his own young family.

1

So Deeply Coveted

Surat — a city that had for centuries ignited the imagination of Mughal Emperors. Descendants of the great Ghengis Khan, they had swept down from the landlocked mountainous regions of Central Asia, never having lain eyes on the vastness of seas and oceans. The greatest of all these Mughals, Akbar, had sat by the knee of his ailing father Humayun as a thirteen-year-old, listening to stories of the glorious Tapti river that flowed through Surat; the majestic Castle looming over the river's banks which was built to repel invading Portuguese; and the enormous ships that sailed out into the Arabian sea to trade far and wide, from Europe to China...

Humayun never got as far as Surat, and so the port remained under the control of the local Sultan of Gujarat. But once the young Akbar became Emperor of Hindustan, he could not resist the lure of seeking to capture the city his father had so coveted. Thus, in 1573, Akbar stormed into Gujarat, defeated the Sultan, and captured the imposing Castle. In doing so Akbar also took charge of the legacy of the man who had constructed the Castle: Khudavand, Surat's former governor, who had perished in battle defending the city against a Portuguese raid in 1546, and whose ornately carved mausoleum a few miles from the Castle had become a symbol of Hindustani resistance to foreign adventurers. Made of stone and large brick slabs, the Castle was equipped with seventeen cannons, four watchtowers, dreadful dungeons and a network of secret tunnels that opened into smaller towns and villages around Surat. To control the Castle was to have mastery of Hindustan's sea trade.

The sweat of Akbar's brow had hardly dried from the heat of battle when he ordered his men to get a few boats ready and sail down the mouth of the Tapti. It is said that as the river waters broke into the Arabian Sea Akbar gasped in admiration of the splendid, seemingly endless waves; and that this encounter inspired him to build the Mughal Empire's first naval fleet for stationing at Surat. So greatly pleased was Akbar by his accomplishments that upon his return to the Hindustan capital of Agra, he constructed the mighty *Buland Darwaza,* or 'Bold Gate' in Fatehpur Sikri, to commemorate his victory.

Mughal influence in the port grew steadily and under Emperors Jahangir and Shah Jahan (Akbar's son and grandson), Surat reached its zenith as Hindustan's most renowned and cosmopolitan emporium of trade – a true powerhouse of commerce. To the Emperors it had come to be known as 'Bandar Mubarak', or 'the blessed port.' The city had given rise to a unique mix of powerful and astonishingly rich merchants – Jains, Hindus, local Muslims, Turks, Parsis, Jews – all owning large shipping vessels that traded in gold, silver, cotton and spices. At the docks under the Castle one would find ships from Arabia, their fine wares offloaded for dispatch to the Imperial Mughal Court in Delhi; ships from Persia bearing exotic fruits, perfumes and robes; and ships from Portugal, Netherlands and England, carrying tobacco from Brazil and bullion.

The bazaars that encircled the docks would be bursting with colour, noise and fragrance. Bargain drivers and *munshis,* with their log books in hand, ensured every item was accounted for. Muslim pilgrims could be seen boarding large vessels bound for Arabia and the annual Haj. For this reason Surat carried the honourable title of *Baab-e-Mecca*, 'Door to Mecca.' The Mughals had also set up their mint not far from the Castle, producing coins in the name of the Emperor that circulated throughout Hindustan.

The cultural fabric of Surat was unique, predominantly Hindu, though the city also had strong Parsi and Muslim communities. The Parsis (who fled Persia in the tenth century because of Arab conquest) were considered industrious and trustworthy, and had built a strong reputation for fair trade. Another thriving community was that of the Jains. Followers of ahimsa, they were a peaceful, tolerant people with an obsessive devotion to the respect and protection of every living organism. Spiritually enlightened, the Jains of Surat were also endowed with astounding entrepreneurial acumen that made them probably the most successful of Surat's diverse merchant mix. Their brilliantly decorated temples could be found across the city, attracting the wealthiest of their number, who nonetheless went barefoot as a mark of humility and gratitude. The stunning Hindu temples devoted to Lord Ram and Lord Krishna were everywhere. The ringing of their bells beckoned the rich and poor every evening as the fabulous *aarti* ceremonies were performed by the Brahmin priests in honour of the Gods.

Baghdadi Jews and Chalebi Turks had also found a place in Surat, having migrated over the years. They traded extensively in carpets and perfumes, and the Jewish merchants had emulated the other faiths in building places of worship: synagogues had mushroomed in the old city. For the Chalebi Turks and other Muslim merchants, spiritual salvation was found at the numerous Sufi shrines that dotted Surat – the white marbled mausoleum of Khwaja Daana Sahib being the most renowned. This remarkable mystic had come to Surat from Arabia in 1549 and established his *khanqaah* or retreat from where he preached universal love, penance and compassion for the poor. His teachings appealed widely and his following grew with time. Following his death in 1607, his annual Urs, or a celebration of the merging of a Sufi soul with the creator, would transform Surat into a spiritual oasis over five much-needed days of contemplation for the otherwise trade-obsessed city.

The European influence in Surat comprised Portuguese, Dutch and English traders. The English and Dutch in particular had become intrinsic to Surat society over time. They had integrated brilliantly, and brought with them a certain sense of glamour. At social events and festivals it was quite common to encounter English and Dutch merchants and ship captains. They, too, had created their own enclaves and established their architectural credentials by building exquisite churches and cemeteries in many parts of the old city. The Dutch and English architects fuelled an intense, competitive and creative culture that drew out their finest talent and eventually added a new dimension to the city landscape as they vied with each other in the size and splendour of the monuments erected over the graves of their company Presidents.

For this heady assortment of international traders, the pleasures of the night were available at the brothels of Shamshad Begum, a renowned courtesan. Her stable of prostitutes provided a source of pleasure for leading European merchants and government officials. Shamshad's brothels offered everything from exotic oriental women to smoky opium cells; from ill-smelling liquor dens to dimly-lit rooms where dancing girls brought all the way from Lucknow would twirl to the beats of the tabla and the tunes of the sitar. These brothels, centres of intrigue where politics and business were discussed openly, were sites for the sharing of secrets by merchants and princes. Like magnets they attracted the Europeans who flocked to them every evening and emerged the next day, utterly dazed but highly likely to return.

European engagement with Surat began with the Portuguese who first commenced trading at the port in 1510. With their superior naval firepower they soon dominated the Arabian Sea and quickly surpassed the Arabs as the most influential force in the region. So belligerent were they that they raided Surat brutally and with absolute contempt, hence the construction of Surat's Castle in 1540. The unpopular Portuguese were followed by the Dutch and the English. Inadvertently the lure of Hindustan's riches set the three European naval giants to fighting with each other. Following some early skirmishes in 1612 the English East India Company's ships under Captain Thomas Best defeated a Portuguese fleet off the Surat coast.

At that time to many it was a relatively insignificant naval victory. It was however to have tremendous consequences, because it threw a lifeline to the fortunes of the East India Company. In 1609 James I, King of England, had reluctantly granted the Company a mere three-year extension of its charter. The King had threatened cancellation if the Company failed to report any profitable ventures in that time. Now, the Company had found fresh impetus in Surat.

Best immediately rushed an emissary to the Mughal governor at Surat, who issued a temporary trading permit subject to approval from the Emperor Jahangir. Word reached England of Best's success in breaching the Portuguese stranglehold over trade with western Hindustan. Seizing the opportunity James I dispatched Thomas Roe as ambassador directly to the Emperor's court seeking permission to trade at Surat. Jahangir preferred the English to the Portuguese, who had acquired an unsavoury reputation for harassing local officers, and issued a *firman,* an order granting permission to the English to set up their first factory in Surat. The factory focussed on refining cotton to meet the demands in Bantam and the Moluccas. Roe declared Surat to be 'the fountain of life of all the East India Trade' and advised his countrymen to 'stand resolute in the face of Portuguese threats and Dutch competition.'[2] From then on began a steady decline of Portuguese influence in Surat and the rise of English trade. With trade reaching new heights, Surat rose to establish itself as the greatest maritime city of Hindustan.

Trade continued to flourish in Surat both for local merchants and the English. But soon, local political power struggles in western Hindustan led to crippling of trade. In 1680 the English East India Company rather betrayed the extent of their ambitions through the use of their naval power when they daringly seized and raided one of the Emperor's vessels, which happened to be carrying his sister onboard. An enraged Emperor immediately issued orders for the closure of all English factories. It took a special mission by English factors to the Imperial Court, and strenuous pleas for forgiveness, before permission to trade was retrieved.

But in terms of their aspirations for trade in the Arabian Sea, the English had not laid their bets entirely on Surat. There was another port that they had been developing, quietly and independently – a port that had fallen into their hands rather by a stroke of luck. When Catherine of Braganza had married Charles II of England in 1662 she had brought with her as part of her dowry seven small island villages 150 miles south of Surat. Charles, not much interested in these seemingly meagre pickings, had passed the villages on to the English East India Company in 1668. By the end of the seventeenth century the English had slowly built them into a trading base as part of a master vision to make a rival to Surat. And these islands, which the Portuguese had come to know as Bombaim, now bore an English name: Bombay.

Blessed with a natural harbour, Bombay would under the English grow into Surat's nemesis. For the English, success at Bombay would mean controlling Hindustan's western trade independently and finally strangling Hindustan of sea trade revenue. And it was in 1687 the directors of the East India Company decided that their seat of administration was to be transferred from Surat to Bombay.[3]

The Mughals had purposely created and nurtured a divided power dynamic in Surat that suited them perfectly. The Emperor would appoint a *mutasadi*, or governor (who would reside and hold and manage city administration in the heart of the city) and a *qilledar* who would control the castle and fleet. The *mutasadi* was responsible for city administration, including civil and criminal jurisdiction, and the *qilledar* was in charge of the Castle and admiralty of the Mughal fleet with the primary job of protecting merchant ships from piracy. This divided power dynamic ensured the Emperor's firm grip on the city and prevented the rise of one supreme authority. But with the death in 1707 of Emperor Aurangzeb, the last powerful Mughal, the authority of the Imperial Court in Delhi began a steady decline. This brought with it a succession of relatively weak *mutasadis* and *qilledars* of Surat.

Trade and commerce had to flourish at all costs, and the wealthy merchants of Surat played a pivotal role in funding and assisting any new *mutasadi*. In the end, however, the merchants would pay anybody whom they perceived as powerful enough to govern the city. Between 1707 and 1733 a series of *mutasadis* and *qilledars* struggled to sustain governance, but there was no real stability and trade began to decline steeply. The English Company watched this developing anarchy intently, nursing a desire to hold yet greater power in Surat. But their time had not yet come. Despite the superior firepower of the warships they brought to dock in Surat, they were recognised as traders rather than administrators, and had yet to win the trust of the city's merchants. With constant internal strife and struggles between failing *mutasadis*, and the Company slowly beginning to threaten a foreign takeover, Surat and its merchants searched desperately for a saviour.

Tegh Bakht Khan was a lean, tall, middle-aged man from the Gangetic plains of Hindustan.* Greatly influenced by the life of Emperor Akbar, he harboured a driving desire for power. He was

---

*These plains are in modern-day Uttar Pradesh, the vast lands through which the Ganges flows.

fluent in Hindi, Persian, Urdu and Arabic and had acquired a basic understanding of Gujarati through a chance encounter with some powerful Surti merchants. Tegh was a soldier of fortune with some connections of merit at the Imperial Court. And as imperial power in Delhi began to wane, Tegh took on the leadership of a reasonably strong band of soldiers and began a life of wandering, moving from one weakening Mughal province to another. Having heard of the prevalent anarchy in Hindustan's greatest port and sensing a possible opportunity, Tegh and his soldiers settled outside Surat and awaited their chance. It was here that Tegh developed his vision for Surat: a unified rule that would bring city administration and Castle control under one command providing a conducive environment for trade.

Soon, excited by what they had heard of Tegh and the forces at his command, the desperate merchant mix of Surat headed out of the city gates hoping to find him. This entourage had barely wound its way out of the northern district when from out of thick woods emerged Tegh on horseback at the head of a thousand cavalry. Following discussions that lasted a week, the merchants decided to back Tegh's entry into Surat, and added their entourage to his forces.

On a bright March morning in 1733, amid a surging sea of fluttering flags bearing his insignia, Tegh – flanked by his brothers Safdar and Begler – arrived at the imposing city gate. As he entered the city to a rapturous welcome from the merchants, his armour glistening in the sunlight, Tegh savoured the sight of the Tapti river and Surat's Castle. He knew very well that if he was to restore order in Surat he would have to grapple with a number of adversaries. Three groups in particular suggested themselves. There were the Abyssinian Sidis who controlled the Castle and were the appointed admirals of the Mughal fleet;[4] the ambitious English East India Company, whose mercantile energies, fighting spirit, sophisticated naval weaponry and position of strength a few miles south in Bombay made them an obvious threat; and the merchants themselves, who had shown themselves to be quite capable of switching loyalties without remorse.

Tegh's procession moved towards Begumpura and into the governor's palace where Tegh took his seat on the *masnad*, an elevated gold platform with large pillows. Power in Surat was his; and without delay he took some swift and forceful decisions. The first was to change his title: 'discarding the official designation of *mutasadi* which was distasteful to him like vine smacking of the cork, he styled himself Nawab.'[5] Since no objection came from the capital, this move elevated Tegh's position almost immediately and established him as Surat's first independent ruler. Then, daringly, he stormed the Castle and wrested control of it from the Sidi Masud, placing his brother Begler Khan in charge. Now the Sidi Masud and the Mughal fleet took their orders from the Nawab. This brought Surat under one supreme command for the first time. 'The division between the castle and town came to an end.'[6] Tegh then appointed his other brother Safdar as deputy Nawab and threw a lavish reception for the city's prominent merchants, bestowing expensive gifts and titles on the most influential of them. Their loyalty was vital. For now, though, the merchants were unanimous in their support.

Tegh then turned his attention to the Company, which he had always viewed as a foreign threat, with the objective of checking its clear and growing ambition. The Company gave him the perfect excuse when they demanded that the *tankha,* or subsidy formerly paid by the city to the Sidis for management of the Mughal fleet should now be paid to them. The Company's argument was that their superior naval forces and experience would better protect the city and merchant ships from piracy. Tegh controlled the revenues of Surat and fully understood that if the Company attainted the admiralty it would be a great step toward their taking over Surat. Instead, with considerable skill, he embarked on a long process of negotiations intended to frustrate the Company, and succeeded in wearing them down to the extent that he wound up retaining the *tankha* for himself.[7] Tegh knew, however, that another confrontation was looming: it was merely a matter of time.

On 8 February 1734 Tegh found the English Company guilty of tax evasion, in that they had claimed exemption on certain trading duties when their entitlement extended only to the Company's own goods from Europe.[8] The Company responded with a trade blockade at sea. Tegh riposted just as fiercely, inciting and ordering the Sidi to engage the English ships.[9] Although inferior in firepower, the Mughal fleet under Tegh's instructions swung into action, causing some initial damage to the Company's vessels. But before long, the Company's ships had unleashed their enormous firepower, killing several Hindustani men.[10] A truce was subsequently reached, as both sides could ill afford a full-scale war. Inevitably this was not the end of the Company–Nawab conflict.

Tegh raised taxes again and ordered custom house officials to increase freight charges on all Company vessels and goods. When the Company refused to pay, he sent in his troops to surround the factory and prevent any further trade. Relations with the Company deteriorated precipitously, and the continued refusal of the Company to pay the higher tax infuriated Tegh to the point where he ordered a raid on the factory. Henry Lowther, the Chief of the English factory at Surat and Head Company representative, instantly ordered all the factors 'to leave the factory and the city and stay on board the ship *Heathcote* at Surat Bar.'[11]

Events then took a yet more dramatic turn: The English claimed they had acquired merchant support. Murmurings reached Tegh that Lowther had persuaded some powerful merchants to see the merit of abandoning Surat and conducting business from Bombay under English protection. In a letter composed aboard the *Heathcote* on 1 February 1734, Lowther made this claim and wrote of Surat's 'inhabitants in general' that they were 'all in our interest' and that 'in case the English withdrew from Surat, they would all follow us down to Bombay.'[12]

Tegh tried to authenticate this claim but also knew well that he could not afford such an outcome. His plans to push the English

Company out and extinguish their factory were dashed, and the English continued to grow their factory and battleship presence in Surat.

While he had brought Surat under a unified command, Tegh had continuously to manage the fragile peace and foster an atmosphere conducive to successful commerce. Although he wanted the English Company out, he desired the prosperity of his city far more. Hoping that he could create a Hindustani alliance against the English Company he secretly opened negotiations with Damaji Gaekwad, the ruler of Baroda, a neighbouring and strong principality who had also set his eyes on Surat. Tegh quickly concluded a treaty with the Gaekwad. While the *chauth* would be a payment made to the Gaekwad, in return the Gaekwad would pay the Nawab a sum called the *moglai*.[13] Having made this agreement Tegh hoped that a unified Hindustani stand might thwart Company ambitions. And, for a time, it seemed to work.

For the next ten years the Company was kept at bay. Tegh's reign was marked by relative peace, however strained, and by prosperity for Surat. He had successfully engineered his legitimacy as the first independent Nawab of a deeply riven city, and with tact and able administration he had checked mammoth English ambitions, and managed merchant expectations well.

Now Tegh turned to indulging in creative pleasures. Being from north Hindustan, his fascination for gardens was obsessive. As a child he had spent a lot of time in his grandfather's orchards where citrus fruit fragrances filled the air. With his grandfather, Tegh had visited the resplendent Shalimar gardens in Kashmir built by Emperor Jahangir and had clung to the image of its wonderful waterfalls. Tegh was fascinated by water and a desire to be close to the sea and so he embarked on his first project of building the fabulous Dariya Mahal, or 'sea palace' on the banks of the Tapti. The site had previously been popular with Mughal governors as a place to build summer houses, and Tegh's palace was constructed facing the mouth of the Tapti to evade the searing Gujarat heat. It was adorned with multiple intricately carved arches and close to five hundred large open windows, all overlooking the river, lit with oil lamps every night. To a sailor drifting by, the palace resembled a glittering jewel, its reflection shimmering across the Tapti's darkened waters. But Tegh was not satisfied with just one palace, and searched for more land on which to build.

Salabatpura, a vast open area, provided Tegh with the ideal space for his second great complex – the Mehmudi Bagh palace. Steep perimeter walls all around ensured privacy, but within lay a magical world. Buildings with intricate wood and stonework housed Tegh's numerous wives, while another *zenana* was devoted to his concubines. At the heart of the garden complex lay two lakes. The larger one was preferred when Tegh and a chosen wife went swimming. It enjoyed a man-made twenty-foot cascade at its south end, and at either side of the waterfall were fountains that created a watery arch through which Tegh and his wife swam to the cascade. The flower gardens laid out in the palace 'were according to season, filled with balsams, poppies and various flowers of an equal height, closely planted and so disposed as to resemble a rich Turkish carpet.'[14] Such was the magnificence of Mehmudi Bagh that 'men pointed with admiration to the imposing palace.'[15]

Throughout his reign Tegh maintained his policy of refusing to entertain Company grievances. One incident that occurred in the twilight of his reign in 1745 reflected his utter disdain for the Company factors. Like many cities, Surat was beset by a colony of vagrant dogs that would attack strangers, snarling and snapping at people's calves. One evening a group of three English Company factors were attacked in this manner. Trying to escape these animals, one of the Englishmen flung an object which, rather than striking the mongrel, managed only to injure one of Tegh's peons. The reprisal for this mishap was brutal:

While returning to the factory, all three [factors] were suddenly attacked by some thirty of the governor's [Tegh's] peons under the orders of two of his officers and were beaten so cruelly that they were with difficulty able to reach the house. The surgeon pronounced the two of them in a very serious condition, though ultimately they seem to have recovered. The Chief naturally lodged a complaint but the records say that no satisfaction for the wrong had been received even two years later.[16]

To the English Company factors whose ambitions were growing swiftly on the back of their superior naval power, it was the first time an independent ruler of Surat was willing to press them on a range of issues – tax evasion, challenging their blockades and even flexing his muscles in the narrow alleys and streets of the city. In effect, with both castle and city administration under him, the hallmark of Tegh's reign was his readiness to send regular signals of strength to his most powerful rivals, leaving them at times utterly exasperated.

———

By 1746 Tegh was advancing in age, yet his zeal to retain a firm grip on Surat showed no signs of diminishing. He was cruelly unaware of how close to him were the events which would turn Surat's fortunes for the worse.

One sweltering summer day Tegh went for a swim, not with a wife but with his brother Safdar. Upon entering Surat back in 1733, Tegh had appointed Safdar his deputy. Now he had made up his mind to strip his brother of those powers. He wanted to break the news gently yet firmly, after a swim and over a kebab lunch.

Ambitious, wild, and unscrupulous, Safdar was a big brute of a man, six-and-a-half-feet tall with the neck of a bulldog. He was routinely to be found either in the wrestling dens of Surat or at the brothels of Shamshad Begum. Prone to drunken fits of extreme rage, the bald and kohl-eyed Safdar had gained a reputation for being a merchant plunderer, and he believed that the loyalty of Surat's merchants could be assured only at gunpoint. Safdar had long harboured daggers of jealousy in his heart towards Tegh's popularity; also towards Tegh's young protégé. Tegh had tried to curb the wild Safdar, but hadn't been able to entirely.

On that fateful afternoon, the two brothers had a heated argument. Tegh reproached Safdar severely for his conduct. Safdar resisted every charge and eventually stormed out licking his wounds and feeling humiliated. Tegh, frustrated and angry, dived into the lake at Mehmudi Bagh and swam hard to work off the afternoon's intense proceedings. Lap after lap the aged Nawab's shoulders and legs sliced through the water. Reaching the cascade at the end of his fifteenth lap Tegh felt a rising sharp pain shoot from his ankle and then grip his chest. Every sinew seemed to be tearing with cramps. The excruciating pain was unbearable. He reached desperately for the banks, clutching at the loose mud, but failed. Each frantic attempt to grasp at the bank became weaker. Unable to resist the currents, Tegh began sinking, water filling his lungs rapidly. Death came by a slow drowning as the Nawab held onto a vision of the fluttering poppies in his beloved Mehmudi Bagh.

Tegh died leaving only a daughter behind him; and immediately after his demise Surat hastened towards anarchy, despair and civil war. The fate of Hindustan's greatest port again stood at a crossroads. But while Tegh had been proved terribly wrong to have trusted and promoted his untrustworthy brother, he would be vindicated in having chosen a protégé who would succeed in restoring order from chaos.

2

Deceit, Blood, Desperation – and the Port Falls

As the Tapti meandered its way from Surat into heartland Hindustan it became a much-needed source of irrigation for barren and parched plains scorched every year by the ruthless summer sun. In this way it also inspired the growth of another major city on its north-eastern banks – Burhanpur. The city had been the headquarters for Prince Khurram, later known as Emperor Shah Jahan, when he was appointed Governor of the Deccan by his father Jahangir. The 'Builder Emperor' had constructed the Shahi Qila, 'Emperor's Fort' on the banks of the Tapti. There, he and his wife Mumtaz indulged in all kinds of pleasures from hunting wild lions to immersing themselves in the exotic hamams specially created for them. Burhanpur had been the town from where this romance would rise and eventually culminate in the Emperor's most heart-wrenching creation – the Taj Mahal at Agra. For it was in Burhanpur's Shahi Qila that Mumtaz died giving birth to her fourteenth child, whereupon her grieving husband swore an oath to build her a mausoleum that would dazzle the world. Burhanpur soon became a great attraction for Sufi scholars from different schools of thought.

Moyeen-ud-deen, was the son of Burhanpur's leading theologian. But besides his academic pursuits, Moyeen-ud-deen had come to harbour a passion for swordsmanship; and his father didn't seem to object to this martial pursuit. Most evenings would find him training on the ramparts of the Shahi Qila. This regular and intense practice had made him an expert in duelling. By his early twenties Moyeen-ud-deen stood five feet nine inches tall and was robustly built, with powerful upper body strength from all his physical rigours.

One cold winter's night in 1740 Moyeen-ud-deen sat with his followers around a fire at his *khanqaah*. Draped in their persian shawls, they discussed the poetry of Rumi, the great Sufi master of the thirteenth century. But the colloquy was interrupted by a speeding horseman who had come with a message for the town. Running west along the banks of the Tapti was Surat, and it was from here that the messenger had arrived. The Nawab Tegh Bakht Khan was holding a duelling competition as part of a quest to find the finest fighters in all of west and central Hindustan. That very night, Moyeen-ud-deen, and a few devoted followers mounted and rode for Surat.

Moyeen-ud-deen entered the Nawab's contest and won. Impressed by what he had witnessed Tegh asked Moyeen-ud-deen to settle in Surat and offered his daughter, Wilayati Khanum, a dark haired, rose-faced beauty in marriage to the victor.[17] Having married Tegh's daughter Moyeen-ud-deen hoped for a quieter life.* In the wake of Tegh's death, however, Surat under his brother Safdar appeared a vicious and deceitful place, as if infected by the poison of treachery that lay ahead. As the new Nawab, Safdar continued his practice of pillaging the merchants without mercy, increasing taxes and collecting the revenues at gun-point. All merchants buckled under in fear. Seeing an opportunity, the English Company reached out to

---

*Some indications are that Tegh got Moyeen-ud-deen married to Begler's daughter. Other sources like *History of Gujarat* by Commissariat Volume III indicate that Moyeen-ud-deen married Tegh's daughter.

some merchants, promising a safe trading environment in Bombay.[18] Unknown to the merchants, though, the Company continued to give tacit support to Safdar, well aware that he was highly unpopular and could be easily ousted from the city administration if the English could obtain the unstinted support of the merchants. Meanwhile they hoped to see Safdar dig his own grave to the greatest possible extent, until the right moment arose to drop him into it – whereupon the merchants would surely fall into their hands and acquiesce to a relocation to Bombay. The English Company's masterplan of taking Surat completely and then paralysing its sea trade would mean their port Bombay would become the unchallenged epicentre of trade. The ramifications of such success to them would be the strangling of revenues to the Delhi court, contributing to a swift decline of the Mughal Empire and their rise backed by enormous revenues coming from their mastery over the Arabian Sea via Bombay. Encouraging the marauding Safdar and making him their aggressive pawn was serving them brilliantly in destroying merchant business at Surat.

Surat Castle, too, had come to seem an easy target for the English Company. It had been under of the charge of Begler, Tegh's youngest brother; but following Begler's untimely death – in which it was rumoured that Safdar was suspected of having a hand – control of the Castle passed to Safdar's alcoholic and inept son Wiqar, who could be observed most nights on the ramparts carousing with courtesans and *nautch* girls. If the English Company now thought the Castle a simple capture, so, too, did the Sidi Masud, who kept a presence around the mouth of the Tapti with armed boats. The interest in the Castle was obvious: the English Company, for one, knew that with it came the revenues of the *tankha*, and such funds 'would enable them to equip and maintain an efficient fleet so that both on land and sea the Company's mastery would be firmly established to the great discomfiture of their enemies.'[19]

Amid this chaotic and poisonous atmosphere Moyeen-ud-deen held his own. Having made Surat his home, he had benefited by time spent with Tegh during the Nawab's later years, when the two engaged in meaningful conversation concerning politics and administration. Tegh had taught Moyeen-ud-deen much, encouraging him to resolve any petty merchant disputes. As a result Moyeen-ud-deen had quickly earned the merchants' trust. Tegh also taught him the importance of building local Hindustani alliances, and to understand Tegh's vision of a unified command in Surat – also the paramount need to contain English Company ambition. It was the enormous growth of Bombay under the Company that had kept Tegh awake at nights. Moyeen-ud-deen had witnessed his father-in-law's anxiety towards rising Bombay power which had the potential to destroy not only the family's rule, but also the eminence of Surat.

Moyeen-ud-deen was by now affectionately called 'Mia Achaey', literally the 'good one'. It was a name he had grown to like. Now, he was being forced to watch Safdar's near-systematic destruction of his father-in-law's legacy. Tegh's vision of a unified and just rule over Surat was in ruins.

Matters came to a head one night when Moyeen-ud-deen was besieged in his own home by a group of Jain, Muslim, Hindu and Jewish merchants desirous of positive action. Amid the hushed tones of an urgent conference in which a few merchants offered a great many promises of loyalty, Moyeen-ud-deen decided to enter the fray. But he was keenly conscious that he had to act swiftly and prevent any Company move against him.

Moyeen-ud-deen's first target was the Castle and its fleet: he knew well that if he didn't take charge of these assets then either the Company or the Sidi Masud would snatch them for their own ends from Safdar's useless, inebriate son. In October 1747 Moyeen-ud-deen, having gathered a reasonable force of three hundred cavalry, led an attack on the Castle and seized it, sending Wiqar fleeing for his life and seeking refuge in the palanquin of one of Shamshad Begum's senior courtesans. So fast was the raid that the Company had no time to react. Having established himself and asserted his control on the docks, the river and the custom house, Moyeed-ud-deen sent a message to the Sidi Masud informing him that he would give him admiralty of the fleet, but under Moyeed-ud-deen's supreme command, as things had been under Tegh's rule. The Sidi Masud reluctantly accepted.

Next, to Safdar he sent a message to surrender the Darbar and the civil government of the city. The message went unanswered and Moyeen-ud-deen didn't pursue the surrender of Safdar with vigour. He knew Safdar was, strategically, not so important, having already done ample damage to himself and forsaken any loyalty he might have enjoyed from the merchants. In the larger scheme of things it was the Company that needed to be kept in check. To this end, what Moyeen-ud-deen did next was nothing short of remarkable.

He first reached out to Damaji Gaekwad – harking back to his father-in-law's policy of a Hindustani alliance – and re-affirmed the treaty, agreeing to give up one-quarter of the revenue of Surat in return for the military assistance of 5,000 Marathas.[20] Then came the most imaginative stroke. A fortnight previous Moyeen-ud-deen had sent out an emissary in the dead of night – a horseman who rode south, stealthily avoiding the Company bastion that was Bombay, and riding with such ferocity and speed that on reaching his destination his horse dropped dead of exhaustion. The destination was the court of His Exalted Highness Nizam-ul Mulk, the master of Hyderabad, Deccan and large parts of central and southern Hindustan. This court duly gave a hearing to a plea that was simple and robust. Moyeen-ud-deen wished for the Nizam to join his Hindustani alliance and so save Surat from both the Europeans and their plundering pawn – Safdar.

The Nizam's written response, in which he addressed Moyeen-ud-deen as 'Your Excellency', was emphatic:

I having being repeatedly informed of the cruelties and oppressions practiced at Surat from the writings of the inhabitants there and the testimonies of persons who have come from that place. Your Excellency is directed if you find it practicable, to possess yourself in whatever manner you can of the city and Castle and breaking the hand of the oppressor that it may no longer distress the poor and helpless ... our army shall be appointed to succour you.[21]

When Moyeen-ud-deen at last made public the news of the extraordinarily powerful alliance he had assembled, the effect upon any wavering merchants in Surat was immediate.

Moyeen-ud-deen now enjoyed essentially unanimous support. The English Company – under their chief factor James Lambe, who had replaced Henry Lowther – quickly realised that their tacit support for Safdar had to end. Knowing well that this was not their moment, and that they had been beaten to the Castle, they were compelled to accept Moyeen-ud-deen (to whom they referred in correspondence as 'Achind') and began ingratiating themselves with him. They informed Safdar of the futility of holding onto the Darbar and the civil administration of the city. Lambe went about this task with great speed, making plain to Safdar the course that would be in his best interests:

Achind [Moyeen-ud-deen] being possessed of the castle and having such powerful assistance, it would be too great a risk for him [Safdar] to contend, as in all human probability he would be driven to the greatest extremities ... and he would have only his evil councillors to blame for any ill consequences that might attend himself... not only as Achind [Moyeen-ud-deen] is so strongly supported, besides his being possessed of the Castle but likewise as the merchants and the whole town in general, from the good character he bears, incline to have him governor and from Safdar it was notorious many of them had received great injuries and oppressions and so considerable a body of people, on proper representations being made in favour of Achind [Moyeen-ud-deen].[22]

Reluctantly, then, the English Company bade Safdar goodbye. He had seemed to them an ideal tool for Surat's destruction. Although Safdar's banishment to Sindh was carried out under the instructions of Moyeen-ud-deen it wasn't done before the English gave him a grand send-off with all military honours, even giving him temporary refuge in their garden house.[23] For the meantime, though, with Moyeen-ud-deen in charge, a unified command once again in place and the merchants much pleased, the English were left to fear that a revival of trade at Surat would pose a genuine threat to Bombay. Moyeen-ud-deen had become the undisputed Nawab of Surat.

At the Mehmudi Bagh palace amid the firing of the state salute by the *Nawab risala,* or personal guards, the new ruler took his seat on the *masnad.* The Sidi Masud ordered his men to one of the terraces and with flaming torches they waved to their colleagues waiting on the ramparts of the Castle. The seventeen cannons then boomed across the Tapti, so setting the court proceedings in motion. Once ministers, police commissioners and custom officials had been appointed, a procession of dignitaries – including the Sidi Masud, James Lambe as Chief of Company factors, prominent merchants and the head of the *Nawab risala* – made their way to the *masnad* offering *nazranas.* As each approached, though, a sense of unease was palpable. In turn they bowed, reached for Moyeen-ud-deen's hand, kissed it and pledged loyalty. But any astute onlooker could see this was but a hollow performance for the sake of a watching public.

For the next three years Moyeen-ud-deen held his unified command over the port and concentrated his efforts on retaining the loyalty of the city merchants. He did so by lowering taxes and changing the hard policy (originated by Safdar and encouraged by the English) of collecting revenues by force. He believed that in the longer run it was the prosperity of the merchants that would revive the city's fortunes and also ensure his reign. But in the shorter term he ran the risk of collecting insufficient tax revenues and being as a result unable to pay his army. As Thomas Marsh, an English factor of the Company who believed in harsh measures for Surat's merchants, wrote on 28 September 1748: 'The people of Surat know but one way of parting with their pice [tax] to the Durbar, and that is by force. This they have been used to, and if Achind [Moyeen-ud-deen] continues scrupulous in this point, I am in great doubt if he will be able to keep his adversaries out.'[24]

Still, the merchants remained in Surat and prosperity seemed to return. English hopes of luring key merchants to Bombay were diminishing swiftly as Moyeen-ud-deen held bravely to his course. The grand Hindustani alliance of the Nawab, Gaekwad and the Nizam had temporarily saved Surat from falling into the hands of the English East India Company.

On a chilly January night in 1751 some merchants were roughed up by the master of the custom house – an officer in charge of collecting duties. He was in the way of taking bribes from merchants to allow their ships into dock after anchoring hours. Moyeen-ud-deen's response to the assault was fast. He dismissed the officer and ordered him to leave the city.[25] Seeking revenge the officer conspired with the Sidi Masud and Company officials to set a larger and more sinister plan afoot – getting Safdar back. The depth of betrayal, though, came to light when one of Moyeen-ud-deen's ministers intercepted letters by the Sidi Masud and Company officials to Safdar, plotting the latter's return months before. In fact the revelation came too late, for ships had already been dispatched to bring Safdar back.[26]

The nexus of betrayal had taken shape, and the plot had gained substantial momentum. Safdar had already landed and in no time, by way of lightning-fast overnight bribes, had secured the opening of the gates of the city and the palace. In a blistering attack with one thousand men behind him Safdar seized the Darbar, compelling Moyeen-ud-deen and a handful of his followers to gallop to the

Castle for refuge but also pushing out the Sidi Masud. Safdar then unleashed his infamous fury upon the merchants. Five hundred houses were burned down and Safdar's lackeys intimidated a number of merchants into parting with payments of up to 40,000 rupees.[27] It was just like the bad old days. The Company sniffed a chance of getting back into the power struggle in Surat. They had successfully engineered the return of their plundering pawn.

Confined in the Castle with his loyal followers, his second-time pregnant wife Wilayati Khanum and young son Hafiz-ud-den, Moyeen-ud-deen sought to regroup. Reserves of faith were provided by his wife. Outspoken and fiercely loyal to her husband, she now urged him on in spite of their straitened situation. Moyeen-ud-deen first sent a message to Safdar urging him to see the looming foreign threat in the form of the English Company to the port if there wasn't good governance and infighting amongst Hindustanis. Safdar ignored him. Moyeen-ud-deen still had the massive firepower of the cannons mounted on the Castle and could disrupt all trade if he wished, thus compelling Safdar to leave. But the welfare of the merchants was foremost on his mind, and it was to this character that the merchants had signed up to when he had become Nawab. So Moyeen-ud-deen turned the cannons not on the ships and the docks but directly at the Darbar where Safdar now sat and at the Company factories.

For months the exchange of mortar continued but the stalemate didn't break. As the monsoons descended on western Hindustan Moyeen-ud-deen's group began running out of provisions: basic necessities including lentils, ghee and bread became sparse.[28] Desperate to feed his pregnant and starving wife, son and followers, Moyeen-ud-deen reached out to the Company. He reminded James Lambe of the pledge of loyalty the Englishman had made at the coronation ceremony and urged him to now lend assistance in the effort to regain control of the city and re-establish peace and stability. But Moyeen-ud-deen was wasting his time: Lambe was under strict instructions from the Company headquarters in Bombay to abet the wrecking of Surat by any means necessary. The Company knew well that it was Moyeen-ud-deen who stood between them and the fall of the port. He had provided an environment for trade to prosper, he like Tegh had held the city administration and castle under a unified command and he had the ability to form strong Hindustani alliances against Company designs. And so, Lambe coldly ignored Moyeen-ud-deen's entreaties and made a pact with Safdar and the Sidi Masud – all agreeing not to provide any help to Moyeen-ud-deen.[29]

Hungry, weary and isolated, Moyeen-ud-deen's group feared further betrayal, none more keenly than Wilayati Khanum. Each night she would weave lucky charms and tie them to her husband's wrist, breathing a special prayer on them. But all manner of malign forces were now being launched against Moyeen-ud-deen.

On a thunderous monsoon night Moyeen-ud-deen and Wilayati Khanum ate a spartan dinner of bread and water with their band of followers and retired to the western wing of the Castle. As they made their way up the stone steps, entrusting the night guards with vigil, Wilayati Khanum looked out of one of the windows that provided a clear view of the western gate and saw that it appeared unguarded. In fact the brothel-keeper Shamshad Begum, under the directions of Lambe, Safdar and the Sidi, had sent a number of her prostitutes to the Castle to use their bodies as decoys; and, sure enough, the guards had failed to resist this temptation. Three other guards, actively complicit in a plot to assassinate Moyeen-ud-deen,[30] then climbed the western wall, their turban tails covering their faces.

As their flaming torches threw shadows up the Castle's inner walls they moved with unsheathed swords from corridor to corridor, hoping to find their intended victims in the highest room of the western tower. Breaking open the door, however, they found the room empty. Swiftly descending, they searched everywhere – the inner compound, the four towers – but, still, could not locate their target. Finally they rushed up to the open air ramparts – only to find Moyeen-ud-deen armed and ready, a most dangerous opponent even without the advantage of surprise. He killed one of the guards and took the other two as prisoners.[31]

As night threw down its blanket of darkness Moyeen-ud-deen gazed at his young son Hafiz-ud-deen and his pregnant wife. The reason for the peril in which they had been placed was depressingly clear: every man had his price. And while this assassination attempt had been foiled, it was obvious that further attempts would follow.

Moyeen-ud-deen made up his mind, deciding to take a great gamble: he would surrender to his enemies, in the hope that the merchants would feel, in due course, that he was the best friend they could have. A truce was agreed with Safdar, the Sidi Masud and the English. A handful of Moyeen-ud-deen's followers surrendered along with his family in July of 1751, and a delighted Lambe made arrangements for these soft hostages to be held captive in Bombay.

From July 1751 to the end of 1757, Safdar acquired some light Dutch support to guard himself against any English betrayal, and continued to rule Surat. The Sidi Masud acquired the Castle. Surat, now with a divided and fragmented command and different pockets of power once again witnessed a steady collapsing of trade. This was playing straight into the masterplan of the Company. The English Company, Safdar and the Sidi regularly fought each other in the streets. Amid the gloom and despair that consumed the city, a murderous act would make for yet another twist in Surat's fate.

In January of 1758, Safdar hosted the English Company factors for a guava fruit feast at one of his orchards hoping to sign a truce. Guavas were a great favourite of the Surtis, usually served with a touch of salt and red chilli powder. While they peaked in summer, that winter some trees in the orchard were still bearing fruit, and to celebrate this unusual happening Safdar decided to have a party. The Sidi Masud and the corrupt master of the custom house who had been sacked by Moyeen-ud-deen years ago were also in attendance. As all gorged on the ripe fruits, the sun climbed to its zenith – and on the stroke of noon, Safdar suddenly fell face forward onto the table, convulsing as he choked on the guava pulp he had been so ravenously devouring. Within seconds he was dead. A select bunch of guavas had been poisoned especially for Safdar. Accusations flew everywhere about the possible murderers – the English Company or the Sidi Masud. Eventually after investigation it was revealed that it was the dishonest master of customs who did the deed.[32] Safdar lay dead at the hands of the man who had brought him out of exile. But what was also whispered around Surat was that it was done under the instructions of the Company. No one would know the truth. The stench of murderous plots once again pervaded Surat's air.

News travelled fast – above all to Moyeen-ud-deen in Bombay, who had left behind some spies in the form of young merchants still loyal to him. 'This is our chance,' Wilayati Khanum urged her husband. 'Our faith has held and we must act fast.'

Wilayati Khanum's extended family had been a source of great support for Moyeen-ud-deen, and now for one final attempt she orchestrated her husband's escape from Bombay disguised as a mystic. This strong-willed woman knew she and her sons would be English hostages, but if her husband could get to Surat and take the Darbar and Castle then he could negotiate their return. On reaching Surat, Moyeen-ud-deen had to act fast. He knew this was the opening for which the English Company had waited so long. Safdar had served his purpose of paralysing trade and making the merchants feel terribly frustrated. A large number of them had, over the past six years, moved to Bombay, and wild rumours were floated by the Company that those remaining in Surat were ready to fund an English takeover of the city.

Moyeen-ud-deen knew the English Company's first target would be the Castle to dock their dreaded warships and then the Darbar to take the entire city administration. He moved swiftly yet again, mustered a reasonable force and took the Darbar. Knowing well English Company ships would soon be sailing on their way to

Surat, he would have to defend the city with all he had. But first he had to get around Sidi Masud.

On a clear day in February 1759, two days after Moyeen-ud-deen had taken the Darbar and the civil administration in his hands for a second time, he summoned the Sidi Masud to a meeting place that he hoped would resonate with any semblance of patriotism that his adversary might feel: the mausoleum of Khudavand. Pigeons fluttered around, picking grain off the cold stone floor. Fresh rose petals were strewn in obeisance to the memory of the great man. Beautiful poetic verses from Indo–Persian masterpieces reverberated in the dome, sung with great passion by the Sufi singers who were gathered. Local Sufis whirled in ecstasy to the beats. Some mystics present carried bowls of *lobaan*, scented smoke that filled the shrine with fragrance. And there, in front of the grave of Khudavand, Nawab and Qilledar came face to face.

'Honour the legacy of the man that lies before us,' began Moyeen-ud-deen. 'The man that built the Castle to defend against foreign invaders. The English Company won't waste time now, the storm clouds from Bombay are gathering and the engines of their war ships have ignited.'

Knowing all this to be true, the Sidi Masud asked meekly, 'But how will we defend ourselves?'

'I have lived in the Castle and defended from there. I know the power of the Castle's cannons. Under my direction, use them as best you can, and take the fleet out to meet the invaders. Your job is admiralty, not administration. Had you learned this sooner, your fate might have been different.'

It was now starkly apparent to Sidi Masud that his time was up. There was no way he could resist the Company artillery and their naval might. Destiny had caught up with him and he found himself utterly exposed, sitting in the Castle with a depleted and jaded Mughal fleet at his disposal. Yet, under the unified rule of the Nawab as it had been in Tegh's time, the Sidi Masud agreed willingly to work under Moyeen-ud-deen's command and resist the Company invasion with whatever means they could muster.

On 10 February 1759 John Spencer, Governor of Bombay, ordered the Company fleet to sail forth with the objective of capturing both the Surat Castle and Darbar. The Company force was a mix of land troops and war vessels, both under the supreme command of 45-year-old Captain Richard Maitland. A battle-hardened leader, brilliant in his use of artillery, Maitland had brought (along with his dreaded artillery companies) a large detachment of the Bombay European Regiment comprising 800 European soldiers and 1,500 sepoys. The navy for this campaign comprised five of the most powerful warships of the Company and a large number of other vessels for carrying soldiers and stores, all under the command of a Commodore Watson.

After a slow passage up the coast, on 15 February the deafening roar of the Company warships ripped through the morning silence as they emerged at the mouth of the Tapti from a lifting fog. Amongst the boats was one *Hibernia,* which carried Moyeen-ud-deen's family including his wife and eldest son Hafiz-ud-deen, especially brought in as hostages and objects of barter.[33]

From the Dariya Mahal Moyeen-ud-deen could see the ships at a distance and he immediately ordered all city gates to be closed. The strength of the defenders reflected Tegh's and Moyeen-ud-deen's vision of a united stand against foreign invasion. Race and religion didn't matter. A total of two thousand Hindus, Muslims, Pathans and others in the service of the Sidi, plus the Nawab's corps, four thousand strong, came together to defend Surat.[34] While numbers were in favour of the defenders, technology was certainly not. Maitland almost immediately went to work with his renowned artillery, pounding the Castle and Mughal fleet relentlessly. The outdated Mughal ships were reduced in a flash. Moyeen-ud-deen then instructed the Sidi to position some men on the left bank of the Tapti about a quarter mile to the west of the outer wall of the city.

From here Moyeen-ud-deen believed if they resisted fiercely with covering fire of the Castle's cannons, the Company's land forces could be held back. However, after a hot dispute of four hours, in which twenty men were lost on the side of the Company, the brave defenders were dislodged.[35]

Maitland then besieged the city around the outer walls from where newly erected batteries began a relentless pounding. For four days a brisk fire was kept up from two twenty-four pounders and one thirteen-inch mortar. But Moyeen-ud-deen and the Sidi defended resolutely, even advancing and occupying the English gardens and wharfs. The Castle's cannons boomed and, for all that they were outdated, they had an effect, temporarily halting any Company advance. After such continued firing without any apparent success, Maitland convened a council of war.

It was decided that a general attack was needed. The Company's twenty guns and four bomb ketches went into action. From the vessels, too, a mighty assault was launched, smashing most of the Castle's cannons. Eventually the boats carrying the troops anchored and the soldiers were landed. Rushing to the city's outer walls, the English troops encountered the last round of resistance from the recently invigorated and resolute Sidi Masud and his men. But so demoralised were these men at seeing the destruction of their batteries and cannons that they eventually took to flight. The Castle still had to be taken and Maitland didn't want to take any chances of encountering lingering resistance. Consequently three mortars were planted seven hundred yards from the Castle. The cannonade and bombardment from these mortars was so precise and devastating that not one response came from the Castle defenders. They had been defeated completely.

Within hours the Sidi Masud came out with his remaining men and surrendered the Castle. The total loss killed and wounded on the Company side did not amount to more than one hundred Europeans. Knowing full well that the next target was the Darbar and the city administration, Moyeen-ud-deen fortified the palace and placed his men in the most strategic places, ready for a street fight. Both sides knew that if such a combat ensued then Surat would go up in flames.

Maitland sent a message to Moyeen-ud-deen to open the gates of the city and surrender the administration in favour of the Company. The plan was to force Moyeen-ud-deen out and appoint a puppet.* The Company demand was met with a flat refusal by Moyeen-ud-deen. Negotiations stretched on for days. The only reason why the English did not simply storm the city was that they harboured a fear of their opponent's alliance-making skills. Previously Moyeen-ud-deen had thwarted their ambitions by persuading the Nizam and Damaji Gaekwad to support his cause; but this time, unknown to the English, Moyeen-ud-deen had no such support. The Marathas and the Nizam both had been plagued with internal problems in their dominions. Nonetheless, knowing no better, the Company still feared that an outright assault on Surat might be met with incredibly stiff resistance.

Meanwhile conditions aboard the ship *Hibernia* on which Moyeen-ud-deen's family was being held hostage began to deteriorate. Moyeen-ud-deen's son took severely ill with fever, and some were suspected of having contracted the lethal smallpox. It was a perilous state of affairs, and the English were conscious, should the standoff continue, that the deaths of any of his family might drive Moyeen-ud-deen to a yet fiercer resistance.[36]

Finally on 4 March 1759 an agreement was concluded whereby Moyeen-ud-deen would continue as Nawab with all civil and criminal administration under him, while the Company would be in charge of the Castle and admiralty and receive the entire amount of the annual *tankha* for maintaining the fleet. It was only after securing

---

*The Company had an informant, Faris, whom they wanted to appoint as their puppet ruler.

administration of the city that Moyeen-ud-deen ordered the gates to be opened. The Company factors were utterly frustrated, not having succeeded in dispossessing Moyeen-ud-deen of the nawabship and replacing him with their puppet.[37] Many accusations flew around the Company headquarters in Bombay; a number of officials now considered the Surat operations to be not entirely successful. However, with the Castle in their control they had muscled their way into a very influential position. From now on encouraged by their enormous naval and military force at the Castle they would be the dominant power in Surat.

Moyeen-ud-deen was heartbroken by the turn of events, and cursed himself daily for his failure to secure a unified command in Surat. It is said that towards the end of his life he rode up to the Castle every day, and then to Tegh's grave, where he asked questions of the dead man and wept profusely at the fate of the city. Providing a conducive environment for trade to flourish was the key to governing Surat and Moyeen-ud-deen, although having tried his utmost, knew well that it was the infighting amongst the Hindustanis that had contributed towards the erosion of that environment. The English Company had done everything to drive divisions between the Hindustanis, cunningly backing plunderers and striking deals that prevented Moyeen-ud-deen from implementing stable rule. And now the Company occupied a position from where they could only advance. Moyeen-ud-deen administered Surat ably until a calm March evening of 1763 when, after the sunset prayers, 'the good one', as he had come to be known to the merchants, passed away in his beloved Wilayati Khanum's arms. He was immediately succeeded by his son.

Hafiz-ud-deen wanted a grand accession to the *masnad*. For this he required the sanction and authorization of the Company, to which he found the Chief of English factors, Thomas Hodges, to be agreeable, and so arranged an elaborate coronation ceremony, its particulars observed and recorded by an English factor:

He was invested by the Chief as governor of the Castle, with the Culgee (feather of the Bird of Paradise set in a golden locket) with diamonds, rubies, emeralds in the shape of a feather, with a large emerald an ornament in the shape of a common sized rose the ensigns of the office, fixed on the turban was led by the chief to the seat of state. Immediately the master of requests called out, "Long live the Nabob Hoffis Deen Annut Cann Bahadur," upon which the Chief of the Castle ordered the great drums to be beat and by a signal 21 guns from the saluting battery round the town were fired. The Nabob being seated in a large chair, the Nabob then presented the Chief with two Arab horses.[38]

And yet, in spite of the auspicious beginnings, trouble between Hafiz-ud-deen and the Company arose almost immediately. Having established themselves as the crowning authorities in Surat the Company flooded the city with their officials: military, naval, and administrative. They were everywhere: commanding the docks, setting up new naval controls, managing the custom house with ruthless authority, even interfering in Hafiz-ud-deen's civil administration. Moreover, they persisted with the policy of seeking to decay Surat by levying new custom duties and freight charges on merchants, taking bribes, and even shutting down the mint – so making trade virtually impossible. The relationship between Hafiz-ud-deen and Chief of Factors Thomas Hodges deteriorated so precipitously that a helpless Hafiz-ud-deen was reduced to pleading, first with the authorities in Bombay and then with the Court of Directors directly in London:

Most illustrious gentlemen Directors of the Superior Council of the Honourable Company of London.

The said gentlemen have entirely broken all our contracts and agreements concerning the government of the city and fortress. I find that they not only govern the fortress but likewise my own district so much that they even command and govern in my own House.

The mint of this city has been shut up without coining by the obstinacy of Hodges to the great prejudice of the merchants occasioned by his not permitting the usual currency of money. Besides this Hodges was the beginning of the ruin of the merchants of the city by not suffering them to carry on their business with their own vessels in order for him to enjoy the profits of the freights it being proved that he received from a merchant Mollam Facorudin 45000 Rupees to grant him leave to navigate his two vessels and all these profits came out of the skin of the merchants and in this manner introducing new customs for his own conveniency so that the merchants and this city are going to utter ruin … I do not know what is the design of these gentlemen, if it is to preserve and benefit the land or ruin it at once.[39]

Predictably there was no reply from London or Bombay. Stifled, frustrated, angry and helpless, Hafiz-ud-deen resigned himself to his fate and flung himself into more creative pursuits. This would be his way of distracting himself from the despair of dealing with the Company authorities. And while nothing could take away the unsettling feeling of power slipping from his hands, Hafiz-ud-deen began taking a personal interest in his estates – his gilded cage, as it were.

Hafiz-ud-deen moved out of the Mehmudi Bagh palace, thinking it was cursed and leaving it to ruin, but he retained the magnificent gardens, adding more waterfalls. For his personal residence he built a massive new palace complex in Begumwadi. The wooden pillars and *jharokas* were inspired by peacocks and everywhere one looked the exquisite carvings of the bird in various forms evoked a sense of being transported to an exotic land. The Darbar hall was furnished with exquisite carved furniture on both sides with crimson satin tapestry and hundred-foot-long Turkish carpets that led to the *masnad*. The ceilings were decorated with crystal chandeliers imported from France and Czechoslovakia. To the right was the *zenana* house for women, and a private wing for the Nawab's personal residence which had its own private audience room called the *Diwan-e-khas* where Hafiz-ud-deen would entertain only the closest and most important guests.

Behind the private residence was the *risala khana* or the cantonment for the Nawab's personal guards and behind them were stables for a large number of horses and elephant garrisons and to the right were the carriage garages.

He then built the stunning three-storey Aena Mahal or Palace of Mirrors. This spectacular exhibition of creativity from some of the finest artisans of Hindustan saw human reflections springing to life. The main hall of this palace had a thousand mirrors of various sizes each hand crafted in Mughal flower designs and placed on the walls. As night would fall and lamps were lit for the best performing *nautch* girls to demonstrate their dancing skills, the Aena Mahal would come alive with a thousand reflections.

To the Dariya Mahal, a refuge for Hafiz-ud-deen in the summer as it had been for his father and grandfather, he added a new Darbar hall and decorated it with exquisite silver furniture. Besides the palaces, Hafiz-ud-deen built ten large gardens and mango orchards, the most prominent being the *Fez Rasul* garden and *Bagh-e-Ver* garden (the former meaning 'Blessing of the Prophet' and the latter 'Garden of the blessed'). Beautifully laid out, these gardens were designed by landscape designers from Delhi and became talking points in western Hindustan. The symmetrically laid mango trees in both these gardens would produce bountiful fruit every summer filling the air with their fragrance, luring the Nawab to lie under their shade on Kashmiri carpets and immerse himself in the aromatic surroundings.

The *Dabholee* and *Seegumpoor* garden was enormous in size with acres upon acres of exotic fruits, from the soft and sugary brown *chikoo*, to pears, guavas and tangerines. The garden was favoured by Hafiz-ud-deen for long evening walks: he savoured the mix of fragrances, stopping by different trees and tenderly massaging the fruit.

Hafiz-ud-deen abided in these beautiful surroundings, most of his life spent desperately trying to keep the Company out of civil administration of Surat, until he suffered from a devastating attack of cholera which proved to be fatal, eventually killing him in May 1790. His eldest son Nizam-ud-deen ascended the *masnad,* again by the consent of the Company. But this time the conditions for accession were even tougher. The Company permitted the crowning of Nizam-ud-deen only after he verbally agreed to pay an annual charge of one lakh (Rs.100,000/£10,000) as additional expenses for maintaining the Castle and fleet.

Nizam-ud-deen's reign was more of the same as had pertained in Hafiz-ud-deen's time: characterised by the frustration of living as a pampered prisoner in a gilded cage, dealing with the unending avalanche of Company officials bent upon diminishing his powers. Nizam-ud-deen died in January 1799, plagued by awful and uncontrollable dysentery for the last two months of his life. A month later, his infant son also died. These untimely deaths gave the Company just the opportunity for which it had waited to take the entire civil administration into its hands.

At this time, a man was rising to become one of history's most famous military figures; and the plains of Hindustan provided the acid test of his potential. Amidst the ruins of the Mughal Empire, he was laying the foundation stones of a new rule in these lands. His name was Arthur Wellesley, later to be Duke of Wellington.

Richard Wellesley, Governor General, was a man obsessed with power. He had locked horns on innumerable occasions with the Court of Directors of the Company in London, trying to pursue them to change their attitude from being mere traders to administrators. Wellesley wanted not merely to trade but to conquer and rule. His passion for acquiring land, cities, forts, palaces and territory was insatiable.

As Wellesley's reputation had grown, so had that of another equally remarkable man – Tipu Sultan. This fiercely independent ruler of Mysore had confronted most local native princes and exhorted them to recognize the one most lethal threat to native rule in Hindustan – The East India Company. Tipu had been the greatest and most formidable threat to Company ambition in central and southern Hindustan. Unrelenting in his distaste for the Company, Tipu and his father Haider Ali had resisted the Company for decades, inflicting severe defeats during the first and second Anglo–Mysore wars. In the third of these wars Tipu had suffered some losses but dug deep to build up to a fourth confrontation, which would bring him face to face with Wellesley.

Tipu had even reached out to Napolean to form an alliance against the Company. In a clash of the giants in May 1799, all of Hindustan watched as the two great military men squared off for a final confrontation. Betrayed by his own generals, who were bribed, Tipu went down fighting, sword in hand. The kingdom of Mysore had fallen to the Company.

The Company was brimming with confidence after this monumental victory. With this momentum behind them, and having learnt that Nizam-ud-deen of Surat had died and so had his infant male heir, the Company decided to now take over the entire civil administration of the city. Nizam-ud-deen though had a younger brother, Nasir-ud-deen, who was desperate to succeed to the Nawabship and wrote to both Jonathan Duncan, Governor of Bombay and to Richard Wellesley, requesting recognition. Sensing Nasir-ud-deen's desperation and not willing to give up his ambition of taking over Surat completely, Wellesley ordered Jonathan Duncan to inform Nasir-ud-deen that if he wanted to be Nawab he would have to pay an additional one lakh annually (Rs. 100,000 / £10,000).[40] A shocked and helpless Nasir-ud-deen did not know how to react to this and negotiations dragged on, with Nasir-ud-deen holding out for as long as he could, pleading profusely that he just didn't have the money.

Nasir-ud-deen had the qualities of a perfectly capable administrator and was well within his rights to succeed. But Richard Wellesley was adamant not to let the rightful succession of Nasir-ud-deen happen.

Finally, after a few months Wellesley's patience ran out. He instructed Jonathan Duncan to go to Surat equipped with a treaty and a large force that would transfer all civil administration into the hands of the Company. Nasir-ud-deen would be allowed to keep the title of Nawab, his estates, a very large pension and a substantial share of the city revenues. The Treaty was thus:

> The Agreement between the East India Company and
> Nawab Nasiruddin Khan and his heirs and successors.
> The Nawab Nasiruddin agrees that the whole civil and military government of the city shall be vested for ever entirely and exclusively with the English Company.
>
> The English Company agree to pay the Nabob Nasiruddin and his heirs of the revenues of Surat and its dependencies, one lakh of Rupees annually (Rs. 100,000 / £10,000). The Company also engage to pay the said Nabob and his heirs in addition to the above mentioned Lakh of Rupees a proportion of one fifth of the annual Revenues now arising or which may hereafter arise (Rs. 50,000 £5,000).[41]

As a measly token gesture and to appease him, the Company would permit the Nawab to have the authority to try his family, servants, peons and managers associated with his estates.[42] That was all – nothing more. The determination in Wellesley's position can be seen in the tone of his instructions to Jonathan Duncan:

> ... if Nasiruddin shall ratify these articles, you shall place him in the station of the nabob. If he shall refuse his acquiesence you will hold your sanction to his succession, assuming however the entire administration of the government of the city and of its revenues in the same manner as if Nasiruddin had ratified the article.[43]

There was no reason to believe the city needed better administration. The judicial system was working well; the administrative services (as in all major cities) had their challenges but generally rose to the occasion; and the police service, too, was relatively efficient. The English warships were already in place under the Castle and were doing their job of providing security to merchant vessels. But the Company had used the excuse of protection and safety to stake a claim to administration, abetted by the fact that Nasir-ud-deen was the brother of the deceased Nawab who had left no male issue.

Nasir-ud-deen was outraged. For a brief moment he considered armed resistance, but the resounding victory the Company had recently achieved over Tipu had sent shockwaves across Hindustan. Powerful native princes sensed that it was only a matter of time before all of Hindustan, including Delhi, would fall to the Company's military might. There would be no assistance from the Nizam, who had witnessed Tipu's fate just next door; while the Marathas were in complete disarray. In the minds of Nasir-ud-deen's ministers, there was no question of challenging the Company. It didn't take much to impress upon Nasir-ud-deen the futility of his fledgling thought, and he resigned himself to his fate.

Jonathan Duncan went in to do business on 10 March 1800 with a desire to conclude matters as swiftly as possible with a couple of military regiments of the Company behind him. A weak and helpless Nasir-ud-deen looked at him and his powerful regiments with profound sorrow in his eyes. He knew well that his local Surat corps which were only meant for policing could not resist the might of Wellesley's army and naval firepower docked below the Castle. Having read the articles Nasir-ud-deen knew he had no option but to sign. But he was especially apprehensive on a couple of counts.

Jonathan Duncan, though his interests were undoubtedly on one side, noted the Nawab's unease in his diary. He told Nasir-ud-deen's secretary Visoonath that he was certainly gratified by what he saw as 'the expediency of the Nawaub's cheerful acquiescence' in quickly signing the new treaty, which Duncan told him:

> would give a security for an honourable provision to his master and his family from generation to generation, greater than they had ever yet, whereas the Company who never failed in a strict adherence to their engagements would now become bound in perpetuity to the support of the Nawaub and his family.[44]

Much later Duncan would, however, acknowledge Nasir-ud-deen's principal concern about the deal the Company were offering:

> All the real objection the Nawaub seemed to have to the signing of the treaty was from the 4th article not having the words "for ever" after the word "heirs" in the second line. I assured Visoonath the, Nawab's agent, that a stipulation for a man and his heirs meant for ever.[45]

On receiving this assurance from Jonathan Duncan that the large pension (£10,000) and the agreed revenue from the city (£5,000) would continue from 'generation to generation' – believing therefore that he had secured his children, family and descendants in perpetuity – Nasir-ud-deen signed the treaty. The port had finally fallen. Surat was annexed. Never again would Surat regain its importance as Hindustan's foremost port. Under the Company, this once thriving maritime trading city would completely lose its significance. The English East India Company officials would successfully strangle sea trade and direct all of it to Bombay. The stripping of the Nawab of his ruling powers would go down in British Indian history 'as the most unceremonious act of dethronement which the English had yet performed.'[46] The proceeding was characterised by tyranny and injustice.[47]

Nasir-ud-deen decided to lose himself to poetry and the management of his magnificent palaces and estates. To the people of Surat, the Nawabship would continue to be a position of respect and much reverence.

—

But the greatest disaster to befall the family was yet to come as Nasir-ud-deen's misplaced hopes would soon be in ruins, destroyed by untrustworthy Company officials. The treaty would soon stand violated by the Company leaving the family and descendants on the edge of poverty. The pension would be ruthlessly stopped and the private palaces and estates confiscated.

It would be one who was yet to be born who would end up fighting for the family's honour. So chilling would be the injustice towards infants that it would take the strongest will endowed in a father to shake the bastion of the East India Company in London. As the last custodian of the House of Surat, this unrelenting Prince would fight not just in Hindustan, but go head to head with the East India Company in Britain's great coliseum of law and justice, its Parliament. Fearlessly his campaign for justice would call for the termination of British rule in Hindustan.

His rise would be such that the highest echelons of the British political establishment would stand bedazzled by his indefatigable spirit. But first we need to understand his origins and the distant lands from where he would emerge to challenge the might of an empire.

3

The Prince, and an Alliance to Safeguard

On a wintry night in 1817 a large caravan of horse-driven carriages and bullock-carts – carrying an eclectic mix of craftsmen, weavers, and a Sufi poet – made its way slowly through the central plains of Gujarat (also known as Kathiawar). The caravan was protected by a band of two hundred armed horsemen, since this was a region infamous for bandits and marauding dacoits, though equally renowned for the large number of principalities that dotted its landscape. Ruled by a number of Hindu and Muslim princes with varied titles – Nawabs, Darbar Shrees, Ranas, Maharajahs and Jam – Kathiawar, Gujarat was in many ways the heartbeat of princely Hindustan.

Astride a white steed at the head of the horsemen sat Syed Meer Sarfaraz Ali Khan, a tall and well-built man in his mid-forties, sharp of nose and cleft of chin, sporting an elegant moustache that twirled at each end. Recently decorated by the penultimate Mughal Emperor Akbar Shah-II, Sarfaraz was one of the many restless and disillusioned fighters of northern Hindustan desperately seeking to carve his own dominions. His ancestors had served the Mughal Court as generals and, by dint of their valour, had for centuries held positions of nobility.[48] Hindustan, though, had ceased to be under the control of the Mughals and the East India Company had taken

Delhi in 1803, thus reducing the status of the titular Emperor to a puppet under many Company officials.

A very select few families could trace their lineage to Modud Chishti the founder of the Chishti Sufi order and from him to the Prophet Mohammad, consequently being much favoured by the Emperor.* Sarfaraz's family was one such.[49] Sarfaraz's ancestor Khwaja Khatir had become the *Vazier* of Hindustan in the 13th and 14th century Delhi Sultanate. And so, when the Company was putting together a coalition force to fight the Pindaree dacoits that were infesting central and western Hindustan, they asked the Emperor to assign a few distinguished soldiers for this task. The titular Emperor, knowing Sarfaraz's desire to seek his own destiny, issued with Company approval a *sanad* or Imperial order granting Sarfaraz tax-free lands and villages in western Gujarat, from where he could launch his military career. The Gaekwad of Baroda was also informed of this and he too gave some of his troops to Sarfaraz. It was to these lands after stopping at Baroda for a few months – and their most prominent town as bequeathed to Sarfaraz that the caravan made its way. It resembled a meandering flame in the depth of a clear and deep-black night.

In the midst of the caravan was a silver palanquin carrying Sarfaraz's wife Raja Begum at the end stage of pregnancy. Servants bearing torches walked loyally in step alongside the palanquin, the torchlight casting shadows onto the drapes that covered the carriage as Raja Begum twisted in anticipation within. The night alone made her nervous and as anxiety got the better of her she went into labour. Engulfed in pain her cries were piercing, and the caravan came to a halt. Her anguish lasted four hours, until the first rays of morning light turned blackness to a dawning crimson – whereupon a great

---

*The Chishti order is one of the oldest schools of Sufi thought. The emphasis on mystical learning, charity and social upliftment through compassion and openness of mind have left an immeasurable effect in India. At the heart of Chishti Sufi meditation is 'Sama' or musical trance.

childish wail was heard the length of the caravan.

Word was sent to Sarfaraz and he galloped to be by his wife. Cutting through the guards that surrounded a hurriedly erected maternity tent, and reaching her bedside, he was presented with the newborn by Raja Begum. For an hour he remained by her, caressing her through the trials of post-natal pain and exhaustion. Then stepping out of the tent which had been surrounded by his loyal soldiers and servants, he held the baby high up in his arms and announced, 'By the blessings of The Almighty – a son!'

Sarfaraz felt a surge of immense joy as he held his child aloft. A great roar tore the air as his soldiers hailed the arrival of the new-born prince.

Mounting his horse, his son in his arms, Sarfaraz looked into the distance. The caravan had come to a halt by the banks of the river Badar and a new day had broken fully. Across the river lay Sarfaraz's newly betrothed tiny principality, Kamandiyah. His newborn, he had come to believe, brought him luck as it was the day when Raja Begum had announced her pregnancy that the Emperor had bestowed Kamandiyah on him.

This part of the Gujarat peninsula had over centuries become home to the Kathis, a people who traced their origins to Sindh and Balochistan and named their homeland Kathiawar. The Kathis were hardy sons of the soil, fiercely traditional, chivalrous and loyal, skilful farmers and, if need be, great fighters, devoted to their swords and muskets. Primarily Hindu, the men wore white turbans with a minimum of four layered rolls covering their heads and foreheads, white short kurtas and tight white cotton *churidar* pants that wrinkled at the ankles. Almost all of them sported big curling moustaches. The women tended toward a shy and demure outward demeanour but weren't confined to their homes. These independent women worked shoulder to shoulder with their husbands in the fields.

As Sarfaraz urged his horse to cross the river, followed by his horsemen and the caravan, he noticed on the other side a line-up of five hundred turbaned Kathi men, some with muskets and some with drums, ready to fire a salute and beat their instruments to announce his arrival. Fording the river, one hand on the reins and the other carrying his new-born, Sarfaraz glanced at his son, and a name sprung into his mind: Jafar, meaning 'a flowing river in paradise that brought abundance.' The name also rhymed with that of the river he and his men were crossing, the Badar.

'Jafar, my son, may you bring abundance to yourself and your future generations,' Sarfaraz whispered in the infant's ear.* Unknown to the father was how the greatest of challenges awaited his son in Surat. The child's destiny would take him to that city as the last custodian of the Royal House of Surat and he in time would have to rise up to honour the meaning of his name.

Kamandiyah resounded with deafening noise as Sarfaraz was placed on a *masnad* and bestowed with the local title of *Namdar Meherban Darbar Shree*, literally meaning 'The Renowned, The Most Gracious, Holder of the Honoured Court.' The East India Company immediately clipped the title down to size and its unglamourised version would simply be – the Ruling Chief.[50] Safaraz's enjoyment of fatherhood and of the newly founded principality would have to wait a little. First, he had to answer the call of the battlefields.

Swiftly an administrative system was put in place and Sarfaraz left his wife and the infant Jafar and rode out with his two hundred men.

—

Between 1817 and 1818 Sarfaraz would be part of two pivotal battles in central Hindustan that would play a crucial role in bringing peace

---

*After much research in Gujarat, particularly in Kathiawar and Baroda, it was established that Jafar was born enroute to Kamandiyah from Baroda. The exact birthplace is unknown but believed to be somewhere on lands that run alongside the river Badar, just past a village called Shrinathgarh near Gondal.

and relative stability to the region. The first was the war against the Pindarees, marauding hordes who had become the scourge of Hindustan. The second was a rescue mission to save the Peshwa, the most prominent of Maratha chiefs. The Peshwa had been held hostage by some of his own Arab troops and mercenaries citing payment arrears and threatening to kill him.[51] Sir John Malcolm, a Company General, was given 600 troops by the Gaekwad to lead the rescue mission. These were placed under the command of Sarfaraz, who led the mission and ensured the subsequent quelling of the mutinous Arabs and the safety of the Peshwa. Malcolm was a distinguished soldier, diplomat and academic who had fought with Wellesley during the Mysore war against Tipu. Unlike Wellesley, however, he had acquired a genuine desire to understand local culture and history.

Malcolm was fluent in Persian as a result of his diplomatic missions to that country. (In due course he would write a *History of Persia*.) His enthusiasms bred in him a real commitment to bringing good order to western and central Hindustan. While he did pursue all East India Company goals with a passionate dedication, he sought also to ensure the rights of the princes of Gujarat and the social development of that region. (In time he worked closely in Gujarat with the Sahajanand Swaminarayan sect of Hinduism to eradicate female infanticide that prevailed in towns and villages.)

Malcolm acknowledged Sarfaraz's contribution in a letter, 'attributing much of the successful issue of the quelling of the mutinous Arabs and Rohillas to the temper, good sense and courage' he had exhibited and informing him that 'the Bombay Government has exempted you from all payment for the Company's share of Kummandia in Kathiawar.'[52]

At the end of 1818 Sarfaraz returned to Kamandiyah having assured tax exemption for his principality and adding a few more villages in Gujarat to his income.[43] As he gained in influence a strong friendship was established with the Gaekwad of Baroda and Malcolm.*

On his return to Kamandiyah, Sarfaraz was delighted with what he saw. The unique mix of travellers with his caravan had slowly settled in their new town. The region had so much to offer and fire their imagination. Amongst the other villages in that region was Rojdi, dating back to 2,500 BC, while to the south west was the Gir forest, home to the Asiatic lion. Both Rojdi and Gir proved to be great inspiration for the craftsmen and weavers of Kamandiyah who, inspired by these surroundings, created beautiful handicrafts depicting ancient and forest life.

The ingenuity of the weavers encouraged by Sarfaraz gave birth to Kamandiyah's first silk-producing encampments around the town. The fertile dark soil would yield the finest quality wheat, cotton and ground nut; all sent to processing mills set up by Sarfaraz in Kamandiyah and subsequently sold across Gujarat. All this revenue, free from the taxes of the Mughal Court and of the East India Company, made Sarfaraz a very wealthy man. Right in the heart of Kamandiyah stood a twenty-foot teak gate which opened out into ten acres of land fortified on all sides; and at the north end of the fortification stood the Darbargadh or court palace commissioned by Sarfaraz.

But with prosperity came a threat. Lawlessness in Kathiawar–Gujarat was rampant. It was Hindustan's wild west. Large bands of armed horsemen often raided the tiny principalities with ruthless savagery, torching fields and raiding granaries, kidnapping local women and demanding huge ransoms. A battle-hardened Sarfaraz, aware of this lurking menace, stationed his garrison of two hundred horsemen in Kamandiyah as a strong warning to any ill-advised

---

*The Gaekwad had large land holdings in Kathiawar and Sarfaraz was given charge of his military operations. For the Gaekwad, Sarfaraz led a series of campaigns in Kathiawar against outlawed bandits.

adventurer. It was amid these fascinatingly fraught surroundings that Sarfaraz's cherished son Jafar commenced his childhood.

—

Brown-eyed, olive skinned and dark-haired, the boy Jafar was also equipped with a loud voice. By the age of 5 he was put on a horse. Jafar learned to trot and gallop and was soon seen navigating through the narrow Kamandiyah lanes, people hurriedly making way as the little Prince was pursued desperately by his guards. Sometimes his riding would disrupt the sleepy town completely. He would burst through the potters' and craftsmen's outdoor workshops sending their earthenware clattering to the ground, or brush past women carrying fresh water in their utensils, often dashing them to the floor. Breaking out into the open country he would be seen galloping through the fields, jumping over fences, storming through barns and plunging his horse into the Badar river, in pursuit of wild geese, cranes and ducks that had till then lazily languished on the banks and were now forced to take flight. Jafar loved his sport.

The fierce Kathis were great marksmen. They had mastered the art of shooting from horseback with one hand, particularly when hunting wild boar (an animal they considered vermin). A couple of Kathi marksmen had been hand-picked by Sarfaraz to accompany him on his campaigns against the Pindarees and the mutinous Arabs of the Peshwa. Staunchly loyal to Sarfaraz, they were now given the job of training Jafar. For the Kathi marksmen it couldn't have been a greater honour. On most days Jafar was made to put on a Kathi turban and then he and his teachers would go into open plains and shoot targets – watermelons, scarecrows and earthenware. With time Jafar learned the skill of keeping the rifle-butt tightly compressed against his cheek and holding his breath till he fired, in order to prevent his hand from shaking on the trigger. But one thing was very observable throughout these training days – Jafar desisted from shooting animal life.

Besides the love for the fabulous outdoors and raw Kathi countryside, Jafar's parents inculcated in him north Hindustani etiquette and *tehzeeb*, aspects of life with which they had been brought up. He learned Hindustani and Persian, besides the local Kathi Gujarati language. He was taught the refined mannerisms of greetings including the Muslim salaam and the Hindu response of folding his hands and slightly bending when the Kathis paid their respects by bowing deep and uttering '*Khamma bappa*'.

Having gone through his Hindustani, Persian and Kathi Gujarati lessons with his tutors during the day, Jafar would sit listening attentively to his mother's words every evening. Deeply pious, she taught him strong values that he would hold onto: generosity, prayer and faith, love for all regardless of religion and creed and, above all, to put family first.

Barely 12 years old, Jafar began to demonstrate signs of a notable compassion. Sarfaraz, an avid hunter, decided to take his son along on an expedition to bag as many antelope as possible. Accompanied by their guards, servants, spotters and meat cleaners, father and son each on horseback raced through the forests around Kamandiyah, searching for the elusive spotted deer or Cheetal, the meat of this animal being the most tender venison. After a few hours of searching the party caught sight of a pair by a small pool of fresh water, albeit at a fair distance. Some of the guards dismounted and loaded a rifle for Jafar.

'It's a clean shot,' whispered a guard, mindful not to scare the antelope away. 'Would your grace please aim and fire?' He passed the rifle to Jafar and placed his arm around the boy for support.

'Go ahead,' said Sarfaraz. 'Shoot'... And then again, 'Shoot!'

After a minute, with impatience growing in the party, Jafar responded, 'I will not.'

The answer was delivered not so loud as to show insolence but sufficient to startle the antelopes who sprung to alertness and darted back into the forest thicket along with their little fawn – which only

Jafar had seen, snuggling behind the mother's rear legs.

That night as lamps flickered around the dining table and servants served the family lamb kormas and kebabs, there was silence. The guards who had been a part of the hunting party had whispered amongst themselves, doubting the Prince's toughness, and Sarfaraz did not like it. He wondered whether his son lacked the stomach for a kill, whether the boy's mother and tutors had made him over-refined, excessively compassionate. Consumed by this doubt Sarfaraz chose to confront his dear son.

'What was the matter today, Jafar? Why didn't you pull the trigger?' he asked tenderly yet firmly.

'The antelopes were protecting their fawn and teaching it to drink. Shouldn't children always be protected? It was the right of the parent to teach and the right of the fawn to learn and drink. Shouldn't rights be respected?'

This answer astonished Sarfaraz – and he noticed his wife wearing a wry smile. He couldn't reason. While the answer showed the boy's compassion, somewhere within Sarfaraz he felt a certain disappointment. He had appointed Jafar his successor. But did Jafar have the right stuff in him? Someday he would have to administer Kamandiyah. How could he do so with such a soft heart? And yet he could not deny that the boy's refusal to gun down the deer was rooted in a strength of reason and morality. In time it would be these qualities of compassion, morality and righteousness that Jafar would call on. They would become the pillars of his character, providing much strength as life would thrust him into the gravest of situations in Surat.

A couple of months passed, in which Sarfaraz ceased taking Jafar on hunting expeditions, still nursing that sense of disappointment. One of the deadliest threats to Kamandiyah folk and surrounding villages came from man-eating leopards renowned for their exceptional size. The beasts would emerge from the forests just when light was fading, whereupon they snuck into villages and snatched children. Wailing mothers would chase and follow the tracks and trails of ripped cloth pieces and bones to the forest's very edges but they dared not go further, as the predators would vanish into the blackness. Whenever Sarfaraz shot one of these fearsome man-eaters he would have its claws drawn out so that he could wear them as a trophy.

He had heard enough of one particularly large rampaging animal and had taken it upon himself to hunt this menace down. Many a night he spent on a *machan*, waiting for this animal to appear, covered with branches and leaves as camouflage and with bait tied below in forest thickets. But even when he did catch sight of the leopard, it always managed to elude Sarfaraz's bullet. Nonetheless, despite half a dozen failed attempts, Sarfaraz remained determined to get him.

One late evening just as Sarfaraz was planning his seventh attempt, his spotters rushed in to say that the beast was on the prowl at the edge of Kamandiyah. Sarfaraz mounted and galloped out, rifle in hand, his party following closely. Just as he approached a thicket of wood and scrub bush, he heard the squeal of a child and the cry of a mother. And then, suddenly, a single shot thundered in the air, followed immediately by a great earthshaking growl. The leopard had been bounding through the thicket straight at Sarfaraz. Yet so precise was the shot that stopped the animal, it had gone straight through the right shoulder to the heart. The leopard fell down dead at the hoofs of Sarfaraz's horse, which reared on its hind legs and threw Sarfaraz to the ground. Several other accomplished shooters also took a tumble.

Sarfaraz got to his feet covered in dust, bewildered, and turning to his equally shocked hunting party he asked who had fired the brilliant shot? He was met with a confused reaction. No-one had the answer. As dust settled and as Sarfaraz and party looked around, a fair distance away they saw a young boy still on one knee, rifle in hand, his Kathi marksman standing behind him.

'Jafar!' exclaimed Sarfaraz.

Hearing his father's call the boy prince got up and approached, looking his father straight in the eye.

'Every action should have a justifiable reason, father,' said the boy. 'When there is abundance in the forest the beast has no right to take a child from our villages. It wasn't his right. But it was my right to protect the infant.' Sarfaraz and his retinue were left understandably speechless.

The incident would become a part of Kamandiyah folklore and narrated for generations. Never again would father doubt son. Although delighted at the shooting prowess of his son and the bravado of confronting a man-eater, Sarfaraz still had questions. From where was his son getting these inspiring thoughts? Yes, his wife was a deeply pious and thoughtful woman, but the boy's verbal reasoning was deeper than he had imagined. Did his wife know something he didn't?

Encouraged by his mother, it was Hasan Shah Pir the Sufi poet and mystic in Sarfaraz's caravan that had taken Jafar under his wings. It was with the Sufi that Jafar would spend hours understanding the life and times of four great Sufi stalwarts: the Khwaja of Ajmer, Ghazali, Farabi and Omar Khayyam. But the lessons Jafar was given weren't the typical ones that he was used to with his other teachers. These were meetings with his master, drenched in mysticism and the philosophy of life.

Sometimes both the Sufi master and student would climb on horseback and ride at a leisurely pace through fields under the open sky, during which excursions the Sufi would elaborate on the life of the Khwaja of Ajmer and his passion for providing relief to the poor and helpless beings – man and animal.

Next for Jafar came the study of Ghazali, the master philosopher who developed the concept of 'inspired intuition' – a mystical method of inquiry and learning that could lead to actions grounded in strong faith and belief. The belief in one's objective had to come from the heart rather than the mind. The searching within with openness of spirit and compassion would justify the belief in the objective. This was the basis of 'inspired intuition'; the mind would then be guided by the heart's calling. In contrast to Farabi, another great scholar who had written on logic, it was Ghazali's works on 'inspired intuition' that appealed to Jafar's searching nature.

And finally Hasan Shah Pir made Jafar study Omar Khayyam, the great mathematician and poet. A great lover of wine, and having borne the savagery of the Muslim clergy for his drinking habits, Khayyam often had digs at the one-dimensional priests, and these verses the young Jafar often recited along with his Sufi master:

> *They say lovers and drunkards go to hell.*
> *A controversial dictum not easy to accept*
> *If the lover or the drunkard are for hell*
> *Tomorrow paradise will be empty.*

> *Oh Canon of Jurists, we work better than you*
> *With all drunkenness, we're more sober*
> *You drink men's blood; we the vine's*
> *Be honest – which of us is the more bloodthirsty?*

Riding into the ruins of Rojdi village where there was quiet and peace, sitting on the rocks of a lost civilization, sometimes under the large banyan trees Hasan Shah Pir decoded the meanings of these magnificent words and then immersed Jafar into this world of inspired intuition, imagination and human responsibility. The crux of Sufism was acceptance of all faiths and so Jafar was encouraged by his master to understand Hinduism and its philosophy of love of humanity. Much time was spent reading ancient scriptures including the Vedas. The Sufi master would often take Jafar to the temples devoted to Lord Ram, sit amongst the chanting brahmin priests and recite versus in praise of the great God.

By the age of 16, Jafar's olive skin had tanned yet deeper from all his outdoor pursuits. His shoulders were broad and he stood nearly six feet tall. His build, then, he had inherited from his father; but his eyes were exactly like his mother's. Soulful and soft brown in colour, seemingly trained upon the distance, they appeared to reflect the searching quality of Jafar's temperament.

But Jafar's life could not be wholly devoted to a spiritual quest. He had to be groomed to administer and fight. Sarfaraz made it his personal responsibility to instil these duties in his son. He kept the boy close to him. Whenever Sarfaraz held court and took decisions, Jafar was made to witness it. On occasion, Sarfaraz got Jafar to read out the sentencing, rather than the local court magistrates. 'Fifteen days rigorous imprisonment for robbery, Extra fines for lapses in tax payment…' Jafar would read aloud, facing the chained criminals.* Sarfaraz thought it vital to demonstrate that his son was tough enough to act against crime. The justice ruling chiefs in this wild country would have to dispense had to be swift and act as a deterrent.[54]

—

Such a diminutive but fertile principality as Kamandiyah, situated on the banks of a river, would always be under threat from the large bands of deadly dacoits and outlaws. By 1818 the Company had more or less brought the Kathiawar region of Gujarat under their control, with all rulers acquiescing to British protectorates. Nonetheless, a large number of outlaws still operated in the region, their small but lethal armies raiding and pillaging villages with inhuman savagery. As a result, Sarfaraz knew the importance of teaching Jafar how to fight. He was trained in commanding men, battle preparation and resource organization, strategic erection of watch towers, sentinel positions and scout recruiting. But Jafar's love for the rifle and

---

*The Kathiawar Directory by Hormazji Kadaka, publ. 1886 indicates that the ruling chiefs of Kamandiyah exercised limited criminal jurisdictionary powers.

sniping was well known, and Sarfaraz encouraged him to spend more time with the brilliant Kathi marksmen.

The most organised and devastating outlaws were ones that had descended into Gujarat from Balochistan: the Makranis. They traced their origins to a town called Makran, and enjoyed a fearsome reputation for cunning, spite, and a commitment to revenge at all costs if they were challenged, refused or otherwise beaten in combat. A while back they had seized a fort not too far from Kamandiyah. They declared they would then sell the fort to the highest bidder. With not many offers coming they forcibly sought employment with the Chief of a principality close to Kamandiyah but the Chief refused to employ this dangerous lot. In turn he made an alliance with Sarfaraz whose experience in dealing with mercenaries was well renowned.'[55]

The Makranis did not forget the Chief's refusal to engage them. Considering this a humiliation, they nursed this grudge, awaiting an opportunity to strike back.

Waori (also known as Vavdi) was a large fertile village on the eastern side of the Gir forest, and very close to Kamandiyah. The annual yield of the village was Rs. 50,000 and the quality of cotton was exceptional. The Chief of the principality who had refused the Makrani's employment reached an agreement with Sarfaraz whereby the village would fall under Sarfaraz's Chiefship in exchange for military and strategic assistance in dealing with the Makranis. When word of the deal reached the deadly mercenaries who had waited several years for an opportunity to hit back, they decided to lay waste to Waori. Jafar's courage in battle was now to be tested.

In February 1833 news reached Sarfaraz of a large number of Makranis approaching Waori. Sarfaraz had already stationed himself there with his 200 men and another 500 horsemen from his petrified ally: he expected a frontal assault from the outlaws. At the edge of the fields to the extreme right of the village, where cultivated ground became untamed forest, Sarfaraz had built himself a series of *machans* high up in the trees from which positions, camouflaged and hidden behind branches and leaves, he would hunt the man-eating leopard. But on the day of battle, there, relatively unguarded, he positioned Jafar and five Kathi marksmen.

As expected, the Makranis launched a full-scale frontal attack, with eight hundred men throwing themselves at Sarfaraz's forces. As a bloody hand-to-hand combat raged and the wheat fields were bloodied with carnage, Sarfaraz signalled to his son. What followed was an exhibition of precision shooting by Jafar and the five Kathis. Thundering through the air, each targeted shot sent Makrani horsemen to the ground. Panic struck the Makrani ranks and a general call to retreat was sounded. As they pulled back, their leader glared up at the *machans* and vowed revenge. Jafar had made a powerful enemy that day in the Makranis, with whom he was fated to tangle again. But that reckoning lay years ahead: for the time being, he had undoubtedly proven himself in battle.

Something had changed, however, in Sarfaraz's outlook: he now believed he needed to get Jafar away for a more culturally enriching life. Having seen his son's first brush with bloody warfare, the possibility of losing the boy made him view life differently. That year Sarfaraz decided to move the family to Baroda for a year. He had already commissioned the building of a house there. For Jafar, though this meant a melancholy farewell to Kamandiyah.

Something inside told him he wouldn't see his beloved Kamandiyah for a long time. The management of Kamandiyah was temporarily put in the hands of the four ministers. On Sarfaraz's arrival in Baroda, the Gaekwad welcomed his friend's presence in his town and as a matter of courtesy welcomed his advice on matters of state, particularly with regard to the army. Sarfaraz agreed to perform this consultancy, and the family settled into their house. As the year progressed it was the question of Jafar's marriage that became an all-consuming fixation for both Sarfaraz and Raja Begum. For Jafar, life was about to change entirely.

Back in 1829 Sarfaraz's friend Sir John Malcolm, Governor of Bombay, had paid an official visit to Surat. There, besides overseeing the administrative machinery, ensuring that courts of justice were operating with efficiency, and that revenue collection was in order, Malcolm also took some time to be entertained by key merchants and, most importantly, by the titular Nawab of the city. Nasir-ud-deen, signatory of the 1800 treaty with Wellesley by which he believed he had secured the fortunes of his heirs and successors, had died in 1821, to be succeeded by his son Afzal-ud-deen. The Nawab threw a lavish dinner for Sir John Malcolm and introduced the Governor to his 8-year-old daughter Bakhtiar-un-nissa. In the Darbar Hall of the Aena Mahal after a spectacular dance performance by the best *nautch* girls and a sumptuous banquet, in front of a large gathering of influential merchants and Company officials, Malcolm 'took her (Bakhtiar-un-nissa, the Nawab's daughter) on his lap from the arms of her father, the Nawab, and declared on behalf of the East India Company that he adopted her as his daughter.'[56]

Afzal-ud-deen not having a male heir, nor a brother, and not even any immediate uncles, made it clear to all in no uncertain terms that Bakhtiar-un-nissa would succeed him. It was Bakhtiar-un-nissa who he believed would inherit his title and estates. Many years later Bhopal would become the state where female succession would be recognised, but when Afzal-ud-deen of Surat had desired it, it would be mocked at by a large number of Company officials. Malcolm, however, having made a proclamation that Bakhtiar-un-nissa had been adopted by him on behalf of the East India Company signalled a sort of vague acceptance of Afzal-ud-deen's desire. But Malcolm also knew that his term as Governor of Bombay would come to an end and the Company could take any course. Looking after Afzal-ud-deen's interests, he knew well the Nawab's cause would need support and in time, the Nawab would be seeking a suitable son-in-law for his daughter. In respect to this, he raised with Afzal-ud-deen the notion of Sarfaraz's son Jafar.

Afzal-ud-deen was a good-natured and intelligent man. He was well read and had a strong creative inclination. Poetry was a passion and with that came generosity. Every Friday the poor would flock to the palace grounds and Afzal-ud-deen would personally distribute alms. And when it came to building on the family legacy, particularly enhancing the estates, Afzal-ud-deen would spare no expense. Caring and loving towards his family and staff, Afzal-ud-deen was in return a much loved man. But undeniably, there was another side to him, one which was rather prone to flights of fantasy, daydreams and indolence. His father having been stripped of power in Surat, Afzal-ud-deen grew up knowing he wouldn't have administrative responsibilities of the city, and focused instead on his household, the numbers of which he added to with great vigour. He basked in flattery and took great pleasure in imagining himself as a champion warrior, though in truth he had never donned armour, much less ridden into battle or witnessed its harshness.

Such were the flights of his fantasy life that Afzal-ud-deen asked the Government to confer on him an extraordinary honorific title modelled upon one that his father had enjoyed. He wished to be known as Jumrood Duola Kishmut Jung Bahadoor or 'The Moon of the State, the Magnificent in War, The Hero.'[57] His application was approved by the Company who viewed it as the mere egotistical trifle of a powerless Nawab and issued orders to confer the title. But when Sir John Malcolm proposed the possible union of Afzal-ud-deen's daughter and the bold son of the estimable warrior Sarfaraz, something in the Nawab's imagination was undoubtedly stirred.

In common with his ancestors Afzal-ud-deen had a passion for building and gardening. With great enthusiasm he had added considerably to his personal estates. To the Aena Mahal he added a new audience room. Then he built a new palace, calling it Hushmut Mahal. To the Mehmudi Bagh, originally built by Tegh, he added more poppies and waterfalls. The Dilfiza Bagh or 'the atmosphere of one which gladdens the heart' was a spectacular demonstration of bringing a single-minded colour vision to life. Afzal-ud-deen was known to love white and in this garden he only had lilies and white roses. The Nagheena and Misri Baghs were a wonderful oasis of palm trees, beautiful coconut trees, almond trees, banana plants, and small lagoons with little boats. The Kadir Bagh had an assortment of roses and around it were three large fields of fresh vegetables. Other gardens that Afzal-ud-deen created were the Afzal Bagh, named after him and rich with pomegranates; Hushmat Bagh, not to be confused with Hushmat Mahal, that produced only mangoes; and the large and small Dad-e-ilahi Baghs which meant 'Praise be to the Prophet' and produced a mix of fruits, vegetables and flowers.

In undertaking all these projects, however, Afzal-ud-deen had overstretched himself, incurring huge debts. Worse, his accountants were mismanaging his pension; and he had developed addictions to opium and women that further worsened his finances. The infamous brothels and opium cells of Shamshad Begum were now in the charge of her great grand-daughters Karamati Begum and Karima Begum, and these venues had steadily sunk to new lows of ill-hygiene. But the opium cells continued to overflow with custom officials, both English and locals, and Karamati Begum carried herself like an eminence of the city. (Her sister Karima, the more demure of the two, preferred to focus on the business's accounts.) While Afzal-ud-deen did not deign to visit these places, his regular supply of opium regularly came by delivery at great expense to the treasury. Middle-aged and chubby with heavy drooping eyelids that seemed to suggest a man overburdened by life's demands, Afzal-ud-deen began increasingly to wear the tell-tale marks of his addiction on his face.

In a brilliant moment of exceptional lucidity Afzal-ud-deen hired a gifted linguist and traveller named Munshi Lutfullah to bring order to his messy affairs. Lutfullah found the Nawab to be keeping the company of 'low, mean and reprobate persons in whose society he passed his time in laughing, joking and nonsense. He had become addicted to drinking ardent spirits in addition to the usual dose of opium,' and was especially ill-advised by a minister who was once a 'bread seller.'[58]

What made Afzal-ud-deen's situation especially delicate was being the only man in a large household of women and eunuchs. He had his wife Ameer-un-nissa and their daughter Bakhtiar-un-nissa; another childless wife, Badsha Begum; and a great number of concubines of whom his favourite was one Ujub Bahar.[59] This household was prone to tremendous and prolonged squabbles over relatively insignificant matters – ranging from the number of servants needed to who was entitled to the Nawab's time and attention, and to the ever-increasing sums dispensed as monthly allowances. The large pension provided for the vast household and the maintenance of the estates, was the only means of subsistence. This cash flow needed to be managed well. But it wasn't.

Despite his weaknesses, Afzal-ud-deen who did not have brothers or uncles understood one thing clearly – after him there would be a vacuum, and without a strong male presence in the household the splendid estates would likely fall into ruin, the household plummeting to the lowest depths of despair. The quarrelling between the ladies of the house, the concubines, the vast number of servants, petty ministers, eunuchs and dependents would erode any semblance of family unity and most likely permit the Company to manoeuvre its way into taking control of the Nawab's personal estates.

Dreading such a prospect, Afzal-ud-deen now committed himself to finding a son-in-law who would have the strength, resilience and boldness to confront any eventuality that could befall the family. He knew well that his daughter would need a husband who could stand by her and ensure her rights were upheld.

His first choices were two princes from the titular Emperor's Court in Delhi. He sent a proposal to the Emperor which was willingly accepted and the two young princes, Mirza Humayoon and Mirza Najaf, duly arrived in Surat. However, unbeknownst to Afzal-ud-deen, their own first priority was to sample some of the famed pleasures of the city. After a few hours in which they submitted themselves to protocol, the two Mughal Princes lost control and as evening fell they escaped from the palace and headed directly for the dingy hospitality of Karamati Begum, who provided them with opium and prostitutes and went so far as to service one of the princes herself, doubtless to her great personal satisfaction. When the princes returned to the palace the next morning, greatly dishevelled, Afzal-ud-deen was appalled. The Mughal princes were given a courteous send-off but any plans for an engagement had been thoroughly torn asunder.*

In 1833, news reached Afzal-ud-deen that Sarfaraz had moved with his family to Baroda. Reminded of Sir John Malcolm's recommendation, Afzal-ud-deen was further struck by a number of factors in respect of Jafar. The young man's distinguished Sufi lineage, his Syedi descent from the Prophet, his father's authority in Kamandiyah as approved by the Company, Jafar's own evident nobility and valour, and Sarfaraz's large tax-free income, all combined to make Jafar a highly eligible suitor.

Afzal-ud-deen wasted no more time and sent a marriage proposal for his daughter Bakhtiar-un-nissa to marry Jafar. Afzal-ud-deen was strategically trying to cover his ground on all fronts. Astutely he had embarked upon and achieved what he believed were strategic successes in securing succession to the title and estates. First he got an assurance from Mountstuart Elphinstone the predecessor of John Malcolm, Governor of Bombay. It specifically read 'Your Highness is the sole controller and authority in all your affairs and transactions and in the inheritance of your family and there seems no reason for the Government to interfere.'[60] Then he coerced the then agent at Surat, John Romer, who had also conferred that ridiculous 'warrior title' on him, to the firing of salutes

---

Mirza Ghalib and the Mirs of Gujarat (publ. 2003) on pgs 16–17 gives an account of this incident and so does *Sukhanvarane Gujarat* by Syed Zahiruddin Madani.

from the Castle in 1826 during the *Bismillah* ceremony of Bakhtiar-un-nissa his much loved daughter.[61] The *Bismillah* ceremony was carried out when a child begins reading alphabets, and could also be taken as a succession ceremony – this was certainly how Afzal-ud-deen meant it. Bakhtiar-un-nissa was to be his unquestionable heir and successor. But while these extravaganzas were playing out, there had been no official acknowledgement from the Company to the succession proceedings carried out by Afzal-ud-deen, or of the verbally declared adoption of Bakhtiar-un-nissa by Malcolm on behalf of the Company. And by 1833 Malcolm was no longer Governor of Bombay, having returned to Britain.

Afzal-ud-deen now feared that the Company might not accept a daughter as successor. If so, he wanted to be in a position to have a male heir. His strategy was to adopt his son-in-law and make him his successor. Sarfaraz initially accepted Afzal-ud-deen's marriage offer but then exhibited some apprehension and hesitancy, unsure in his own mind of quite what Afzal-ud-deen had in mind for Jafar. Aware of how absolute anarchy could consume Afzal-ud-deen's household after his death, and having received nothing in writing, Sarfaraz began considering other options. On being informed of Sarfaraz's seeming cold feet, a worried Afzal-ud-deen wrote to him:

> As the season of the grand and august festival of marriage has approached, I write to you in clear terms that you should have no anxiety of any kind and should not imagine the wedding to be the usual ones, for I adopt your child to be my son and appoint him my successor. The ceremonies of the nuptials are to be mutually performed. After the consummation of the marriages* your son shall be mine and shall live in my house.[62]

---

*Afzal-ud-deen had another daughter, Najib-un-nissa and Sarfaraz had another son, Akbar. These two would also get married on the same day but both would die within the lifetime of their respective parents.

This was in many ways an attractive proposal. If the Company rejected Bakhtiar-un-nissa's succession on the grounds of gender, then Jafar as the adopted son and successor to Afzal-ud-deen could be the next titular Nawab of Surat. As a couple, Jafar and Bakhtiar-un-nissa would inherit the pension, the share of city revenues and the vast estates. Jafar would also in time inherit Kamandiyah and all the villages Sarfaraz possessed, with the paternally inherited title of Darbar Shree. Visualizing his son in this position and the joint wealth the couple stood to acquire, Sarfaraz finally agreed.

The Company gave consent to the marriage but continued to remain noncommittal regarding succession. Afzal-ud-deen, though, believed he had secured the family on all fronts and succession was bound to happen. In the first instance it would be he hoped, Bakhtiar-un-nissa, if not, then his adopted son, Jafar. Delighted with what he had achieved he began preparations for the wedding celebrations. The date was set for 11 March 1834. As the day approached, hundreds of servants swung into action at the palaces, climbing up scaffoldings to wipe of any dust from the wooden peacock carvings, polishing every furniture piece, cleaning the tapestry, brushing the Turkish carpets, hands carefully navigating their way through the brushing of the crystal chandeliers. Stable boys and elephant *mahouts* ran across the compounds bringing order to their animals, brushing their coats, polishing their saddles and the howdahs.

The Dariya Mahal, as it did during Tegh's and Hafiz-ud-deens's time, was a spectacle that continued to astound the inhabitants of the city. This time its balconies were graced with Kashmiri carpets and cushions for the wedding guests. A special set of women, cherry-picked for their soft hands, were sent to the Aena Mahal to clean each mirror and the delicate glass carvings. Experts were brought in to decorate the Hushmat Mahal.

The Mehmudi Bagh glistened with the newly added waterfalls and cascades lit from the edges of the flower beds. The Dilfiza Bagh came alive with its rows of white lilies and the Nagheena

Bagh, which had a pond at its heart with blooming fresh lotus, was delicately nurtured to make it the most romantic setting. Afzal-ud-deen seated himself on the most prominent balcony of the Dariya Mahal as he and his entire household waited in silent anticipation for the groom's procession to arrive at the gates.

As day gave way to dusk, the silence of the Dariya Mahal and its surroundings was shattered by the sound of cannon fire. After a few seconds of renewed silence a relentless and thunderous firing commenced. These weren't the cannons of the Castle; and Afzal-ud-deen's ill-informed household went into panic thinking this must be an attack of sorts, until they realised that the firing was from Sarfaraz's cannons. He was announcing the arrival of his son.

Hearing the earthshaking blasts the women at Dariya Mahal dispersed to the windows and balconies to observe the advancing procession. A thrilled Nawab now couldn't wait to see his counterpart and his son-in-law. His impatience was about to be answered.

It was dark by then, and as if to bring light to the proceedings forty men entered holding flaming torches. Behind them were fifteen drum beaters who began a slow pounding as they poured in through the gate. The beat then slowly gained momentum and all eyes of Afzal-ud-deen's household strained towards the gate. Soon emerged a huge elephant with an open-air howdah. In front of the howdah sat the *mahout* guiding the beast's slow progress. In the howdah sat Jafar with an attendant behind him.

At 17 Jafar was having his first experiment with a moustache, which he wore with a slight twirl. He was dressed in a crimson silk *angarkha* and a long Hindustani coat also in crimson, the colour of his birth. A golden cummerbund was fastened at his waist. Around his neck were three large uncut diamond necklaces (a gift from Afzal-ud-deen) and a fabulous *serpench or* crown piece with a large Columbian emerald in the centre, (also a gift from Afzal-ud-deen). All around the elephant were Kathi horsemen with rifles in hand. On the left of the elephant was Sarfaraz – astride his favourite white horse, dressed in a white *angarkha*, white turban and brown tanned leather boots that ended just under his knees, one hand on the reins and the other on the hilt of his sword. Behind the elephant was a palanquin carrying Jafar's mother Raja Begum and behind her a retinue of servants carrying gifts for the bride ranging from jewellery, clothes and silver ware; and behind them the finest of Jafar's horses.

After the nikaah was performed against the backdrop of stunning fireworks that lit up the city, celebrations went on for another five days: dinners in the various candle-lit orchards, poetry sessions in the gardens and lazy boating excursions for the newlyweds. Afzal-ud-deen's joy at having secured what he thought was the finest possible son-in-law and successor was communicated in a letter to James Williams Esq, the English East India Company's Resident.

> In this time, by the grace of God, the marriage of my daughter has been completed with all propriety. The illustrious Syud (Descendent of the Prophet) Meer Jafur Ali Khan incomparable in dignity and ability. I am exceedingly pleased and appoint him my successor. I shall request the same of the Honourable British Government, and for the same reason I beg of you to keep the matter in your reflection.[63]

James Williamson responded.

> In this matter I write to you as a friend that I will use all the endeavours in my power with the Honourable Government on the object above cited. You should think of no omission on my part as a sincere friend.[64]

Settling into marriage, Jafar at first found Bakhtiar-un-nissa a source of much intrigue. He hadn't met a more demure person in his life. Rather petite, with long black hair, full lips and small eyes, she had depended entirely on her father, emotionally and monetarily. Growing up under strict *purdah*, hidden from outside presence, she had led the most sheltered and unadventurous life, the complete opposite of Jafar's. Traumatised by her father's addictions, so long surrounded by quarrelling women, she found Jafar's boldness and love for righteousness highly refreshing – likewise his regard for spiritual knowledge and his understanding of the works of the great Sufis, though this overwhelmed her at times. Jafar realised as much, and resolved to take the introducing of his bride to the works of Omar Khayyam at a more leisurely pace. In the meantime their romance proceeded apace: while walking in the gardens, lounging on rugs in the balconies of the Dariya Mahal overlooking the Tapti and under the waterfalls of the Mehmudi Bagh. Their carriage could be seen carrying them to Nagheena Bagh where they would relax in the reclining benches overlooking the lotus pond. This was an entirely new life for Bakhtiar-un-nissa and very quickly she came to believe that Jafar would be the source of love and all new adventures.

Afzal-ud-deen and Jafar also developed a fondness for each other. While Jafar was exasperated with Afzal-ud-deen's opium addiction and found him weak, they shared a passion for poetry and found a common hero in Khayyam, often discussing his works and reciting them together.

> *Why ponder thus the future to foresee, and jade thy brain to vain perplexity? Cast off thy care, leave God's plans to him – He formed them all without consulting thee.*
>
> *Drink wine. This is life eternal. This is all that youth will give you. It is the season for wine, roses and drunken friends. Be happy for this moment. This moment is your life.*

Afzal-ud-deen would recite the last with great enthusiasm, eager that his son-in-law drink with him, and Jafar obliged. Afzal-ud-deen, though, more commonly would get completely drunk, hands flying all over the place, and collapse face-first into the soft Turkish pillows, leaving young Jafar to escort him back to his private residence.

Exasperated with his father-in-law's behaviour once intoxicated, Jafar would at times be left with no choice but to seek more meaningful company with Lutfullah and complain about Afzal-ud-deen's excessive addictions and conduct in life.[65]

In this setting, Jafar, besides his poetic bent, also longed for the call of the wild. He wanted the smell of spent cartridges and smoking metal in his nostrils. And so he organised hunts of man-eating tigers in the forests and districts around Surat, Bakhtiar-un-nissa always by his side. The few years after marriage were filled with such thrilling activities led and undertaken by Jafar. Afzal-ud-deen's bickering household, plagued by petty politics, felt the great rush and uplifting energy of the young man.

But things would soon start taking a more serious turn at the estates. A series of events would embroil Afzal-ud-deen in laborious and troubling affairs. It began in 1835 when a drunk English official and two police peons in a similar state were found languishing at the gates of one of the gardens. When asked to leave by Afzal-ud-deen's guards, they responded with a volley of insults. Unable to bear the affront, the guards seized the peons and the English official and assaulted them. Afzal-ud-deen exchanged letters with the Company explaining the situation and the reason for the behaviour of his guards, but he received the strongest possible remonstrance from the Company and was warned not to cross an English official – so leaving him helplessly swallowing his pride.[66]

By 1836 the first real signs of dreaded Company interference in the private estates began to emerge. A consignment of mangoes were seized by the Collector of Customs, one Mr Pelly, who claimed that the fruits weren't exempt from duties, and further alleged that they had been sourced partly from gardens belonging to the Nawab that fell outside of city limits, but also from certain gardens that were not his. An infuriated Afzal-ud-deen decided to protest. In a fractious correspondence that went on for a couple of years, a determined Afzal-ud-deen eventually proved that the gardens were his and were exempt from duty. In this laborious affair he had an unusual ally in G.L. Elliot, the Agent to the Governor in Surat. Elliot was a man of courage and conviction who had become close to Afzal-ud-deen and had relished many a wonderful evening at the palaces, enjoying the dance performances of the finest *nautch* girls at the Aena Mahal. A meticulous and hard working civil servant, Elliot saw no grounds for Pelly's claims, and his word proved more influential.[67]

Afzal-ud-deen kept Jafar close and the adopted son began learning first hand how to manage these tricky relations with Company officials. For Afzal-ud-deen, though, such chicanery was sadly typical. He did not believe that all of the English were treacherous. Some were honourable and some not. It was a question of the individual. The rapidly changing Agents to the Bombay Governors were an unpredictable mix of British characters: some the Nawab could work with, others less so. It was purely a matter of luck if the Agent was sympathetic to the Nawab's cause or not. A new Agent inevitably brought with him a new mindset and much depended on that.

Afzal-ud-deen harboured great sorrow over the loss of Surat in 1800 when his father was forced to sign the treaty. Still, the enormous pension and share of city revenues promised by the same Company for generation to generation allowed him to pursue a life of leisure and pleasure which he absolutely loved and hoped that his successors could do the same. The lessons of how to manage the Company officials he now passed on to Jafar, who had grown up on stories of how Delhi had fallen to the foreigners now controlling the destiny of Hindustan; but Jafar also knew of honourable men such as Sir John Malcolm. Again, it seemed to come down to the calibre of the man himself.

The continuous pressure of managing the estates, the household and the English was taking a toll on Afzal-ud-deen. His health began deteriorating rapidly, exacerbated by the opium addiction.

A terrible incident in 1840 would bring the Company again

meddling in the affairs of the household. Abdulla Beg, Afzal-ud-deen's friend and minister, had been found guilty of corruption, embezzlement and all sorts of nefarious dealings. Afzal-ud-deen had by the treaty of 1800 acquired the right to try his servants and relatives; and so with a heavy heart he carried out a somewhat ridiculous trial of Abdulla. Abdulla managed to escape and took refuge with some Company officials, declaring himself an English subject. Afzal-ud-deen demanded the return of Abdulla. The Company initially refused and after much persuasion handed Abdulla back to Afzal-ud-deen who issued orders to throw him in a grisly dungeon. But there Abdulla took his life, driving a dagger through his intestines. Afzal-ud-deen was completely distraught that his old friend had met such an end. The Company took severe offense, and tried to unearth the case. Afzal-ud-deen resisted, saying it was a matter of the household and by the treaty of 1800 he was within his rights.[68]

Surrounded by all this despair and gloom the household craved joy and some excuse to indulge in festivities that might lighten the heart of Afzal-ud-deen. It was the birth of a child that did the trick. In 1840 Jafar and Bakhtiar-un-nissa had a daughter and such joy and love did the child bring with her fabulous gurgles that the parents named her Ladli, meaning 'the urge to cuddle'. The baby brought great delight to Afzal-ud-deen, who began managing his drinking habits a bit better – avoiding his morning indulgence in order to be with Ladli. Sarfaraz and Raja Begum rushed to Surat to see their granddaughter and presented her with jewellery and silk baby clothes. Jafar eagerly asked Sarfaraz when he could bring his family to Kamandiyah and Baroda, but Sarfaraz was sensing something amidst the festivities – something so catastrophic that it would need his presence in Surat – and so he dashed any plans Jafar might have made to go to Kamandiyah.

Celebrations lasted a month and the clouds of despair seemed to have temporarily dispersed. As a father now, Jafar felt yet more responsible and a certain sense of protection towards the household gripped him. He was witnessing his father-in-law fade and now with Ladli's birth the instincts to look after his own and nurture them for the future took a deep root. Jafar, Bakhtiar-un-nissa with the energetic Ladli in her arms and Afzal-ud-deen would go for long morning walks in a chosen garden, breakfast there and spend the entire day observing and playing with the new bundle of happiness. By 1842 Jafar and Bakhtiar-un-nissa had another baby girl and named her Rahimun, meaning 'the merciful'. She, too, was a lovely infant, of a quieter disposition, but with a perpetual smile.

In the same year, though, it had become evident to most that Afzal-ud-deen was struggling. His immune system was in shambles and it left him prone to any ailment. Weak and drunk on most occasions, he finally fell victim to the most dreaded disease in Surat – cholera. It struck Afzal-ud-deen's frail body with the velocity of a storm. On the night of 8 August 1842 the inevitable happened and Afzal-ud-deen died, surrounded by the entire household. The wailing that night was frightening. Women tore at their clothes and smashed their bangles, concubines and eunuchs cried and struck their heads against the pillars of the palace, each one trying to out-do the other in melodramatic displays of love for the departed Nawab. Some genuine in their grief, others not quite. Within hours of his death, what Afzal-ud-deen feared, happened. The women attacked each other physically and verbally. The vast number of concubines accused each other of all kinds of conspiracies, the wives hatched plots against each other and against the concubines. Both, the wives and the concubines hoping they would get a share of the pension and the private estates.

Jafar immediately took charge, ordering the stable boys and guards to send messages to merchants and city folk. He took a trembling Bakhtiar-un-nissa into their private residence, the Hushmat Mahal, where she could mourn in peace. The entire night she held onto her husband with the two little girls fast asleep in their cradles. Next morning, the palace grounds were swelling with mourners. People from all walks had flooded through the gates. The confusion, chaos and noise were maddening. Along with Lutfullah, the great scholar, Jafar began preparations for the funeral, only to be confronted by a horrifying truth, as Lutfullah noted:

> At dawn we broke the seal of the treasury, to take up some money for the funeral expenses, but to our astonishment we found in the money chest, nothing but vacuum, Mir Jafar Ali got from his own banker five hundred rupees for the funeral expenses. It is a most remarkable thing that a man having an income of nearly two lakh rupees per annum, had not, at the time of his death sufficient money in his treasury to defray the charges of his own first stage to the other world.[69]

It was a tough night as Bakhtiar-un-nissa, confined to her private residence, was so overcome by grief that she fainted in Jafar's arms. The entire night he nursed her back to senses amidst reverberating prayer chants.

The following morning people in the Hushmut Mahal grounds woke up sore-eyed, tired and still nursing their raw grief. At mid-day the sun's rays bathed one of the balconies of the palace in brilliant sunshine. Looking up towards the balcony they saw Jafar dressed in princely finery, hand resting on a state sword looking serene accompanied by Bakhtiar-un-nissa holding little Ladli in one arm and Rahimun in the other. Behind them stood Bakhtiar-un-nissa's mother and behind them all stood Badshah Begum. The silent crowd erupted. A unanimous and resounding roar went up: 'Nawab Zindabad. Nawabshahi Payindabad' ('Long live the Nawab. May the dynasty live forever').

But unknown to Jafar a letter from the Governor of Bombay, George Arthur was making its way to Lord Ellenborough, the Governor-General of Hindustan. This missive contained a frightening prospect:

> We deeply regret to state that His Excellency Afzuludeen Khan Kamrood Daulah Hushmut Jung Bahadoor Nawab of Surat died of Cholera without having any male issue. For the convenience of reference we beg to annex an enclosure to our present despatch, copy of the Treaty with the British Government in May 1800. From the 4th Article in this Treaty your Honourable Court will observe that the late Nawab was entitled to receive the sums of One Lakh of Rupees (Rs. 100,000/ £10,000) annually and in addition thereto, one fifth of the remaining revenues of Surat and its dependencies which we believe has averaged about 50,000 Rupees per annum (£5,000). We are unable to state whether these sums now revert to the British Government or whether under the provisions of the Treaty they are to be continued.[70]

After a few months of deliberations between the Governor General Lord Ellenborough, George Arthur and G.L. Elliot, the latter two recommending that the pension be paid to Bakhtiar-un-nissa, Ellenborough overruled them and made clear that the pension, would now not be paid anymore, and the only way Bakhtiar-un-nissa could be entitled to such a payment was as a bounty. And there was no reason to give the bounty. It was a clear signal to the Bombay Government not to make the payments. This is precisely what happened.

The Government of Bombay declined to make any provisions either as a bounty or as a right.[71] Ellenborough had, in effect, rejected Bakhtiar-un-nissa's succession on the grounds of gender; Jafar's succession rights as an adopted male heir also stood rejected. The large pension, the only source of sustenance and means for managing the vast estates and which was meant to continue from generation to generation was now in one brutal move stopped. Afzal-ud-deen's strategy lay in tatters. Nothing mattered to Ellenborough – Malcolm's verbal adoption of Bakhtiar-un-nissa on behalf of the East India Company in front of a vast number of Company officials in Surat, Afzal-ud-deen's unquestionable appointment of Bakhtiar-un-nissa as his successor by the firing of the cannons from the Castle and Jafar's adoption as a son and male heir and successor – Ellenborough, in one despotic move had swept it all aside. They did not concur with his vision for Hindustan. Every opportunity to loot the foremost families of the land would be his top priority.

The news hit the family like a crushing thunderbolt. Bakhtiar-un-nissa, who hadn't yet recovered from the death of her father, felt the full force of the predicament and fell gravely ill, leaving Jafar to nurse the infants.

Now surrounded by women of the house Jafar found himself in the same quandary as Afzal-ud-deen. At 26, he was facing his greatest challenge, one that would define the purpose of his existence. His frail wife and young offspring had been stripped of their means of sustenance. The rights of the family stood violated. Hounded by terrible thoughts of what might befall his girls and the estates, Jafar passed innumerable sleepless nights, sometimes pacing down palace corridors, on other occasions mounting his horse and galloping down the banks of the Tapti. His thoughts flew in different directions. Would the household crumble? How would the estates be managed without the pension? Would his daughters inherit dust and ruin? Aware that he risked becoming a prisoner of his fears, he still could not withstand an anxiety that loomed largest of all. He had heard it put into words, albeit in hushed tones, by one of the attendants as he paced the palace corridors one late evening. 'If he doesn't have a son, the Company might take Kamandiyah too.' Bakhtiar-un-nissa's ill health was worrying. For days she wouldn't eat and shake with fever. A few weeks later she was diagnosed with galloping tuberculosis. Jafar felt life closing in.

Unsettled by this terror, most days he would sit by the cradles of his daughters wondering bleakly what the future had in store. In fact, worse was to come immediately. A new Agent to the Governor had taken over from the compassionate Elliot. His name was Robert Arbuthnot and he would be the bearer of looming calamity. His first move would be the seizure and illegal sequestration of the private estates with the objective to publicly auction them and fill Company coffers. This would immediately lead to the confinement of Jafar and his family in miniscule quarters. Jafar would soon have to fight for the honour of his wife and infant children.

4

The Challenge, and Beginning of the Rise

Robert Arbuthnot and Lord Ellenborough, unlike Sir John Malcolm, were two men driven by a single goal – self-enrichment. In keeping with Wellesley's aggressive policy, Ellenborough desired conquest at all cost and wished to annex Gwalior and other large principalities. In due course he would be sacked by the Court of Directors in London for his high-handed and arrogant behaviour towards Indian princes, suffering public humiliation upon his unceremonious return to Britain.[72] However, in 1842 by rejecting Bakhtiar-un-nissa's succession claim to the Surat pension based on gender and Jafar's claim as the adopted male heir and successor, Ellenborough was laying the framework for the most lethal and destructive policy the East India Company would initiate and execute against Hindustani princes.

In time (by 1848), emboldened by the audaciousness of Ellenborough's actions in Surat, Lord Dalhousie as Governor-General would give the finishing touches to the most dreaded annexation policy, terming it the 'Doctrine of Lapse'. At the heart of this policy would be the motive of ruthless conquest. It would be a great tool that would aid the expansion of Empire. A Hindustani ruler not having a son as heir would have to hand over his territory to the English East India Company in entirety. There would be no hearing for any claims, no recognition of female rights of succession and no acceptance of adoption. Furthermore, under this policy if it was felt a local prince was not managing his state in accordance with Company methods, the Company could depose him. In other words the Company empowered themselves to usurp large chunks of Hindustani territory if the ruler did not have a male heir or if they opined that he was not the right person for the job.

The Company's reputation as a war machine towards the mid-nineteenth century was terrifyingly formidable. Having landed in Surat with a few hundred men in 1612, by the 1840's its army numbered quarter of a million, excluding its allies which included a considerable number of fearful Hindustani rulers, who, afraid of confrontation chose to ally with the Company. The annexed territories of Bengal, Surat and Carnatic allowed the Company to raise cash and handsomely pay its native sepoys and British troops.

As a build up to the 'Doctrine of Lapse' which would come into play in 1848, Robert Arbuthnot as Agent to the Governor of Bombay in Surat in 1842 regarded the pension as a pampering of the princely family, and saw his appointment as Agent in Surat as an opportunity to rise through the Company ranks. The timing of his appointment in Surat struck him as highly propitious. The Nawab had died, his daughter Bakhtiar-un-nissa had not been recognised as successor and neither had his adopted son Jafar, the pension had been stopped, and the fabulous private estates seemed to be there for the taking. Arbuthnot's primary objective was to do a great financial deal for the Company by auctioning off the estates for the best price. But in order to do that, he first needed possession.

As Arbuthnot waited for the right moment, Jafar busied himself in looking after the palaces, gardens, stables, mosques and dependents, with such resources as were locally available. He gave special attention to the three palaces – Dariya Mahal, Aena Mahal,

Hushmut Mahal and the large number of gardens including the Mehmudi Bagh, Misri Bagh, Nagheena Bagh, Dilfiza Bagh and others; originally built by Tegh and Hafiz-ud-deen and further beautified by Afzal-ud-deen. All eyes were now on Jafar. Within the palace the list of those who looked to him hopefully ran from the gardeners, managers, guards, scores of servants and ridiculous ministers appointed by Afzal-ud-deen right up to the close circle of those he held dearest: his ailing wife, two infant daughters, and his mother-in-law. From the outside, though, Jafar also felt the intensely watchful gaze of Company officials who had begun their interference in the estates during Afzal-ud-deen's time. Prominent citizens of Surat engaged in gossip every time Jafar's carriage passed: the talk was of how it could only be a matter of time before the Company made its next move. Keeping his nerve, Jafar began work with the wise Lutfullah to streamline the household accounts, taking stock of all assets and lifting the sagging morale of the underpaid staff.

Arbuthnot now began putting his designs to take over the estates in motion. He first put pressure upon Jafar to reduce the family's grandeur. For Jafar and Bakhtiar-un-nissa this was an insult: they were the successors and heirs of Afzal-ud-deen and the parents of his granddaughters. Their pension had been stopped and now they were being instructed on how to manage their estates. Jafar would have none of it. He had Arbuthnot's messenger physically thrown out of the palace gates with a message for Arbuthnot to interfere no further. Arbuthnot's ego had been punctured and he complained to Ellenborough of how Jafar had 'protested strongly against Company interference [in the family estates] and positively refused to be guided by my opinion.'[73]

Word reached Sarfaraz about the Company's impetuosity. Wasting no time, he hastened to Surat to watch over the interests of his son and daughter-in-law.[74] Of great importance to Sarfaraz was the cause of his granddaughters. As it stood, they were the heiresses not only to Surat's royal pension pledged from generation to generation by the Company but also to the private estates. Furthermore, they were heiresses of Kamandiyah too; and if the argument for female succession had to be won, then Sarfaraz would have to act. Sarfaraz's presence at the Surat estates provided much relief to Jafar. Bakhtiar-un-nissa had been fast slipping into a state of irrecoverable ill-health. High fevers, coughing blood and reluctance to consume food had led to a very weak immune system, and overcome by regular bouts of depression, she regularly sought solitude. But with father now backing son, a certain sense of renewed strength was felt at the estates.

Arbuthnot knew well that Sarfaraz was cash-rich. In a letter to the Governor-General he described Jafar as 'the son of a person possessing considerable wealth.'[75] So for a few months Arbuthnot held back, waiting and watching as Sarfaraz funded the upkeep of the estates. Sarfaraz had known this effort would hurt him financially because he had to keep Kamandiyah cash rich and also put money into Surat. It was becoming difficult. The Surat estates were proving too rich even for Sarfaraz. But it had to be done: Sarfaraz had to demonstrate that the family was running and managing the properties. Both Jafar and Sarfaraz were soon forced to borrow from local money lenders and debts began to rise.

Towards the end of 1842, however, Arbuthnot decided he had waited far too long. Having not lost sight of his objective to auction off the estates and keep the lion's share for the Company he soon got an excuse he could use to take control. There had been a flimsy and dubious inquiry by bribing some Company officials about the state of the estates and a possibility of a piece of the pie from some disingenuous people, trying their luck by claiming a remote and distant relationship to Afzal-ud-deen. Using this excuse and conniving with them – citing vague property laws regarding divisions, Arbuthnot, now decided to dislodge the real heirs – Bakthiar-un-nissa, Jafar and the two infant granddaughters of the last Nawab and bring the estates under Company possession. Rumours abounded about how the Company would get kick-backs from the auction. The *Times of India* would sum it up 'Instead of being quietly admitted to the succession, the daughter and son-in-law (and granddaughters) of the deceased Nawab were shortly after his death, informed that no further allowances from the British Government would be paid to them and that the refusal of the annuity was only a preliminary to the sequestration of the personal estates'.[76]

Arbuthnot's decision flew in the face of Elphinstone's assurance as Governor of Bombay of noninterference in Afzal-ud-deen's decisions regarding succession, inheritance and management of his estates. The Company had disregarded John Malcolm's adoption of Bakhtiar-un-nissa on behalf of the Company and completely cut-off the infant grand-daughters. The Company contemptuously now ignored the fact that the Nawabship had been hereditary for five generations. That they had 'no jurisdiction over the estates'.[77] That for 'several generations the estates had devolved entire and undivided from one (successor) to another without question'.[78] That the Nawabs of Surat as rulers, royalty and titled princes 'never adopted any code of inheritance to their family'[79] except of one successor down to the other. And most importantly that these so called relatives were utterly 'remote.'[80] Infact so far flung were these pretentious relatives that they failed miserably to demonstrate how they traced their relationship to Afzal-ud-deen. But to the Company these people were a brilliant excuse and tool through which they could take control of the estates. The Company knew well that these disingenuous people would never be able to prove their relationship to Afzal-ud-deen but through their ridiculous and weak claims the Company could take charge of the estates, auction them off and make money through kick-backs and a share of the sale. Bakhtiar-un-nissa, the only surviving child of the last Nawab who had been appointed successor along with Jafar, her husband who had been adopted by the last Nawab as a son and also appointed successor, would now have to watch as their infant daughters' birth-rights would be systematically torn to shreads. Jafar knew well of the bribing that was rampant in the Company offices at Surat and Bombay. He now feared the worst.

And so in December of that year (four months after the death of Afzal-ud-deen) Arbuthnot issued a public proclamation for the seizure of all the property of the late Nawab, including the gifts made out to his daughter and Jafar.[81] Arbuthnot had crowned himself as the sole authority over the estates. Every palace and garden was to be brought under illegal sequestration. Stables, horses, elephants, farm lands in villages and even jewellery were to be seized. And the operation was conducted in the most forceful manner, Arbuthnot hiring a 'native agent' who in turn sent out officials and peons in large numbers like raiding parties, forcibly tried to enter the properties. These invaders would come clamouring at the gates waving orders from Arbuthnot, on the pretext of providing security to the property. Loyal palace guards, unable to bear this insulting behaviour, would invariably end up scuffling with the officials. These attempted incursions became a weekly ritual and a stern test of Jafar's nerve. They included threats, appalling behaviour towards the family and blatant disregard for decency. Jafar would later write to the Governor-General, complaining that he had 'offered to the agent security to account for all property, yet when ample security was tendered to him he declined to receive it and persisted in seizing everything.'[82]

Having received no response, Jafar would desperately write again and go onto describe the Company Agent's despicable behaviour:

> I cannot better manifest the manner in which my family were treated. On the 2nd of June 1843 the agent wrote to the daughter of the late Nawab [my wife] to the following effect. "Forward me quickly a correct list of all the property of the late Nawab, should you not comply with my request, I shall be under the necessity of resorting to measures as will probably not please you."[83]

Within a year, Jafar having received no assistance from the Governor-General, Arbuthnot had succeeded in seizing all the properties. Arbuthnot's men entered each palace and went through every single piece of clothing and jewellery as Jafar, Sarfaraz and Bakhtiar-un-nissa watched helplessly. Soon all palaces were sealed, jewellery boxes were confiscated and new locks applied. All garden gates were locked and entry restricted. Every stable was sealed and horses and elephants taken away. Jafar and his young family were now confined to living in small quarters in the Hushmut Mahal with keys to only one part of the Dariya Mahal that housed certain personal belongings. These keys Jafar had successfully managed to hide from Arbuthnot's prying men.

Now having possession of the estates, Arbuthnot believed the Company was in charge of them; and that, so long as he could demonstrate for a couple of years that the Company was occupying and managing them, he would be in a position to auction them off with ease. Still, Arbuthnot knew he had to be seen to be doing this as legally as possible. So on 29 December 1843 the Company Agent asked Jafar, Bakhtiar-un-nissa and Jafar's mother-in-law to make an application and submit proofs within two months that they were the heirs.[84]

To add insult to injury, as Jafar was preparing the application the Company decided to conduct another terrible raid. The Agent wrote to Bakhtiar-un-nissa on 15 February 1844, stating that on the following day he would call at the palace, 'and everything which may be there you must deliver over to my care.'[85] As Jafar read this, Bakhtiar-un-nissa summoned strength and came and stood behind her husband. Holding him from behind and feeling nauseous after hearing the Company Agent's words, she began a slow decline towards the floor. Jafar held her in his arms as they both sank on the rug that caressed their feet. He then carried her back to her room.

Having received the Company Agent's latest letter, Jafar's and Sarfaraz's patience began running thin. Not only was the Company showing utter contempt towards the family, the officials were blatantly expressing a desire to rob the family of their possessions. Sarfaraz and Jafar both knew now that, whatever their response, Arbuthnot would reject all claims.

Seeking to out-manoeuvre him they decided on a split response: Jafar and Bakhtiar-un-nissa would jointly reply, but Amir-un-nissa (Jafar's mother-in-law) would do so separately. In this way they believed they would diminish the chances of complete rejection of all claims. Arbuthnot would have to be seen as giving in to something, and that could be enough to live and fight another day.

Jafar and Bakhtiar-un-nissa jointly wrote on 21 February 1844: 'Amongst the property sequestered by the Government belonging to us both and as guardians to our daughter a list is appended', they made plain, 'with a view to a speedy release of the same from sequestration.'[86] This exhaustive list included Hushmut Mahal, Aena Mahal, Dariya Mahal, Hushmut Bagh, Dilfiza Bagh, Misri Bagh, Mehmudi Bagh, Nagheena Bagh, Bagh-Junn, Village of Aontadra and a description of the State Jewels.[87] The Hushmut Mahal Palace was very dear to Jafar and Bakhtiar-un-nissa. It was the place into which they moved after marriage in the Dariya Mahal, and it was where Jafar kept his favourite Kathiawari horses brought along with him from Kamandiyah. As he would express himself:

On my first entering [The Hushmut Mahal], the Nawab presented it to me saying "I give you this place, may it be propitious to you", and I have ever since continued in the exclusive occupation of it. I needed a stable for my horses and the late Nawab built a stable outside the palace gates for myself.[88]

In another application made later Jafar would make a claim for his confiscated personal elephant called 'Hygauze', which was 'the property of myself and children and protest against being retained or disposed of by the Agent.'[89]

Amir-un-nissa's list, meanwhile, would include Kadri Bagh, Afzal Bagh, Seegumpoor Dubholy gardens, Dariya Mahal, a piece of land in Salabatpur and Daad-i-Ilahi large and small gardens.[90]

A few days after making these applications – which the family believed were doomed to failure – Jafar and Sarfaraz sat together in the allocated living room. There was a sense of desperation. The evening was fading fast, nightfall descending. Bakhtiar-un-nissa lay in the small adjacent room, sick and frail. She called out to her husband, and both Sarfaraz and Jafar went in. Taking Jafar's hand in hers, she uttered meaningful words: 'Let not the ordeal consume you. But let your struggle for justice define you.'

Sarfaraz knew what she was hinting at. They had discussed a certain matter keenly the previous day. Bakhtiar-un-nissa now looked closely at Jafar, who sat by her bedside.

The only way out of this is for you to claim all the estates and the re-instatement of the pension for our girls in Calcutta. Go there. Now! Arbuthnot is but an Agent. Let Ellenborough in Calcutta see you, hear you. Time is short. I want to see you win. Win it back for our girls.

Jafar could sense a certain sense of premonition in her fading voice, and yet he couldn't conceal his pessimism. 'I have written to Ellenborough,' he replied, 'and there hasn't been a response, not even an acknowledgement. 'But never shall I give up the rights of our girls. Never shall I give in to the Company.'

Unable to bear his wife's suffering, he urged her to close her eyes and rest. Leaving her side, Jafar and Sarfaraz went for some air in the little compound they were permitted to use, and Jafar pondered his wife's urgings. One amongst the others being that he should claim the title. Bakhtiar-un-nissa was reflecting on her father's strategy of covering all grounds to face any misadventure from the Company. Afzal-ud-deen's appointment of Jafar as successor was something

Bakhtiar-un-nissa wanted her husband to pursue. Bakhtiar-un-nissa believed that Arbuthnot was doing what he was only because there was no Nawab and while her recognition had been dashed, she believed her husband's adoption and appointment had merit and strength. And if he were recognised the girls inheritance could be saved.[91]

Jafar was now conscious that every possibility had to be explored to try to save the girls from losing their birthright. But nothing much was discussed during the short evening stroll that father and son undertook, before Sarfaraz retired to his room. Jafar sat alone on the courtyard steps looking into the dark night that he now found suffocating. Leaning against a pillar he shut his eyes; and in the silence his mind opened, a realisation firing in his head like a flash of inspired intuition. As a child his study of Ghazali's iconic method of education based on inner calling had signalled something to him in this most testing time of his youth. He had been aware of rumours to the effect that come the middle of the year Ellenborough might be recalled back to London by the Company, his arrogance having got him on the wrong side of the directors.

Suddenly Jafar knew what he had to do. It was past midnight but he stormed into Sarfaraz's room, waking him up by flinging open the door. Sarfaraz leapt out of bed.

'I will not go to Calcutta,' said Jafar.

For an instant Sarfaraz couldn't help but think of the moment when Jafar had desisted from pulling the trigger at the deer in the forests of Kamandiyah. Was Jafar backing down? Didn't he have it in him? But before Sarfaraz could continue in this vein of doubtful thinking Jafar spoke again: 'I will go to England. The Court of Directors there has had enough of Ellenborough. He will be sacked sooner rather than later. This is the time to go and be heard there. And I need to do this before Arbuthnot takes a decision of public auction.'

Sarfaraz quickly realised that his son had come to a powerful decision, a plan that had a chance of working. He walked up to Jafar, grasped him by his shoulders and exclaimed, 'Go my son. Let England hear you!'

Sarfaraz would ensure Jafar got to England. For the next three weeks preparations began for this most extraordinary journey. Sarfaraz got busy in getting introductory letters organised for his son, recipients including Mountstuart Elphinstone, G.L. Elliot, the Agent who had saved Afzal-ud-deen's mango orchards; and other Company officials he believed might be compassionate to his son.

Bakhtiar-un-nissa, however, was in no way favourable to her husband's plan. Overcome by Hindustani superstitions that the long voyage could be perilous and her husband might not return, she plunged into days of relentless crying. The household was a large one – Amir-un-nissa, servants, stable boys and the guards would gossip for hours, filling the ears of Bakhtiar-un-nissa's female servants with grim imaginings of how turbulent Jafar's passage to England by sea was liable to be. This, after all, was a land thousands of miles away, the other end of the world. What if the ship sank? What if Jafar fell gravely ill on board and didn't survive the journey? What if some Company officials hatched a conspiracy and murdered him on board? Even if he got there, how would he communicate with home? And what would he eat? English food was bad enough in itself, cold and flavourless, but what if Jafar's meals were poisoned?

As the day of his departure neared, Jafar dedicated most of his time to his family. Bakhtiar-un-nissa would lie in his lap with raging fever and a look of despair in her eyes as he caressed her head gently. And yet, slowly she was coming around to the fact that his leaving was inevitable. He had to go. Soon Bakhtiar-un-nissa demonstrated great strength in understanding Jafar's decision.

Jafar saved his kindest attention for his little girls for whom he was going to fight. Ladli was now four years old, and Rahimun, two. He made it a point to play with them for hours each day, chasing them around the small compound and putting them to bed every night. All along, he lived with a thought that he hoped to see them again. When spending time with Bakhtiar-un-nissa, he couldn't help think of those few years immediately after marriage. Such a delightful time it had been for the two of them. And now there was fear and anxiety within. Would he see his wife and children again? All this emotion he hid under a stoic disposition.

At this time in 1844, hardly any Hindustani prince had voyaged to England. It was almost unheard of. Most consumed by fear and superstition preferred to have agents engage with the Company both in Hindustan and if need be in England. By deciding to personally go, Jafar's decision in many ways was rare. He was going to challenge the actions of Company officials in Hindustan and to make a bold demonstration to their bosses in London.

Sarfaraz, in the meantime, had handpicked a team to accompany his son to England. The most wise and illustrious amongst them was Lutfullah, the great linguist, fluent in English, well-travelled, and a man with a strong track record in dealing with the English Company officials. T.J.A. Scott, a Briton, had been hired by Sarfaraz as Jafar's personal secretary and interpreter. Scott was advancing in age and had spent a healthy portion of his career with the Company in Hindustan as a civil servant. He had a passion for the country and had come to love it. Now in his early seventies, Scott had retired from the Company a decade ago, but had chosen to extend his stay, travelling to Kashmir, Punjab and Madras. His family were with him too, but his wife had put immense pressure on him to bring up their children in England. And so when this assignment came up to accompany Jafar to England as his personal secretary, Scott and family decided to seize the opportunity to relocate to their home country.

On 12 March 1844 at the crack of dawn Sarfaraz woke up and got busy ensuring all was packed and ready for this momentous journey. Jafar's wardrobe included silk Hindustani *angarkhas* lined with golden embroidery, his favourite crimson robes, and cashmere shawls to protect against chilly evenings. The Surat state jewels having been seized, Kamandiyah jewels were packed in deep indigo velvet bags, including diamond and pearl necklaces and *bazu-bands*, arm bands with emeralds and rubies. The night before, Jafar had slept in a bed made up next to his daughters, in an attempt to make as much as possible of the time he had with them before his departure. But on that morning as the sun's rays crept through the curtains into the room, Jafar stood pensively over the beds of his sleeping offspring. The two girls whose birthrights had been snatched by the Company slept unaware that their father towering over them now was about to go away on the longest possible voyage across the seas to fight for them. When they would wake, he wouldn't be there. Then Jafar bent over, kissed their foreheads, and turned away swiftly before the pain rising from his heart could reduce him to tears.

He went to his room, where Bakhtiar-un-nissa, too weak to rise, lay in bed surrounded by her servants and maids. He stooped and kissing his wife's brow then sat by her bed for a few minutes. These were moments of silence. Jafar looked around the small room. Afazl-ud-deen's portrait hung above the bed. Through the window Jafar saw the branch of a mango tree, bearing its first spring flowers that fluttered in the breeze. This seemed to him a hopeful sight, and he sprang up from the bedside, resisting the urge to look back at his wife for fear of possible weakness, and left the room, rushing down the stairs. With each step fear pangs began tearing at him. What if he didn't make it back from the perilous journey? Worse, what if Bakhtiar-un-nissa didn't survive the galloping tuberculosis and died too. His infants would be orphans. Searching deep within for strength he made it to the compound.

Lutfullah, T.J.A. Scott and the local physician Badruddin awaited him in the compound, surrounded by the entire household staff. Chief gardeners, accountants, the heads of stables and of the Nawab's *risala*, Hindu priests and Sufi mystics – all of them took a turn and approached Jafar, kissed his hand and garlanded him, presented him with lucky charms, blew prayers across his face and gave him words of courage. Sarfaraz held Jafar and felt his son's pounding heart, sensing the mixed emotions in his chest – anticipation, fear, enthusiasm, uncertainty.

Then Jafar's carriage sped out of the Hushmut Mahal gates, bound for the harbour, where the team duly boarded the steamer *Sir James Carnac*. The route had been mapped. The steamer would take them to Ceylon, where they would board a second, larger vessel, the *Bentink* to Cairo, from which point a third, the *Great Liverpool*, would carry them to their final destination.

The first few days at sea were fraught, as the steamer hit massive storms and turbulent waters while passing through the Adams Strait on the way to Colombo. Jafar, who had known such a charmed and joyous life through his childhood and young adulthood, was acutely conscious that he was leaving the comforts of the past behind and voyaging into grave uncertainty, for the sake of his fading wife and his children.

At Ceylon, Jafar's party boarded the *Bentink* for Cairo; and as the massive steamer turned north, its great iron prow cutting through the surging waves of the Arabian Sea, Jafar went out to stand on deck. Surveying the seemingly unending waves as they rose threateningly only to be countered by the will of *Bentink*, Jafar felt his spirits lift. The Hindustani shores were now distant; gazing behind him he could no longer see a semblance of the coast. Ahead lay Eden, Cairo and then England. Inspired by the drama of his surroundings, he felt a certain sense of happiness and anticipation. Being outdoors always brought out the best in him, and he looked forward to the challenge ahead, sensing that to break free from the stifling environment of Surat might yet bring out his best.

Jafar's revived spirits became contagious among his team. Lutfullah and he played chess on the deck. They learned how to eat with cutlery, and Lutfullah began tutoring Jafar in the language of the country of their destination. He also encouraged Jafar to learn from observing the English passengers aboard the ship: one thing that was abundantly clear, Lutfullah later wrote, was that the English were 'first-rate eaters and drinkers.'[92]

The long voyage threw up some delightful surprises. On one occasion while out on deck Lutfullah and Jafar observed flying fish springing from the water to land near where they stood; they excitedly grabbed some of the fish and requested the chefs to prepare them for supper.[93] On another occasion, as they sailed past the island of Socotra off the Arabian Peninsula, a large number of Boston birds flew in. Lutfullah had waited to see these birds, having heard of their powers of flight. Much to the excitement of Jafar, Lutfullah began a mathematical calculation of their flight capacity and concluded that they were capable of an astonishing five hundred miles a day.[94]

On 12 April 1844 the *Bentink* docked at Suez. Jafar and his team were itching to get out and see grand Cairo. Having loaded their luggage onto camels they took off for a tour. Lutfullah noted:

> It was the most enchanting scene to see, just at the verge of the wilderness, the lofty edifices and the golden spires of the domes and palaces shining brightly over the houses of the population of this city, the capital of Egypt ... Men and women are strong and robust and fair: and the eyes of the Egyptian ladies are remarkably handsome and most enchanting. Donkey riding is not considered a disgrace.[95]

Then came a chance to meet the ruler of Egypt, Mohamad Ali Pasha, and to share in a discussion on government. Word had reached the court of Jafar's arrival. Lutfullah noted:

> Our young master received a visit from a Mr J. Tibalde a man of rank and wealth and proposed he meet Mohamad Ali Pasha .... This morning I asked leave to see the Pyramids but to my dismay I was refused under the plea that I could not be expected to return on time ... Two pairs of valuable Cashmere shawls were presented by Mir

Jafar Ali Khan and then my young master observed about the well regulated government.[96]

The next few days were filled with adventures, including a visit to Alexandria and the hiring of a boat to sail down the Nile, a journey that offered thrilling sights of alligators chasing their prey.[97] Jafar loved it. He felt the same adrenalin rush as he did in the outdoors of Kamandiyah. In many ways he needed this burst of energy to re-ignite his zest for life and his cause.

Having spent a dozen days in Egypt the team boarded the *Great Liverpool* which would carry them from Alexandria to England. Engines ignited, the *Great Liverpool* stormed ahead. With each passing day the excitement in the team grew, Jafar rushing on deck every time a milestone passed – first Malta, then Gibraltar. While much activity took place on the *Great Liverpool*, including tea parties and lunches on deck, Jafar and Lutfullah remained watchful of the changing behaviour of the English. Closer to home they seemed endowed with politeness and civility, and appeared to question the attitudes of their countrymen towards Hindustanis back in India.[98]

With England approaching, Lutfullah accelerated his early morning tutoring of Jafar, running through what would be his conduct and clothing for each occasion, The list of appointments were reviewed: with Elphinstone, Elliot, and, most importantly, the Chairman of the East India Company, John Shepherd.

The morning of 11 May began with a slight chill, but Jafar rose early in great anticipation. As he had expected, this was the day when the English coast was at last sighted. The ship slowly turned and gave him a full view of the beautiful lush mainland on the left, and, to the right, the Isle of Wight. He took a deep breath, shutting his eyes and filling his lungs with fresh, crisp English air. This was the land to which he had come in search of justice, to win a hearing for his story.

Upon reopening his eyes and looking around a little more closely, Jafar noticed a number of other smaller vessels in the vicinity of the *Great Liverpool*, and so struck was he by the sight of a number of women aboard these boats that he sent a friend to wake and fetch Lutfullah. When Jafar's trusted companion joined him on deck, wrapped up in a cloak against the chill, he was indeed gratified to see 'several fresh and fair damsels of England of very dazzling beauty'. The only disappointment for Lutfullah was that there was no way to make the acquaintance of these delightful ladies. 'To see everything marvellous without being permitted to have any intercourse,' he wrote, 'is a state most disagreeable to man.'[99]

The *Great Liverpool* docked at Southampton. After couple of days of quarantine Jafar's team proceeded to the Union Inn to settle before their journey to London. Badruddin, Jafar's physician, overcome by the excitement of getting out into the city and seeing its markets, decided to embark on a discovery of his own. The poor physician in his Hindustani robes was stared at and followed closely by a mob that gathered around him, compelling him to return hastily to the Inn complaining to Jafar about the 'ill mannered over curious white devils whom he wanted to pelt with stones.'[100]

Come the morning, horses were harnessed to two carriages, one carrying the team and the other their luggage. They set out for London, and en route they were treated to beautiful if fleeting views of the English countryside, breathtakingly green and well-watered by silvery brooks. Lush meadows dotted with white sheep. Similarly they took note of each fine village, town and parish through which they passed. The journey took four and a half hours, including a couple of stops to water the horses. Wary of attracting unwelcome attention, Jafar resisted the temptation to step out of the carriage, choosing instead to peer curiously through his window. He observed bakers bringing out their fresh loaves – 'Coburg loaves,' named after Prince Albert, as Scott informed him. He took note of the farmers in long rubber boots, transporting their wares in sturdy carts; and little pubs serving local ales to the local people. But the beauty of the quaint stone parish churches charmed him most of all – one so much that he was moved to step out and study its architecture and surrounding graveyard at closer quarters. Moving on towards London Jafar's party opened the neatly packaged lunch prepared for them at the Union Inn. But the contents – seven lamb and mustard sandwiches, one for each – were a profound disappointment, and Jafar and Lutfullah ate their cold English luncheon grudgingly, hoping to get to London at the earliest.

As the carriages entered the city Jafar, Lutfullah and Badruddin marvelled at how street after street and square after square were paved and spotlessly clean; and at how the large homes of the nobility were distinguished by their large porticos and superior construction. The carriages then made their way to the magnificent Mivarts Hotel,* London's finest lodging, the exquisitely furnished destination of choice for visiting European aristocracy.

For three days Jafar and his team enjoyed the charms of their magnificent hotel. They knew a tough few months lay before them and their stay in the Mivarts provided the team with just what they needed to settle their nerves and acclimatise. Indulgence was the order of the day. Kindly advised by T.J.A. Scott, Jafar experimented with his first taste of sumptuous English breakfast: porridge with honey, and eggs, poached or scrambled or fried and runny on crisp buttered toast. Lunch was roast chicken or lamb chops with boiled vegetables. With his Hindustani palate inclined to well-done meat and spiced side dishes, Jafar was dismayed to find that the English seemed to prefer their meats nearly raw and their potatoes unseasoned, thus inedible. He found solace, however, in the quintessential English 'high tea' served at four in the afternoon: scones, thick cream and luscious strawberry jam, relished along with rich chocolate and carrot cakes. Looking up from his plate Jafar would see the English gentry nodding their heads in acknowledgement of the delights before them, and here, at least, Jafar had begun to see

---

*Later to be known as Claridge's at Brook Street.

some refinement in the culinary habits of the English.

Dinner would be a lavish spread on candle-lit tables laid with white lace tablecloths, accompanied by a musician softly playing the piano or harp. Jafar appreciated the customary starter soup of pea, spinach or pumpkin: his taste buds detected a similarity to the lentil *daal* he was used to. Main course would be game – rabbit, antelope or duck – served with the finest red wines of France and Italy. When dining, Jafar's party observed a strict protocol: Scott, Lutfullah and Badruddin took their seats first at a specially reserved table and waiting for the entrance of Jafar, who would duly appear in his robes and turban walking ahead of three personal attendants. On his arrival to the table his team would rise, bow, and perform the Hindustani salaam, after which Jafar took his seat while his attendants stood behind him. The curiosity his presence aroused amongst other guests was understandable; and requests to find out more about him began to mount.

Jafar, however, was conscious of what had happened to Badruddin in Southampton, and on advice from Lutfullah he desisted from public interactions, keeping his distance from the English, using his two secretaries and his physician as the first medium of engagement.

On the third morning at Mivarts, however, Jafar received a gentle-but-firm wake-up call by a hotel attendant that he had no choice but to acknowledge. The attendant had brought the bill for his three-day stay, and the sum was astonishing. The young man's indulgence had made a substantial dent in the strict budget his father had allocated. Immediately Jafar decreed that his party should check out, and private lodgings were taken up at 7 Sloane Street.[101]

This new address was where Jafar settled down to work with his team. The building did not boast a grand exterior. Its fascia had large cream bands, and the decorative arches did not seamlessly merge with the red bricks. The lounge on the ground floor was small, with big gold-framed portraits of Victoria, Albert and other members of the royal family. Two apartments were hired: one with two bedrooms exclusively for Jafar and the other a four-bedroom apartment for the team. The ceilings had ornamental mouldings, and Jafar's living room benefited by a natural fireplace (which he would use even in May to keep his Hindustani body warm during chilly nights) as well as two large leather armchairs upholstered in his favourite crimson and a large rosewood Victorian writing table.

Here, in these less lavish surroundings, work became the primary focus. Jafar laid out the strategy and got approval from his team. The primary objective was to meet the Chairman of the East India Company, John Shepherd, and to present a factual and passionate argument against the actions of Ellenborough and Arbuthnot. Success for Jafar would mean an assurance or an order from the Chairman to the Government in Hindustan to restore the pension and lift the sequestration of the estates. In addition to that pivotal meeting, however, T.J.A. Scott suggested a second-level approach, or parallel offensive – since no one could anticipate how the Chairman would react. Thus, according to Scott it was important to get the word out to London's high society about Jafar's presence in town and the nature of his cause. A proactive social calendar was drawn up, Scott spearheading this soft but specific PR strategy. The first meeting was with G.L. Elliot, predecessor of Arbuthnot in Surat. Elliot came to Jafar's lodgings in Sloane Street and the meeting over high tea was warm and affectionate, the two embracing each other for a few minutes. Elliot offered all possible assistance. Scott pushed for confirmation of the appointment with the Chairman, and other influential introductions. Elliot said he would ensure both. In due course the meeting with John Shepherd was confirmed for 30 May 1844, and another social meeting arranged with Robert Pulsford MP.

The days ahead would be crucial and tense. Jafar and Lutfullah began collating the papers they had carried with them for the demonstration to the Chairman. Locked for hours in their large apartment, the two assembled evidence relating to the Treaty of 1800, the assurances from the Company to support the Nawab family, the list of applications to Arbuthnot and details of his contemptuous behaviour. Scott advised Jafar on how to begin the discussions – namely, with courtesy and greetings, to be precise yet passionate and not sound too complaining but, rather, confident of his cause and the injustice done to the family. He emphasised the need for Jafar to communicate in a manner that the company Chairman would appreciate. This meant doing away with the Hindustani habit of interrupting when others spoke, instead allowing others to complete their sentences. Also Scott knew well that Jafar's voice, when excited, could become quite loud. He would have to be mindful.

Scott aligned Jafar's arguments. It was an appointment due to last precisely half an hour, and the most had to made of it. First Jafar had to begin with the predicament he faced and the perilous position his wife the only child of the Nawab and infant daughters found themselves in because of the stopped pension that had constituted a breach of treaty. Scott wanted Jafar to then give the Chairman the background story of Surat and the city and how it had fallen. He wished for Jafar to finish the argument with the illegality of Arbuthnot's possession of the estates, and to support this assertion with his applications, concluding by requesting a letter from the Chairman to restore the pension and lift sequestration of the estates. This was intense study for Jafar: days of rehearsing what Scott taught him, and poring over the treaty of 1800. Lutfullah, seeing the intense coaching that Jafar was undergoing couldn't help but lament the ill fortune that had befallen Hindustan, its fate now controlled by a few inhabitants of a tiny island:

> Coming from the middle of the globe to the end of the world, where the sun appears far in the south, as weak as the moon and the polar star nearly vertical where the country all over is fertile and the people ingenious, where the language and manners are entirely different to from our own; where the destiny of our sweet native land lies in the hand of some twenty-four men. It cannot be I'm sure without the will

of that Supreme Being that this small island which seems on the globe like a mole on the body of a man, should command the greater part of the world and keep the rest in awe.[102]

Scott then went to work in getting Jafar exposed to London's society. On the 24 of May, at the request of G.L. Elliot, Robert Pulsford MP organised a day of scenic drives and sightseeing. Earlier, on the Great Liverpool, Scott had asked Jafar which sights he was most eager to see and Jafar, who had heard much about English engineering, had enthusiastically mentioned the bridges of London. Thus on 24 May Jafar sprung out of bed early in anticipation: a four-horse carriage awaited him outside 7 Sloane Street. Dressed in a cream kurta and a long similar coloured Hindustani cloak Jafar rushed into the carriage and Robert Pulsford greeted him with a broad smile and vigorous handshake that endured for rather longer than either wished, since neither man wanting to end it first for fear of rudeness. The carriage then trotted down Sloane Street. It was a brilliant day on the cusp of spring and summer and as Jafar looked out of his carriage window he sighed in delight at the sights of the clean and beautifully laid-out roads lined with lush green oaks, lamp posts with flower hangings of bright pink busy lizzies and purple petunias, squares carved out for the yellow daffodils and blue lavender. The flowers reminded him of the Mehmudi Bagh, the Misri Bagh and the Dilfiza Bagh. What also struck him during the drive was the disciplined and orderly progress of traffic. Every carriage driver manoeuvred his vehicle with care and utmost consideration for pedestrians. As ladies passed, drivers gently tugged at their hats. Some pedestrians, recognizing the MP's carriage, acknowledged Pulsford with a similar greeting and the same was returned.

Then came the bridges: first the enormous iron bridge at Hammersmith and then the swinging bridge. It astonished Jafar greatly to see large masses of cast iron regularly fixed and cemented together. England, Jafar and Lutfullah came to believe, surely had inexhaustible mines of iron. On their journey to the bridges they had eagerly noted how every house appeared to boast iron railings and iron bars, and even gardens were hedged in with iron.[103]

Parking just before the bridge Jafar, Pulsford and Lutfullah stepped out and took a walk, Jafar eagerly racing forward to look over the bridge. Elliot had already apprised Pulsford of Jafar's predicament. Pulsford watched Jafar standing in his flowing cream Hindustani robes, gazing out into middle-distance as the Thames flowed below and St. Paul's stood majestically in the background. The Thames reminded Jafar of the Tapti in Surat. But the sight of the 'wronged' Prince in an alien surrounding struck a chord in Pulsford. Walking up to Jafar the MP assured him of any help he might need in the future. Pulsford informed Jafar that the Company was not unassailably popular in England – that, indeed, it had strong critics, some of whom were powerful MPs. While Jafar was not convinced he would require parliamentary assistance in his cause, the idea occurred to him that such help could surely do no harm; and so he accepted his new friend's offer courteously with another long and vigorous handshake.

At St. Paul's, Jafar and Lutfullah admired the majestic workmanship and compared it to the mausoleums and temples in Hindustan. Jafar and Lutfullah inquired with Pulsford about the purpose of sculptures and paintings in a protestant cathedral. Surely Protestants believed that worshippers should not be distracted from their attention to the sermons and Bible readings recited by the Vicar?[104] Pulsford suggested to them that the craftsman, too, was expressing his love of God by his works.

The following day's adventures involved a different sort of spectacle. Pulsford and Alfred Latham, a wealthy businessman, invited Jafar and his team to an Italian opera. Much was discussed that day about Jafar's entrance, his seating, and the clothes he would wear. Preparations began from morning. A light blue carriage was ordered with four black horses to carry him to the venue. Behind the carriage two of Jafar's attendants would stand, with Jafar seated inside, T.J.A. Scott, Lutfullah and Badruddin sitting opposite him. At precisely 8 pm when the sun was beginning its slow decline the carriage left for the Opera House. There was much excitement within as Scott briefed the visitors on what to expect. But nothing could prepare them for what they were about to experience. Jafar was received at the entrance by his hosts and entered wearing a black ruby-buttoned *sherwani* that ended at his knees, together with white tapered Turkish trousers. Around his arm was a *bazu-band* of emeralds.

The fabulous interiors of the hall were built up in splendid style. Five tiers of boxes wide enough to hold four to five people were on either side and ran in semi-circular lines. Jafar and his team were escorted to one of the boxes, opposite that reserved for the Queen. After much anticipation, Victoria and Albert entered. Jafar looked at the majestic couple and rose in honour along with all who were present. The brilliant gas lights that Jafar had been admiring for their strength were then dimmed and the curtains pulled up. What followed next was exciting to Jafar, but offensive to Lutfullah:

> Two very handsome ladies very indecently dressed and an old man representing their father appeared on stage. They sang a historical ballad in conjunction with instrumental music and danced very expertly. Whilst the females whirled around in their dancing their short gowns flew upto forbidden heights. Tantalizing the assembly being the principal aim by such a violation of decorum. We enjoyed the music well but couldn't understand a word.[105]

Jafar, though, was pleasantly stunned at what he had witnessed. His staying on long after the concert and engaging with other dignitaries was precisely what Scott had wanted. Jafar was working his charm, greeting new introductions with an erect body but a raising of the hand in an acknowledging salaam.

Jafar was also now realizing the attention he was getting from English ladies. A few of them had glanced at him flirtatiously at the Opera and had sent feelers to Scott, enquiring about this charismatic young Prince. Scott and Lutfullah knew that Jafar had been exercising a degree of personal self-restraint according to the gravity of his mission: he had crossed the oceans to fight for his family's rights and future wellbeing. He was, however, a flesh-and-blood male of 26, and one who had, perforce, been denied the opportunity for physical intimacy for over twelve months. There had been no intimacy with Bakhtiar-un-nissa since she had been diagnosed with tuberculosis. His sojourn in England clearly proposed the opportunity of an affair; and such an opportunity duly presented itself.

A few days before the most important meeting with the Company Chairman, an appointment was made by Scott for a meeting with Thomas Postans and his wife Marianne. The two had been in Hindustan, Postans working in Surat and Bombay for the Company, in their infantry. Jafar had met them in Surat briefly and Scott, learning that they were now back in England thought it prudent to strengthen another English contact.

Marianne Postans would bring another friend along with her – Rose Underwood. Rose too had been in Hindustan with her husband who had been posted in Calcutta. Rose was, in fact, utterly disheartened to have returned to England, for she had loved everything about Hindustan: the colour, the warmth of the people, the food and languages. (She had good basic knowledge of Hindustani and Persian.) A meeting was arranged with the Postans over lunch at 7 Sloane Street followed by a walk in Hyde Park. Rose entered with her husband dressed in a cream crinoline with faint peach flowers, cinched elegantly at her waist. She had a delicate round face, ruddy cheeks and a smooth spotless white neck. She lined her hazel eyes with kohl, knowing fully well this was a gesture to the Orient that only enhanced her appearance. Her light brown hair was tied back in plaits and further fastened at the back in a neat bun.

Her nails were painted rose-pink. Lunch was prepared by specially hired English chefs: the usual bland chicken roast and potatoes. While Scott and the Postans relished it, Rose had hoped for a more fragrant, spiced meal, possibly a Hindustani korma. Throughout the meal Rose watched Jafar struggle, too, with the local cuisine. The two exchanged coy smiles.

In the carriage on their way to Hyde Park Rose sat beside her husband but opposite Jafar and with enthusiasm she pointed out to Jafar the landmarks as they sped towards the site for their afternoon stroll. The carriage drew up at one of the grand entrances to the park, the Wellington Arch. As the party disembarked, Jafar stopped to reflect. Before him was the triumphal arch and a grand statue of the Duke astride his horse. Jafar slowly walked towards and then under the arch, looking up at this statuary tribute. The sun cast the master strategist's shadow on Jafar as the young Prince surveyed the image of Wellington.

The stroll proved to be a magical experience. With Scott, Marianne Postans, the two husbands and Lutfullah engrossed in deep conversation about the Company and the future of Hindustan, Rose and Jafar walked together. Hyde Park was at the peak of its spring powers. Pathways of stone were distinct and broad and alongside them were flowers of all kind. The display of colour was brilliant and it brought much cheer to Jafar and Rose. They walked past clusters of roses, some circular, others square. Around the flower clusters the lawns were lush and bright green. Fresh water sprang from ornate carved stone fountains as the walk continued under a bright London spring-summer sun. Of particular interest to Jafar were trees that drooped low, their leaves and gentle branches seeming to kiss the waters of the newly laid ponds. Rose explained that these were weeping willows. Exchanging glances, they both sensed a connection with the other.

Rose had wanted the presence of Hindustan back in her life, and Jafar was a compelling embodiment of her longing. He boldly proposed another afternoon meeting the next day, knowing well that her husband would be at work. Hesitatingly, she nonetheless agreed. The next day Lutfullah, Badruddin, Scott and the attendants were ordered to leave 7 Sloane Street for the day with instructions only to return at tea time. The afternoon was theirs.

The affair was conducted with a mutual understanding and respect for each other's station in life. Neither would expect more than what transpired that afternoon at 7 Sloane Street. Whatever were Rose's feelings about the gravity of the marital infidelity, Jafar was not about to be consumed by guilt. He was able to compartmentalise his emotions, permit himself the gratification and release of the tryst, and then return to the great matter of his real business in England. Rose, for her part, exercised a similar practical restraint. She wanted to now watch and admire Jafar from a distance. Spending much time with her friend Marianne she would learn about Surat. Marianne was more well read and academic than Rose and had a passion for understanding local culture. (In time she would write about Jafar's life in her book *The Moslem Noble, His Land and his People* – as Marianne Young, having remarried after the death of Thomas Postans.)

As the 30 of May 1844 approached, Jafar, Scott and Lutfullah accelerated the process of fine-tuning Jafar's presentation to the Chairman. The night before, Jafar sat with Scott. There were nerves. The meeting was with the man who controlled the destiny of 200 million Hindustanis. Sitting in the lobby of 7 Sloane Street as they watched the porter dim the gas lights, Jafar saw his past. He thought of Kamandiyah, and of 'the good English': Sir John Malcolm, who had orchestrated his wedding; of his father, Afzal-ud-deen the helpless; of his fading wife and his little daughters. The thought of Arbuthnot, too, came unbidden and made him even more determined. That afternoon he had received a message from Rose. She wanted to see his carriage charge towards East India House: Marianne too wanted to capture this moment, and record it in her diary. Jafar was amused and ordered the detour which meant swinging past the ladies at the Strand, where they would be standing.

On the morning of 30 May 1844 Jafar wore his lucky colour: a crimson cloak over a cream Hindustani round-necked shirt, with white tapering trousers. He carefully twirled the edges of his moustache and draped a black cashmere shawl on his right shoulder. Departing Sloane Street the carriage kept to its plan and sped past the Strand where Marianne and Rose duly noted this dash to his destination. Swirling then towards Leadenhall Street the carriage, making up for lost time because of the detour, tore along the thoroughfare and reached its destination on time. East India House was a palace, imposing in size with six gigantic pillars at the front entrance and a great statue of the Sovereign on top of the triangular fascia held up by the pillars. It had a great number of apartments, huge halls and long corridors. Taking a few deep breaths Jafar and his team walked up the stone steps to meet with the prime movers of the government of Hindustan.

On their arrival, the team was ushered in by two state attendants to a large room with huge windows, red drapes and a large gas chandelier. Sitting behind a large Victorian rosewood desk was Captain John Shepherd, the Chairman, and standing by a temporarily dormant fireplace, smoking a pipe, was Sir Henry Wilcock, the Deputy Chairman, who understood Persian well. Shepherd, 52 years old, wore a navy blue suit. Both Company officials greeted Jafar with courtesy and took their seats. Scott and Lutfullah then translated Jafar's compliments and greetings.

Speaking in Persian, Wilcock translating, Jafar began by putting forth his predicament and inquiring if the Chairman knew about the breach of the 1800 treaty by Ellenborough. When Shepherd replied in the negative, Jafar explained the details: the despotic stroke of a pen that resulted in the stopping of the pension and the outrageous actions of Arbuthnot that had compelled him to come to England to seek justice.[106] The fall of Surat and the details of the treaty were then explained by Jafar. Wilcock began to find translating rather a chore and asked Lutfullah to take over the role of interpreter.[107]

It was finally explained that the rights of the daughter of the last Nawab, and those of his infant granddaughters, now stood completely violated. Jafar hoped to stir the Chairman's and his Deputy's emotions. Neither Shepherd nor Wilcock said a word. For half an hour they merely listened. Wilcock seemed irked by the entire demonstration and, looking at the clock, pushed for closure of the meeting. Fixing Jafar with a look he told him he was better advised to continue his efforts in Hindustan, and proceeded to characterise the act of coming over to England as imprudent.[108]

Jafar and his team were shocked by Wilcock's reaction. Jafar once again explained that his efforts with Ellenborough had got him nowhere and that, besides, Ellenborough had done much to harm the reputation of the Company amongst Hindustan's princes by planning the forceful annexation of Gwalior, another large principality. Wilcock would have none of it and rose from his chair, walking back to the fireplace and lighting his pipe, continuing to resist Jafar's urging and telling him that he had wasted his money by undertaking such a long voyage to London.[109] Jafar didn't know how to react; Scott began to sense Jafar's impatience mounting. His voice was showing signs of frustration and he had begun interrupting and cutting off Wilcock's sentences. Something had to be done. Scott looked at Shepherd who was also clearly feeling the unease in the room. Shepherd then stepped in and took control of the meeting. He asked Jafar what would satisfy him and make him feel his visit to England was successful? It did seem to Shepherd, at least, that the injustice was completely flagrant.[110]

Jafar requested a letter that he could take back with him to Hindustan that would instruct the Government there to restore the pension and lift illegal sequestration of the estates. Shepherd, rising from his chair as if to signal an end to the meeting, held out his hand to Jafar and gave his personal assurance that only a small portion of the pension would be kept with the Government and the remainder would be restored.[111] Shepherd did caveat what he said with the need for a Board of Directors approval that he would have to obtain; he also made clear there would be no immediate issuance of the letter that Jafar sought. Jafar would have to wait.

Jafar and the team were left with a certain sense of half-baked accomplishment. The Chairman had given a personal assurance but it had been caveated carefully, with nothing put in writing. In seeking to lift the mood of the visitors and make them feel as if they had accomplished something, Shepherd had also bought time for the Company and rather deflected the spirited charge of his visitors. To further distract from pressing matters Shepherd hurriedly changed the topic and arranged for a tour of the East India Company museums within the building.[112] Waving them goodbye, Shepherd and Wilcock then held a second closed-door meeting. It was apparent to Shepherd that the injustice was appalling but, according to Wilcock, any act that went against the decision of the Governor-General could send out a signal to other grudging Hindustani princes to bring their cases to London. Thus the overruling of the Governor-General's decision might begin a trend. The Company had no wish to encourage such a tendency. But Jafar had begun something by voyaging to England and his case could not go unaddressed.

For Jafar and his team the next few days at 7 Sloane Street were all about analysing the meeting. They had mixed feelings, believing they had received a verbal assurance but nothing more. All they could do now was wait for a letter from Shepherd. Scott once again encouraged Jafar to attend to his social engagements and seize those opportunities to spread the word of his case. The social calendar was again ignited.

Scott arranged for a meeting on 1 June 1844 with another nobleman: retired Colonel Theodore Wood was an MP and knew Pulsford well. For Jafar this was an afternoon spent at the Colonel's house in the leafy suburb of St. Johns Wood, a charming stone cottage with a white fence, surrounded by large oaks and chestnut trees. The Colonel's wife had begun preparations for roast pork when she realised belatedly that Jafar was Muslim and hastily changed the menu to lamb stew. Amidst the soothing sounds of English songbirds and a running brook in the background, Jafar briefed Wood about his predicament. There was, however, a minor awkwardness to be managed. Lutfullah nursed a desire to emulate Jafar and enjoy an illicit tryst, either with the Colonel's elderly wife or, if luck would favour him, one of Wood's two daughters, as Lutfullah would describe them 'exquisite in beauty and adorned with accomplishments obtained from high education.'[113] Nothing came to pass in this line: all that Lutfullah received was a strict remonstrance from Jafar for his ridiculous attempts at flirting with English ladies. Lutfullah naturally rated this as utter hypocrisy from his young master, in light of the affair with Rose Underwood.

Then an opportunity arose to visit the Chancery Courts, which would be a notable first for a Hindustani Prince. Scott believed this would give Jafar exposure to and understanding of the English judiciary, as well as enabling contact with leading London solicitors. Word had begun spreading fast around town of this swarthy Hindustani who had crossed the oceans to challenge the injustice of the Company. But as of now, more than his cause, the press were interested in Jafar himself. Jafar's entry to the Chancery Courts was suitably dramatic. On learning of the arrival of his carriage, solicitors, barristers and lawyers streamed out of doors to catch a glimpse of him. In the courtrooms they even climbed on chairs and tables to see him enter. The Lord Chancellor received him with full honours and welcomed him as 'His Asiatic Highness.'[114] The *Times*, which had heard of his impending visit, would declare him to be 'a very good looking fellow.'[115] 'Certainly he is a princely-looking personage,' the paper further opined, 'and his features are of a fine cast.'[116] Jafar then spent half the day at Chancery listening to the proceedings of a case, seeking to understand the arguments and counter-arguments.

Behind the growing attention paid to Jafar round London remained the constant of his cause. Pulsford, the well-meaning MP sympathetic to Jafar, who had urged patience had also, in the interim, begun a soft lobbying on Jafar's behalf. Pulsford had spoken to other influential MPs and peers who were already aware of the wrongdoings of the Company and disliked the utter ruthlessness with which the corporation was going about business. It was the general opinion of these MPs that a large number of officers in Hindustan were menial men from lower middle-class backgrounds who had never known the meaning of good living, let alone luxury; and so in Hindustan their access to servants and large homes had made them newly arrogant and vain, inclined to treating locals and natives with complete disdain. On their return to England, having made a decent fortune, these officers would tend to embark on a pathetic effort at climbing the English social ladder. (A striking example was Robert Clive who, following the annexation of Bengal, returned to England a rich man yet failed to get entry into the aristocracy, these frustrations contributing to him allegedly taking his own life.)

One influential person who knew well of these menial officers was Sir John Bowring, an MP and leading economist. He disliked the Company, kept a close watch on news from Hindustan, and was among a number of MPs who were vocal critics of the Company's conduct. Jafar met Bowring through Pulsford and gave him a detailed account of his cause. Bowring was moved and, wishing to give Jafar a sense of the seat of England's great law-making procedure, took him on a guided visit to both Houses of Parliament, where he had the opportunity to listen to legislative questions and debates.[117] Jafar was not to know that this was a portent of how his own mission would reach its final, crucial stage

Days were going by without sight of the promised word from the Company Chairman. Matters seemed in a limbo. Summer peaked in England. Jafar would spend his days looking out of the large windows of 7 Sloane Street watching carriages go by and wondering if he would ever get anything of what he desired in writing. At times, utterly frustrated, he would take a drive to Hyde Park and sit until evening by the weeping willows pointed out to him by Rose Underwood. With light lingering in the sky until 9 o'clock, Jafar had time to contemplate the future of his little daughters. He was sure that Ladli and Rahimun must have been looking for him forlornly ever since the last night that he had slept in their room prior to his departure for England. What must they have been told of their father's voyage? The distance he had been forced to put between himself and his loved ones was a poignant thing for Jafar; and his reflections were personal to him, as he made these excursions to Hyde Park very much alone, without Scott or Lutfullah.

But he could not falter. There remained important places to go and eminent people to see – none more so than Victoria and Albert, whose acquaintance he would have the opportunity to make at one of the lodestar events of the English social calendar: Royal Ascot.

5

A Divided England

Queen Ann had a passion for riding; and it was when she rode past Windsor Castle one cold misty morning in 1711 that she first paid serious mind to the vast surrounding open fields and heath. Thinking of these as perfect riding country she commissioned the building of England's most magnificent race course. Over the years Ascot had grown to become the most luminous gathering of English high society. The Sovereign took a personal interest in Ascot, racing her own thoroughbreds. But Royal Ascot really came into its own with the introduction of the Gold Cup. Presented by the reigning monarch, this was the feature race of the day in which the Sovereign's horse would compete with special zeal. In many ways Ascot was the pinnacle extravaganza that brought English aristocracy together. Dukes, Earls, Lords, MPs, landed gentry and foremost, the Sovereign – all made grand entries at Ascot. Preparations for the great day began months in advance. Men polished their knowledge on the competing horses, and brushed up, too, on their current affairs. Ladies spent days fussing over their elaborate crinolines, specially designed hats meant to create a stir, and luring veils made to make a man's heart beat faster.

Here, as the thunderous hooves of galloping horses kicking

up dirt and sharply elevated the heartbeats of cheering onlookers, a great deal of varied business was also discussed. Ascot was the ideal hunting ground for matrimonial alliances among English aristocracy. When the race card was interrupted for lunch, tea and picnics, gossiping ladies would speculate on everything from the lost fortunes of a once-eligible Duke to the rising powers of a young Earl. Mothers of English maidens would keep a close eye on new prospects. Titles, land and property were all highly favourable factors. If good looks happened to be thrown into the bargain, then the package approached perfection. For their part, the English maidens endeavoured to glide around Ascot, making their way through chatting clusters, managing their flowing crinolines with grace, hoping to attract the attention of eligible suitors. The turf purists, meanwhile, debated betting odds, horse pedigrees, and new training methods emerging round the country (particularly in the counties of Gloucestershire, Oxfordshire, Somerset and Dorset). The most powerful attendees would discuss politics, elections, recent debates and new acts passed in Parliament, and the state of the Empire and its colonies.

Pulsford ensured that Jafar was seated in a private box not too far from that of Victoria and Albert. The hope was that the oriental team would catch the eye of the Prince Consort, a contact which could then be developed into an introduction. Jafar, his team and his attendants began drawing attention immediately upon arrival, just by their robes, turbans and sparkling jewels. For Jafar, watching the horses being led out of the stables and paraded before each race brought back memories of his own horses that had been confiscated by Arbuthnot. And as the magnificent beasts stormed towards the finishing line, he was reminded, too, of his carefree riding days in Kamandiyah.

Just before the main race – The Gold Cup – a break was announced, allowing for socialising and picnicking. As Victoria and Albert moved among the gathering, being introduced to several

Top and middle: The eighteenth-century Dutch (top) and English (middle) cemeteries in Surat. Both English and Dutch architects eagerly competed to outdo each other, adding a new dimension to Surat's skyline.

Right: Rising on the banks of the river Tapti, the Surat Castle was built to resist Portuguese invasions and stood as the foremost symbol of Hindustan's maritime trade. It fell to the East India Company in 1759.

Engraved for MILLAR's New Complete & Universal SYSTEM of GEOGRAPHY

A PROSPECT of the Castle of SURAT, a great City of INDOSTAN, commonly called the Mogul Empire, in INDIA.

Above left: Nawab Hafiz-ud-deen (r. 1763-90). His petitions to London regarding the corrupt practices of the Company went unanswered.

Above right: Nawab Nasir-ud-deen (r.1799-1821). Signatory of the Treaty of 1800 that guaranteed a large pension and his private estates to him and his successors from generation to generation.

Above left: Richard Wellesley, Governor General of Hindustan 1799–1805.

Above right: Nawab Afzal-ud-deen, titular Nawab of Surat (r.1821-42). He appointed his daughter Bakhtiar-un-nissa and son-in-law, Jafar as his successors.

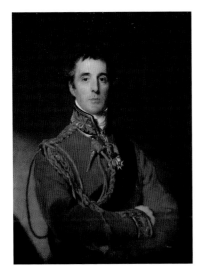

Above left: Arthur Wellesley, later Duke of Wellington.

Above right: Mountstuart Elphinstone, Governor of Bombay (1819-1827). He gave written assurances to Afzal-ud-deen that the Company would not interfere in inheritance, succession and management of his estates. Despite this the Company did the exact opposite.

Below left: Sir John Malcolm, Governor of Bombay (1827-1830). At a lavish dinner in Surat he adopted Afzal-ud-deen's daughter Bakhtiar-un-nissa on behalf of the Company and proposed Jafar's name for her future marriage.

Below right: Lord Ellenborough Governor General of Hindustan (1842-1844). He violated the Treaty by stopping the Surat Royal pension and paving the way for the usurpation of the estates.

Above left: Darbar Shree Syed Meer Sarfaraz Ali Khan, the Ruling Chief of Kamandiyah State. Also known as the old leopard hunter. Notice the leopard claws worn as trophy.

Above right: Darbar Shree Syed Meer Jafar Ali Khan. The Last Custodian of the House of Surat. He led the greatest legal counterattack against the Company to safeguard the birthrights of his daughters and expose its malpractices.

Above left: An ageing Ladli Begum. Jafar's older daughter and the granddaughter of the last Nawab.

Above right: Queen Victoria and Prince Albert. Jafar met Queen Victoria and Prince Albert first at the Royal Ascot in 1844.

Above left: Sir Richard Bethell, also Lord Westbury, and Solicitor-General of the Queen was amongst the strongest critics of the East India Company. His closing arguments in the heated debate in the Commons ensured Jafar's victory. Later nominated as Attorney General.

Above right: Sir Vernon Smith, President of the Board of Control, East India Company and MP from Northampton. Fearing defeat he pleaded with Jafar on the floor of the Commons for the Bill to be withdrawn.

Below left: Sir Fitzroy Kelly, MP from Suffolk, was one of the most revered lawmakers in England. His arguments in favour of Jafar destroyed the Company's stand in the House of Commons.

Below right: Sir James Weir Hogg, MP from Honiton and a Director in the Company. He tried to defeat Jafar's Bill in the Commons.

Left: Jafar's son from his second marriage, a young Meer Zulfikar Ali Khan in England.

Below: An ageing and garlanded Meer Zulfikar Ali Khan surrounded by his fierce Kathi fighters in Kamandiyah. Notice some with sabres tucked in their waistbands.

Right: Jafar's mausoleum in Surat bearing testimony to his Syedi descent from the Pophet and Chishti-Sufi lineage. In time it became a 'dargah' or shrine for the people of Surat.

Below: The mausoleum of Hasan Shah Pir in Kamandiyah. The sufi mystic's teachings had influenced Jafar immensely and inspired him to challenge the might of the British Empire.

Below right: It was on 30th May 1844, at the East India House at Leadenhall Street, London, the colonising corporation's headquarters that Jafar led a bold protest against the injustices practiced by Lord Ellenborough and other Company officials against his family.

Left: The Houses of Parliament 1857. Illustration after the completion of the Big Ben. It was on the floor of the House of Commons, Britain's bastion of law and justice that Jafar inflicted the first and only defeat of the East India Company at the hands of a Hindustani Prince when his Bill passed with a thumping majority.

Below: The Royal Society of Arts where Jafar sat besides Prince Albert during the celebrations of its 57th anniversary. It was at this event that Prince Albert first introduced Jafar to Sir Richard Bethell.

dignitaries, they noticed Jafar's Oriental entourage that stood out from the crowd.[118] Victoria had a fond regard for Hindustan and its people; and while she had not been actively involved in monitoring the Company's activities, a few murmuring of wrongdoings had reached her ears also. Now her eyes fell on Jafar.[119] As she and Albert approached, and Jafar and his attendants stood ready for an introduction, the monarch wore an unusually warm smile. Jafar and his team greeted the royal couple with the Hindustani salaam. Albert then inquired about the business that brought them to England. Jafar spoke quickly but crisply of his case. After hearing out Lutfullah's translation patiently, the royal couple moved on, but not too far before Victoria commented softly to Albert, who then turned slightly and whispered to his attendant. The attendant rushed back to where Jafar still stood and extended a personal invitation from Albert to attend the 57th anniversary celebrations of the Royal Society of Arts. Albert, clearly, wished to hear more of the visitor's story.

Located at the Strand on John Adam Street, The Royal Society of Arts had been founded in 1754 to champion the cause of innovation in British manufacturing, mechanics, sciences and arts. Its annual awards ceremony was an elaborate affair with Albert presiding and distributing the honours. The building enjoyed a spectacular staircase with inlay work that led to the 'Great Room' on the first floor. The walls surrounding the Great Room were arrayed with paintings by the famous English artist James Barry depicting the progress of human knowledge. Jafar, a keen student of Omar Khayyam and Vedas, was conscious that the Asian contribution to scientific advancement was now overshadowed by that of the West, and so the Royal Society function held much interest for him: the chance for an insight into how the West encouraged innovation and discovery in these fields.

On the afternoon of the event, Jafar timed his entry to perfection. Guests knew of his impending arrival. From seven in the morning the 'Great Room' began to fill up and by noon – the scheduled start-time for the event – it was overflowing with nobility,[120] including the likes of the Marquis of Northampton, Earl and Lady Dartmouth and the Duke of Sutherland. Jafar bided his time and then picked his moment. As the *Morning Chronicle* and *Morning Post* would report:

> shortly before the arrival of His Royal Highness, Meer Jafar of Surat accompanied by his secretaries entered the room and took their seats on the left of the platform prepared for his Royal Highness[121] The Eastern Prince Meer Jufur [Jafar] Alee Khan Bahadoor was attended by two native officers, all three being attired in the most splendid eastern clothes.[122]

A great hubbub arose in the 'Great Room' as people scrambled to catch a glimpse of Jafar while he took his seat next to that reserved for Albert. Seconds later, as Albert entered escorted by the Duke of Sutherland, the Prince Consort wondered about the noise that had preceded his arrival and the Duke informed him about the Eastern Prince's arrival just prior to his own. Jafar and Albert then exchanged greetings and the proceedings were set in motion with Jafar at Albert's side. Albert addressed the gathering, praised all efforts, and distributed medals for improvement of the workings of microscopes to machines that made ridged tiles.

After the prize distribution was over and social mingling began, Albert turned his attention to Jafar, enquiring about how he liked England and wanting to know more about the business that brought him so far. Jafar elaborated. Albert didn't give away much in his facial expressions. It was apparent that Jafar had struck a chord but Albert couldn't be seen to being too sympathetic. After all, the Company was English. But what he did next was to prove his empathy for Jafar: a significant introduction, made in the most tactful manner. First Jafar presented Albert with two gifts – a book on the works of Omar Khayyam and the Vedas – which Albert received gratefully.

Taking his leave Albert invited Sir Richard Bethell to inspect the presents and then, having effected the introduction, proceeded out. The simple social interaction would, in time, assist Jafar's cause immensely.

Sir Richard Bethell was one of the most influential lawmakers in England. A brilliant solicitor, he had gone up to Oxford aged 14 to read Mathematics and classics. A few years previously he had attained the elite status of Queen's Counsel. In time Bethell would go on to become the most powerful lawmaker in England being appointed Lord Chancellor and Solicitor General to Her Majesty, besides being an MP and the title holder of Lord Westbury.

In person Bethell was a portly man with a fast-receding hairline and long sideburns that gave him a distinguished appearance. He listened to Jafar's brief outline of his case and advised him to wait for a formal response from the Company. If the answer was in Jafar's favour, Bethell suggested that he implement it in Hindustan. But if the Company were not to respond, then Bethell assured Jafar of all possible help.

While hopes ascended after these meetings, two separate and subsequent meetings specifically arranged for Jafar by Scott did not produce such promising outcomes. These were with powerful executives of the Company, and Scott hoped they might have some influence on the much-anticipated letter from the Chairman. The first was with George Fredrick Robinson, Lord Ripon, the President of the Company's Board of Control (and second son of former Prime Minister F.J. Robinson). Lord Ripon, though, was a fierce Company loyalist, and he heard Jafar out with evident coldness, his final response being a mere shrug of the shoulders and the opinion (echoing Wilcock's) that Jafar was wasting his time in England. The second meeting – with W.B. Baring, Secretary to the Board of Control, was yet worse. When questioned by Baring on the state of affairs in Hindustan and what he thought of the Company's governance, Jafar and Lutfullah's candid views did not go down well.[123]

The tension of the situation had begun to wear Lutfullah down. He had a ravenously inquisitive nature and, feeling strained and burdened by the extensive lobbying of which he was such an integral part as translator, he pressed Jafar on the need for recreation. Thus, visits to Westminster and Windsor were organised during weekends, besides the long walks in Hyde Park. The team also went to see the fascinating Diorama at Regent's Park, a particular object of wonder in Victorian London. This beautiful exhibition consisted of pictures brought into view by an ingenious mechanical contrivance. The interiors, which resembled a theatre, enjoyed a revolving floor that gradually withdrew certain pictures and brought others to the fore. A judicious introduction of light and other contrivances enhanced the visual effect of the pictures, helped also by actors, making an optical illusion of sorts. It was a magic house, and Jafar's team found the whole experience thrilling, if also a little unnerving. Lutfullah recorded his experience like so:

On our arrival at this place of incantation we were conducted by the keeper into a room as dark as an infidel's heart and kindly seated on chairs. I say kindly for having placed ourselves at his disposal he might have maltreated us in this dungeon. In the meantime, our sense of hearing was gratified with distant music, and then a beautiful scene of frosty morning gradually presented itself to our deceived vision in which we saw a rough clownish vegetable vendor seated in his boat on the river, shrivelled with his wife and children. The motion of water of the river was nature itself and in the background was a palace whose inhabitants were engaged in various employments. In the meantime the sun shone brilliantly and extended his rays all over; and then the vegetable seller was metamorphosed into a pretty woman, the stars became visible and the moon rose casting her serene light over the scene. Then the sun rose again and we were presented with a scene of an empty church which filled up within minutes and then it became morning again and night within minutes, as they kept changing it was all beyond our comprehension. Thus half satisfied and half puzzled we returned home. Surely I would have the house to be under the power of evil spirits.[124]

The team also visited the National Gallery, and were further entertained by a renowned English juggler known as Herr Dobler. Much was done by Dobler to impress the Orientals. He produced pigeons from dry fish, set handkerchiefs alight then produced them intact – all kinds of tricks. Amused but not convinced, Jafar and Lutfullah compared him to Hindustani jugglers who performed without the assistance of light and sound in open plain settings. They were used to seeing such stunts as a snake being fed to a mongoose, its bloodied mouth seeming to devour the reptile – until, to the utter amazement of onlookers, the juggler would pull the snake out from the mongoose's tail. On special occasions Hindustani jugglers would appear to slit the throats of their wives in public view, only to produce the ladies for inspection, alive and well. By comparison Herrr Dobler could only be a disappointment.[125]

Agreeing to Lutfullah's urging to keep the recreation going, Jafar ensured regular visits to the theatre. Prince Alexis Soltikoff of Russia, whom Jafar had met at the opera, had interested Jafar with his knowledge of Hindustan acquired on visits Travancore, as well as with his great collection of art. The Prince was invited to Astley's Theatre by Jafar, and a private box engaged. During the performance Lutfullah couldn't control his customary excitement at watching the 'very pretty fairy-like damsels with smiling countenances that jumped on horses and stood on them smiling all along.'[126] Jafar was displeased with Lutfullah's exuberance and warned him, once again, to get a grip on himself.

Entertainment done for the time being, the team then began preparations for another vital engagement: one where Jafar would meet his strongest English allies.

Lord Ashley (later to become Earl of Shaftesbury) was a highly distinguished Tory MP. Jafar had met him at Ascot and now had an invitation to a select evening party at the Lord's residence. Tall, lean, and sharp-featured, Ashley was a loyal supporter of the Duke of Wellington. Lobbying Ashley's support would be crucial. Scott knew how important this meeting was and began preparations well in advance. He coached Jafar on what needed to be said, the way it should be said, and whom he should address, keeping in mind that other MPs would be present. While certain lawmakers were evidently sympathetic to Jafar, the example of powerful Company loyalists like Wilcock, Lord Ripon and W.B. Baring showed that many others were not. So it would be important for Jafar to first try to gauge the views on the Company of anyone to whom he spoke.

Arriving at 6.30 pm Jafar was personally received by Ashley and his wife with great courtesy.[127] As the evening gathered momentum out in the garden and deep discussions began with regard to politics and the state of Hindustan, Jafar and Scott listened closely. There seemed to be some indications of discontent with the way the Company was conducting its affairs. While Ashley maintained a restrained silence, two rather distinguished-looking Englishmen launched a tirade against the Company. An opportunity presented itself, and Scott, looking first at Ashley and then Jafar, mentioned that the Eastern Prince's opinion on the matter might be of considerable interest.

Jafar then took centre-stage, with Scott by his side for translation. He spoke boldly about the Company's misconduct, knowing well that he was now talking to a sympathetic audience while taking care not to offend English sentiments. He drew a distinction between the Company and the English in general. Diplomatically mixing his words and examples, he spoke highly of Sir John Malcolm who had worked tirelessly with local Hindustanis in Gujarat to drive out the ill of girl-child infanticide. But he was scathing about the Company's practices when it came to the honouring of treaties, which led him naturally enough to an account of his own case. He was soon surrounded by eager guests wanting to know more. The two Englishmen who had already made plain their disapproval of Company conduct now heard Jafar out with rapt attention.

They were Sir Fitzroy Kelly and Sir Erskine Perry. Kelly, MP for Cambridge and on the way to becoming Solicitor General to the Queen was a 48-year-old Oxonian with a receding hairline and large tufts of silver hair hanging from the sides of his head. He enjoyed the finest reputation as a practitioner of criminal law but was kept most busy with cases of a commercial nature. His passion for law was demonstrably immense and he was famed as an impactful orator.

Sir Erskine Perry, meanwhile, was a Charterhouse School and Cambridge man, and a former judge in the Supreme Court in Hindustan, now 38 years old. Immensely knowledgeable about the affairs in Hindustan and the Company's rise, Perry knew well about the practices of Lord Ellenborough, whom he didn't much like and whose imminent sacking he was aware of. What made Perry a yet more useful contact to Jafar was his speciality in cases regarding property rights for women.

Jafar, having captured the attention of these two powerful lawmaker–politicians, then moved round the room with Scott and Lutfullah and was introduced by Lord Ashley to others: among them Viscount Jocelyn, one of the youngest MPs in the Commons, from King's Lynn. Having fought in the Opium Wars Jocelyn was known to be a brave soldier, and he engaged in deep conversation with Jafar about Hindustan. After a dinner of pumpkin soup, venison steak and Eve's pudding made with baked apple and rich cream dressing, the men were led by Lord Ashley to the smoking room. Here Jafar was approached anew by Sir Fitzroy Kelly and Sir Erskine Perry. All three, helped by Scott's translating, fell to a deeper discussion of Jafar's business. Listening closely, both politicians were mortified to hear of how the Company had behaved in Surat, and of the tragic fate that might befall Jafar's infant girls being stripped of their inheritance. Every detail was discussed, key points of the treaty strongly emphasised by Jafar. Both Englishmen immediately offered him legal help if necessary. But first, just as Bethell had recommended, they felt he was best advised to wait for the Company Chairman's response and then get it implemented in Hindustan if it was in his favour. The discussion was concluded with handshakes as coffee and chocolate was served. But just at the same moment the strange sound of some kerfuffle seemed to emanate from the adjacent room, accompanied by female laughter.

The seriousness of the smoking room gave way to curiosity and the men investigated next door, there to find Lutfullah prancing around the young Viscount Jocelyn's wife in the most ridiculous manner. Having played a couple of games of chess with the wife whom Lutfullah thought was 'loveliest of English beauties' and claiming to have purposely lost the chess game to this nymph of paradise' Lutfullah, with a few drinks under his belt, had embarked on the most bizarre attempt at outright flirtation.[128] He had executed a number of Hindustani dance steps in the hope that this performance might incline the lady to see him again in private. Happily, the gathering saw the funny side of Lutfullah's outlandish behaviour.

In the carriage back to 7 Sloane Street, however, Lutfullah had to face Jafar's wrath. His extraordinary manners had to be reined in, his blatant and desperate desire for an affair with an English lady needed to be suppressed, lest it have an adverse effect on Jafar's mission in England. Lutfullah riposted by reminding Jafar of his affair with Rose Underwood while his wife lay so gravely ill in Surat. Exasperated and angry Jafar whispered to Scott who in turn ordered a change of direction for the carriage. But as they sped onward, Scott began to look nervous. Even the carriage driver hesitated and re-checked their intended destination: Covent Garden, and the nearby Seven Dials.

This was a notorious 'red light' district where prostitution was the main activity for the nocturnal, with the attendant presence of criminal gangs and muggers. As Jafar's carriage neared Seven Dials, the air of dirt, deprivation and depravity grew visible and palpable: dead cats strewn in open sewers, the odour of gin and rotting vegetables overflowing from sacks made the air unbearable. Prostitutes lining the pavements lunged at the carriage with such aggressive gestures that it seemed like an attack. Looking out of the window Lutfullah broke into a cold sweat. At the other side Scott saw a gang of menacing men approach. Jafar then produced a five-pound note, pressed it into Lutfullah's hand and ordered him to get out and find the means to satisfy his urges. Panicking, nearly in tears, Lutfullah begged forgiveness and vowed never again to chance his luck with a married English woman. To the relief of all, not least the driver and the anxious attendants standing at the back of the carriage, Jafar gave the order to head home.

—

August was far advanced yet still there was no letter to Jafar from the Company. Expenses were mounting. Jafar was exceeding Sarfaraz's budget. Frustration mounted at 7 Sloane Street. Lutfullah confined himself to loitering the streets aimlessly, keeping a distance from Jafar. The Hindustani Prince spent his days wandering in Kensington Park, admiring nature as a means to counter the turbulence he felt within. But the immense pressure that came with being heir apparent to Kamandiyah and the last custodian of the House of Surat was telling on Jafar. His consternation began to express itself both through a marked indulgence in food and alcohol, and in flashes of quick temper.

Whitebait was a culinary craze at the time. Large shoals of little whitebait fish could be fished from the Thames, then fried with vinegar and served for consumption whole. It had become a fashion for politicians, among others, to take steamers up the river and to lodge at popular inns and taverns on the riverbank where whitebait dinners were a speciality. The Company had built its very own Brunswick Hotel and Tavern for such a purpose. Politicians who opposed the Company, however, would be more likely found enjoying whitebait at the Trafalgar Tavern in Greenwich, built on the site of the Old George Inn in the year of Victoria's ascension in 1837, with river and bay views from the balconies and dining room. Nelson's statue was at the entrance and portraits of His Lordship hung from every wall. It was at the Trafalgar Tavern that Robert Pulsford entertained Jafar and Lutfullah, who each consumed a couple of kilos' worth of the little fishes.[129]

Most evenings Jafar would read Omar Khayyam and drink wine steadily, a mixture that put his head in a spin. Lutfullah would hear Jafar reciting the master poet's verses and then screaming out loud in frustration. Fearing Jafar's growing anger, his usual practice was to leave the building awhile and take long walks; otherwise to confine himself to his apartment and avoid engagement with Jafar unless specifically requested. It was uncharacteristic behaviour on Jafar's part, not how he had been raised. He was of Sufi incline and yet circumstances were bringing out an unhappy dimension to his personality.

Scott spent a great deal of time listening to Jafar vent his inner furies, typified by a barrage of expletives aimed in the direction of the Company officials, Arbuthnot and Wilcock most especially. Scott's preference was to let the young Prince expend his feelings in this way, a form of therapy, after which Scott could calm him and encourage him to press on with the duties of further lobbying meetings that Scott was arranging. One such was with Lord Bloomfield, 80-year-old former MP for Plymouth and private secretary to George IV. Aged and frail but wise, Bloomfield gave Jafar a courteous hearing and categorically proposed taking legal action against the Company.

By the end of August, having still not heard from the Chairman, Jafar wrote to him:

It can never be the intention of your Honourable Court to cause the descendants of an ancient house to be reduced to poverty. The circumstances afford the reason why the Begum [my wife Bakhtiar-un-nissa] and her family should enjoy a really liberal pension. On the occurrence of the death of the Nawab, I undertook the maintenance of the dependents, attendants, servants, horses, elephants &c. belonging to the estates. In this great expenses were occurred and it became necessary to borrow money. The Nawab being in debt. Under the circumstances I confidently hope that the allowance assigned to the Begum [my wife Bakhtiar-un-nissa] will be granted in perpetuity I make the following requests which I recently made in a verbal consideration to you. – The family to be treated on all occasions with respect and distinction and the property of the begum's [my wife Bakhtiar-un-nissa's] father both real and personal be made over to her and released from sequestration.[130]

Early September brought with it the shades of autumn, the turning of the leaves to orange, red and yellow and the gentle shedding of the trees as to make thick coloured carpets around the base of every tree trunk. Summer had faded, and a crisp chill attended London's misty mornings and quickening nights. Jafar and Lutfullah walked in the parks every day, draped in their cashmere shawls, with Badruddin the physician and the attendants. For one such walk in Kensington Park Scott invited Marianne Postans and her husband. Thomas Postans, who had a great interest in archeology, spoke at length to Scott and Lutfullah about Egypt and Hindustan and his desire to go back to the latter. But the topic soon turned to Surat. Marianne had loved the port-city and wished to return. She wanted also to dedicate the next few years to pursuing her writing interests, paramount among them a work concerning life in Surat. There was reason to hope these dreams would be realised, and that Marianne's relations with Jafar would deepen, albeit in a platonic manner.

The walk was suddenly interrupted by a rushing attendant. Instructions had been left with the porter at 7 Sloane Street to send an errand boy to find Jafar if ever a letter from the Company came. Such a letter had now arrived. Bidding the Postans farewell, Jafar rushed back. There were, in fact, two letters: one from the Chairman and the other from the Court of Directors. Jafar and Lutfullah clustered around Scott in Jafar's apartment as he opened the Chairman's letter (addressed to the Government in Bombay and to Jafar) and read aloud, Lutfullah translating:

4th September 1844

We transmit a copy of the letter that has been addressed to us by Meer Jafur Alee Khan with regards to the requests preferred by Meer Jafur Alee Khan on behalf of his wife, Bakhtiar-un-nissa Begum, the extent to which they can be properly complied with will depend upon the rights according to law or usage of the Begum. You, will we have no doubt deal liberally with the family. We are not anxious that any larger portion of the pension Rs. 150,000 (£15,000) should be saved to Government.

Signed John Shepherd and Henry Wilcock, Chairman and Deputy Chairman[131]

Jafar's instant reaction was a kind of restrained joy. Hoping to hear more, he urged Scott to carry on reading. But there was nothing else of note to the letter, and certainly no mention of lifting the illegal sequestration of the estates. Grabbing the other letter from the Court of Directors, Jafar handed it to Scott, who tore open the envelope and began reading:

Whilst the Court must decline any discussion respecting the grounds of their decision against the claims of Bakhtiar-un-nissa Begum to inherit the dignity, stipends of the late Nawab of Surat, they are most desirous that the relations and connexion of his late Excellency should not only be liberally provided for but treated with consideration due to the high rank of the family.

Court of Directors[132]

Disappointment now descended on Jafar. The Company had acknowledged that the family needed to be treated with dignity but there was no specific amount mentioned regarding the pension. The full pension, it seemed, would not be restored. The word 'liberally' had been used, the interpretation of which was left to the Bombay Government – to the likes of Arbuthnot, in other words. There was also no mention of the pension being re-instated for perpetuity per the provisions of the Treaty of 1800. What was most crushing, though, was the way the letters had completely ignored the matter of the sequestered estates.

The letters contained honeyed words but nothing more substantive. It seemed that all of Jafar's efforts had been futile. It was also apparent that while Shepherd, the Chairman, had felt for Jafar's cause and recognised a clear injustice, he had been prevailed upon to uphold the Governor-General's decision by his vigorous deputy Wilcock – the man who had so aggressively rebuffed Jafar during the meeting on 30 May, insisting he go home and pursue his claims in Hindustan. Wilcock surely seemed to have got his way in ensuring the Company Directors did not heed Jafar's plea. It was quite plain that Wilcock did not want to set a precedent of Hindustani princes coming to London to successfully claim on grievances; and that he had impressed this point hard upon the Court of Directors.

Ripon and Baring, too, had played their parts. As President of the Board of Control and Secretary to the Board they had agreed with Wilcock and worked towards ensuring the Directors did not overturn the decision of the Governor-General in Hindustan. Still, they had reckoned with the exceptional circumstances of a Hindustani Prince voyaging to London to petition the Chairman, and had worded the letters with sentences intended to appease Jafar. In the end they left it to the authorities in Hindustan to decide the amount of pension that needed to be re-instated, and had drawn a veil purposely over the question of the estates.

Jafar swiftly called for a meeting with Pulsford, Sir Richard Bethell, Sir Fitzroy Kelly and Sir Erskine Perry. The venue was the Trafalgar Tavern, preferred meeting place for the strongest critics of the Company. A steamer carried Jafar and his team up the Thames to Greenwich where they got off and walked into the Tavern. The atmosphere, however, was fraught, as Jafar's party immersed themselves in the re-reading and analysis of the Company's brief letters.

All were in agreement that what had been extended was an attempt at appeasement rather than redressing injustice. Bethell, Kelly and Perry were particularly appalled. Kelly in no uncertain terms suggested legal action against the Company in England, immediately. Bethell and Perry agreed. But with that proposal came a big question. Could Jafar afford to stay on in England any longer? His funds were running low and he had exceeded his father's budget. He would have to borrow in England. Jafar requested a break in the meeting and stepped out onto the balcony overlooking the Thames, to confer with Scott and Lutfullah. Jafar wanted to stay, borrow and fight the Company in England. Scott and Lutfullah were more cautious: they recommended a return to Surat, to fight the Company there. Jafar disagreed vigorously. He told his associates there would be no justice in Surat. The Company being all powerful, the Courts were completely prejudiced to any case against them. In England, however, Jafar believed he had a strong chance. Having lobbied hard and come to realise that there was much dissent towards the Company, Jafar insisted he should mount a legal resistance on his opponent's home territory.

Lutfullah and Scott, however, could not see how Jafar might get anything more from the Company in England. Besides, how would he raise the money? But Jafar simply didn't trust the Company's indication that it would restore most of the pension to the family. Moreover, he had come to England to get a decision in his favour before Arbuthnot took a decision on the auctioning of the estates; and that objective had not been achieved.

The discussion grew more agitated in its clear differences, Scott and Lutfullah seeking to calm Jafar and take him back indoors in order to discuss the true picture of how he might cover the legal costs of fighting on in England.

Back at their seats where Bethell, Kelly and Perry awaited them, a wood fire had been lit especially for a chilly Jafar. But when his friends gave him an estimate of possible costs for proceedings against the Company, Jafar felt a new coldness within. The indication ran into thousands of pounds annually. It would mean hiring an exceptional English law firm and the services of Kelly and Perry. And there was no obvious time limit: the case might go on for years. Thanking his English sympathisers, Jafar closed the meeting by telling them he would come back to them in due course.

Back at 7 Sloane Street Jafar, Scott and Lutfullah continued their debate for some days. It was apparent to them that the upper political echelons of England were deeply divided with regards to the Company. Jafar believed he had attained a position that no other Hindustani Prince could hope for. He had broken into the circles of the powerful elite of political England. He had got the most influential lawmakers on his side, willing to stand by him against the Company. He wanted to take full advantage of this unique position, for his own good but also as a stirring example for other Hindustani princes who might challenge the Company in England. With the benefit of first-hand witness Jafar had come to believe that the British judicial and political system was robust and impartial and would give him a fair hearing in England – unlike the Company in Hindustan that chose to run its own courts. He simply didn't believe he would be heard in the courts in Surat.

What soon became apparent was that the Company was utterly divided in itself. What was brought to light after a few days of extensive lobbying led by Sir Fitzroy Kelly was astonishing. The Court of Directors had:

decided by a majority of one that the Governor-General's opinion should be sustained. At the same time the injustice of the case seemed so flagrant that the Chairman assured that only a small portion of the pension would be resumed by the Government and the remainder paid to him [Jafar].[133]

On learning this from Kelly, Jafar again sought counsel from Scott and Lutfullah. He urged both of them to see the unique position he occupied in England. He could really push the Company hard and lobby his cause with the Directors who had voted for him. To be defeated by one vote was an outcome Jafar thought he could contest and reverse. He called for another meeting with Bethell, Kelly and Perry. This time they met at the Mivarts Hotel, and over dinner Jafar restated his view for this new audience. However, Kelly and Bethell emphasised that once a decision was taken within the Company, it was final. Jafar simply did not accept that this should be so. Surely, he insisted, such a narrow defeat could be reversed by another round of voting? Bethell, Kelly and Perry explained to Jafar how voting worked – that a matter decided by even a single vote meant a decision nonetheless. If he wanted to challenge the Company it would have to be in a court of law, not within the internal machinations of the Company.

The next few days at 7 Sloane Street were coloured by utter despair. Jafar took to drinking. So frustrated was he that he locked himself in his apartment for days. After a few days of self-imposed solitude he re-emerged to be met by Lutfullah, once more pleading for entertainment, at breaking point amid all the stress and tension. Having heard of a brilliant dwarf conjuror in London, Lutfullah wanted to see the entertainer's show with his own eyes. Scott was also keen to seek out this amusement, and at length, Jafar agreed. Lutfullah would record the spectacle like so:

> He was 16 lbs in weight and 28 inches in stature, aged thirteen years. He was called General Tom Thumb and on receiving rational answers to our questions from him we found his reason to be quite sound. He was dressed in a military uniform with a cocked hat upon his head and a small sword buckled to his side which gave him the most ludicrous appearance and brought much laughter to the visitors specially when he danced with a girl somewhat bigger than him.[134]

Jafar had come to find Lutfullah's desire for such amusements annoying; and though, admittedly, they did lift his spirits for a while, he nevertheless had come to enjoy Scott's company more than Lutfullah's. Scott spent the next few days with Jafar philosophising about life. They walked in Hyde Park every evening. Scott knew his time to part ways with the young Prince was drawing near: there was no way that Jafar could sustain himself in England much longer. During one such stroll Scott got Jafar to see reason and return to Surat. Though Jafar resisted still, Scott urged him to understand that it would be impossible to raise money in England for a legal resistance to the Company. Creditors simply wouldn't lend money to a Hindustani without adequate assurance of the ability to repay; even less so if they realised that Jafar's formerly wealthy father was also in debt and the family estates sequestered. Scott's affection for the young Prince had grown as they had spent these months in England and it pained him greatly to see Jafar's plight; but as of now, according to Scott, Jafar's only real option was to return, regroup and fight in Hindustan.

Despite his reluctance, Jafar did take Scott's point that back home he could conceivably raise the money for an immediate return to England. If not, he would have to pursue his claims in Hindustan.

Jafar asked Scott to come with him to Surat, so invaluable had been the Briton's support. While Lutfullah had over time come to view this mission as rather a joyride, Scott had been the one who had brilliantly managed Jafar's affairs, orchestrated his strategic PR drive, and tutored him in the ways of handling English aristocracy and politicians. Most importantly, he had understood and related to Jafar's pain. Scott, however, could not acquiesce with Jafar's wishes by returning to Surat. He had spent much time in Hindustan and now wanted to devote the rest of his life to England, where his wife and children insisted he remain.

Jafar had one last meeting with Bethell, Kelly and Perry. All four tried to get Jafar to reconsider his leaving for home. Bethell, Kelly and Perry really believed the time to challenge the Company was now: if Jafar could only raise the money he could build on his momentum. But Jafar knew the reality. Thanking them for their support he then instructed Lutfullah to make bookings for the journey back.

On 3 October 1844, Jafar, Lutfullah, Badruddin and the retinue left for Southampton, from where they boarded the ship back to Hindustan. As the vessel pulled away from English shores Jafar knew well within himself that he would come back and challenge the Company in England. Something never attempted before by any other Hindustani. For the moment though, he was not sure how or when he would return to England. But return he certainly would.

In Surat his dying wife was holding onto her last breaths in order to see his safe return. His infant daughters for whom he had begun this resistance awaited their father with desperate eagerness. Jafar had spent his last few days in England seeking out gifts for them. He had bought trinkets and little English frocks with pretty lace and flower patterns. Sarfaraz, his father waited too, to hear of the outcome of his investment. And then there was Arbuthnot, the Company man whose designs had driven Jafar and his young family to such desperate measures. Arbuthnot was waiting, most anxious too, to know exactly what Jafar would come back with.

6

Courage and the Chosen Battleground

Back in Surat, Jafar faced a situation nothing short of catastrophe. Immediately upon his return he received an account of the miserable state the estates were in under Company officials. Gardens were in an appalling state, the lakes and lagoons had dried up, and some palaces were in a terrible condition with no maintenance work being done. Worst of all by far, within a month of his return, the inevitable happened. His wife lost her fight with tuberculosis and died, clinging to him and urging him to carry on the struggle he had started. Seeing Bakhtiar-un-nissa die in his arms was torturous for Jafar. While they had such different childhoods, they had come together in matrimony to safeguard for the future. And now having lost the mother of his children, Jafar felt enormous pain. It was for the first time he had witnessed the death of a close one and it took him months to recover.

Sarfaraz was disappointed by the visibly meagre outcome of the English mission, and desperately tried to rally creditors to raise money for Jafar's return to England. But this proved difficult. He was struggling to repay his creditors. Kamandiyah had been struck by drought and yields were painfully low in 1844.

With Bakhtiar-un-nissa's death, Jafar not having a son, the

Company could now begin preparations for taking Kamandiyah too. Sarfaraz was ageing. If Jafar didn't assert himself in Kamandiyah the Company could seize the Prince's local powers under the pretext of mismanagement of the princely state. Jafar pressed on Sarfaraz the larger strategic objective and the path to victory for the family: defeat of the Company in England. If he was able to do that, and so long as female succession was accepted, then his daughters might in time assume the estates in Surat and Kamandiyah. Desperate, Sarfaraz again commenced negotiations with creditors and Jafar began astute preparation in locating a good English teacher to instruct him in the language.

In the interim Jafar forwarded the letters he had received in London to the Company authorities in Bombay, expecting to secure the re-instatement of the pension. What followed was nothing short of humiliation for him. The Company officials in Hindustan had waited anxiously for his return. Some, including Arbuthnot, were afraid of what he might come back with. Jafar had dared them, going over their heads to challenge their judgement in England. Now, motivated by the desire for vengeance, the Company authorities in Hindustan decided to do everything in their power to make an example out of him such that no other Hindustani prince would dare try to follow in his footsteps.

Having digested the content of the letters from London, they knew nothing was binding and that they were allowed the freedom to make their own decision. The first matter was the pension of £15,000. In closed-door discussions in Bombay and Calcutta the Company decided to disregard the letter from Shepherd and 'offered to pay him, instead of the large residue promised by the Chairman, only £2,400 annually, and this sum only for life, and on the condition that no payments would be made until they were accepted in satisfaction of all claims. As final.'[135]

The affront in this derisory offer could not have been plainer. Jafar was livid and simply refused to accept this, carrying on without a pension rather than accepting such an insulting fraction of a settlement.

Arbuthnot moved to a more powerful position in Bombay, but with Surat – and particularly the affairs of the Nawab's family – still under his jurisdiction. A new Agent was posted to Surat reporting directly to Arbuthnot. The new Company Agent, having been assured that the London letters were impotent, now unleashed devastation. The magnificent Dariya Mahal had been sealed as part of the illegal sequestration but the keys to one wing that Jafar had hidden away contained gifts from Afzal-ud-deen, the last Nawab to his now dead daughter and little granddaughters. These included jewels, furniture and clothes amongst the gifts Jafar had brought from England. The Company through its Agent now demanded the keys to that wing and all that it contained.[136]

This led to an intense exchange of correspondence between the Company Agent and a furious Jafar.[137]

Company Agent: *The effects of the late Nawab which are in Dhurria Mehel [Dariya Mahal] it is requisite for me to take inventory and put in my care. Send me the keys.*[138]

Jafar: *There is no property belonging to the late Nawab in the Dhurria Mehel [Dariya Mahal] but there is property that belonged to Bukhtyaroonesa [my late wife].*[139]

Company Agent: *Should you fail in doing so, I shall order the government servants under my charge to open the same. You had better send me a quick reply.*[140]

Jafar: *Again. The property deposited there is the Begum's [my late wife]. You state that should I not deliver the keys you shall open the house. [I Recommend] persons on the part of each party should be present and take down an inventory.*[141]

Company Agent: *I have issued orders to call on the Durrieh Mehel*

[Dariya Mahal] tomorrow, open the place and take down the accurate inventory of the effects deposited there.[142]

Jafar: *I point out that the Agent has no lawful claim on the Durrieh Mehel [Dariya Mahal]. I have now very reluctantly sent you the keys according to your very imperative request.*[143]

What followed next was despicable. Company officials ransacked the Dariya Mahal, leaving it in tatters, stealing whatever they could lay their hands on. Angry and frustrated, Jafar found himself doing the same thing that he had done before he left for England – writing to the Company authorities in Calcutta, detailing the incident, quoting the London letters to the effect that his family should be treated with dignity and highlighting the miserable state into which the estates had fallen under the Company's illegal sequestration:

Your memorialist in order to avoid the disgrace of having his property violently seized by the agent, was compelled to comply with the agent's threatening demand. It has been recently ascertained that a considerable portion of the property valued at 6,000 rupees was stolen. The (Company) officers in assuming the management of the estates, were not at the trouble of taking care of the gardens and estates which was essentially necessary for their preservation and a very considerable loss has been sustained. The fruit trees and flowers in the gardens, required careful supervision and the rules of gardening and to ensure their being regularly irrigated but by the neglect of the officers have withered, destroyed and [are close to being] worthless.[144]

Nothing had changed. No response to Jafar's complaint was forthcoming. Over the next few years the Company methodically closed every recourse to justice for Jafar. First was Arbuthnot's awaited decision on the estates. It duly followed. He outright rejected the claims of the little girls on the Dariya Mahal, Hushmut

Mahal, Aena Mahal, the Mehmudi Bagh, the Dilfiza Bagh, the Misri Bagh, other large gardens, stables, elephants and jewels, the taxes called Wakhyanagree fees that the Company paid to the family on certain produce would also not be re-instated.[145] To Amir-un-nissa, the widow of the last Nawab, he gave a couple of gardens. This was immediately followed by what the family had feared most – in November 1845, Arbuthnot officially recommended to the Bombay authorities to auction the estates.[146]

So grave was the injustice Arbuthnot was proposing that even the Governor-General of Hindustan, Sir Henry Hardinge (who had replaced the sacked Ellenborough) hesitated in implementing this recommendation. Instead he kept it on hold for a while, fearing the possible ramifications. It might, he believed, push Jafar to yet more radical measures in response; and if word reached London there could be an investigation into the affairs of the Company.

For his part Jafar spent the next few years frantically moving between Surat, Kamandiyah and Bombay, trying to raise money from creditors in Surat, to demonstrate his presence in his paternal principality, to gather further funds from his father's villages, and to engage with the Bombay authorities in the hope of preventing the auction. It was desperate stuff.

In his despair Jafar's excessive drinking habits accelerated. He had, as a result, begun to gain weight. The fine features of which the London *Times* had written admiringly were being overshadowed by double chins.

He vented his temper, too, on the lethargy of his servants, further induced – he saw clearly – by their own growing addictions to opium and prostitutes supplied by the two best known brothel-keepers of the locality, Karamati and Karima. During Jafar's absence the servants of the palaces had begun flocking to the brothels, sometimes 'on the sly' even inviting the prostitutes in their own quarters inside the palace compound. Karamati and Karima were more than happy to provide the service. But once an enraged Jafar understood the scale of such activity he furiously demanded its cessation and sacked the indulgent ones.

Jafar's one solace was the peace and joy he sought with his girls, for whom he reserved his tender affections. They were growing fast. Both loved to hear the stories Jafar could tell them about London, and these were repeated time and again. They wanted to know about the inhabitants of distant England: their ways, their clothes and their manners. Jafar would be harassed into retelling tales of the magnificent bridges, the carriages, the opera, the second-rate juggler Herr Dobbler and the fascinating Tom Thumb. But what got the girls really excited were accounts of delicious English puddings, rich and creamy with frosted sugar. On one occasion while narrating the story of the great Royal Ascot, Jafar described the crinolines, veils and hats he had seen the English ladies wearing, even the pounding of hooves as the horses thundered toward the finishing line. All these stories he typically told the girls during English lessons with his tutor by his side. He encouraged the girls to practise a little English on him in turn. On one occasion Ladli innocently enquired about the family's horses and stables, and when they would get these back? Jafar had no answer.

The day came when Marianne Postans and her husband Thomas arrived for their return to Surat. Lutfullah was assigned to them and he ensured they enjoyed all the comforts required. Marianne would visit Hushmut Mahal's tiny quarters where Jafar and his little girls resided. Shocked and saddened at seeing the fate that had befallen the family, Marianne felt especially for the girls. When Jafar could take time from his gruelling meetings in Surat and Bombay, he and Marianne would spend some hours together, their meetings lightening his sense of burden. Discussions would range from history and the works of such English poets as Wordsworth and Shelley to Omar Khayyam and Ghazali, the master of inspired intuition.

Their renewed acquaintance, however, was not to last. It was now well known in Company circles about Jafar's acrimony with their officials; and so, at Thomas Postans' insistence, Marianne pulled away from Jafar. She continued to pen her diary and subsequently wrote her book in which she was careful not to indict the Company but showered praise on the young Jafar.

1848 descended carrying with it ominous prospects. Lord Dalhousie as the new Governor-General put into action the policy of 'Doctrine of Lapse.' In the same year, the damages that the estates were sustaining under Company sequestration were so severe that Jafar wrote to the Chairman and the Court of Directors in London. The Company authorities in Bombay now realised that if the estates became so dilapidated as to be near worthless then they could face legal action in Bombay. In any event, such damaged goods wouldn't fetch a good price in any auction of the sort that Arbuthnot was recommending. Thus, before the Court of Directors in London could reply – and in order to be seen as conducting matters justly – the Bombay authorities proposed to raise the pension marginally to £5,200 per year. But what they would do next through utter cunning would isolate Jafar completely. In 1848, the Company secured the passing of a Special Act through the Legislative Council of India affording themselves exemption and immunity from being sued. In effect they invested themselves with an *ex post facto* immunity.[147] It read:

> No Act of the Governor of Bombay in respect to administration to and distribution of such property from the date of the death of the nawab shall be liable to be questioned in any Court of law or equity.[148]

The Company had in effect closed all outlets for justice to Jafar and his daughters. There was no hope for redress in Hindustan. The fears he had expressed to Lutfullah and Scott on the balcony of the Trafalgar Tavern in London had been realised. Word reached Shepherd, the helpless Chairman, in London, and he could only sadly lament for Jafar: 'It was impossible to imagine that the legislature would pass as act for the purpose of depriving a native Prince of India of his legal rights.'[149]

Jafar was in Bombay when the Special Act was passed and he only found out about it through newspapers. He dispatched his peons to the Company offices to verify this. It was true. He was cornered.

To rub salt in the wound, while being seen as keeping up the ridiculous appeasement of Jafar, one Mr. Frere was given the job of conducting a farce of a review of the estates and the rights of the girls. His recommendation in 1851 was that only one half of the properties should be given to the girls.[150] The rest would remain with the Company. In the Surat and Bombay offices of the Company there was much rejoicing. The jewellery, animals, gardens and palaces were ready to be auctioned, potentially providing much enrichment to the Company. They seemed to have finally got around the unrelenting Prince. While they would give him one half of the estates, they believed they would keep the best ones and hand back to him a few of the crumbling buildings and barren gardens. Jafar would have to accept the measly pension too, which would never be enough to manage the properties. In time if the Company could prove that he was not managing the properties given to him well enough in the limited pension allocated to him, the Company could take them over and auction them off as well. The Company officials were sure they had won this long game. As a result of the Special Act the young Prince could not legally fight them in Hindustan. With his father who once had surplus cash but now (like the last Nawab) having to deal with creditors, Jafar, they believed would have to accept their offer. And yet at this crux moment Jafar would summon a response that was steeped in courage and which would stun the Company.

Unbeknownst to the Company officials Jafar and his father would locate a fresh source of hope and funding. Sarfaraz on a fateful day took his son to Kamandiyah. Hundreds poured out into the narrow alleys as Sarfaraz led his son into Kamandiyah. Holding him by the upper arm, Sarfaraz took Jafar to a place which he did not know existed. The shrine of Hasan Shah Pir, the young Prince's Sufi master. The Shah had died. Jafar was unaware. As the throng gathered around and a sea of humans surrounded Jafar, Sarfaraz and his guards closed ranks around him and thrust him in front of the simple mausoleum. Sufi mystics sitting by the grave swinging to the beats of the 'Qaul to Ali', sung by *qawwals*, looked at Jafar and holding him by the arm dragged him to the ground.* Jafar fell in obeisance to the rustic spiritual master. Seeing his master now manifesting himself in a shrine, Jafar succumbed to spiritual devotion. There was nothing to say but he soon rose and then looking at the shrine, uttered words…

'Shah-Az-Karam.
Suh-ae-ma-yak-nazar.'

These were words of the great Indo-Persian poet Amir Khusrau which meant 'Oh master, I now beseech you to look at me with grace.' Sarfaraz and Jafar then moved to the Ram Temple. There he sought moments with the enlightened Brahmin priests. They urged him to continue his struggle.

Sarfaraz then took his son to the Darbargadh. In closed doors father and son discussed their options. The 'Doctrine of Lapse' policy had been implemented in Hindustan which meant pocket sized Kamandiyah would surely be swallowed in time either under pretext of the Prince not being present for most of the time or because Jafar did not have a male heir. Infact both father and son's long periods of absence from Kamandiyah had resulted in it

---

*'The Qaul' are Sufi verses written in praise of Imam Ali, the Prophet's son-in-law who many consider the first Sufi. Written by Amir Khusrau it is sung with great reverence at most Sufi shrines.

being marked for annexation. Furthermore, Sarfaraz knew well that the grandest of the Surat estates seemed lost to the Company, the pension would never be restored in its entirety and the Special Act in place prevented his son from prosecuting the Company in Hindustan. The ravaging of his granddaughter's estates and the farce of conducting an investigation into their rights and then deciding to hand over to them a few dilapidated buildings had mauled his sense of honour. Furious at the injustice of the Company, Sarfaraz now wanted revenge. He suggested extreme measures. He and Jafar could station themselves in Kamandiyah he believed, and lead a guerrilla war against the Company. He asked Jafar to bring the girls to the wild terrain of Kamandiyah from where the family could launch this campaign and if it came down to the worst, he believed the family should go down fighting.

Summoning some of his fiercely loyal Kathi snipers, Sarfaraz even went as far as suggesting a secret mission to gun down Arbuthnot. The vast lands of Kathiawar were still infested with outlaws and the jungles provided a sanctuary of sorts. Quite clearly for Sarfaraz, it was better to live and die with honour. But Jafar had witnessed something across the oceans that his father had not. He had seen the British judicial system at work in London and most importantly he had created an impression in Britain and built a set of powerful English contacts prepared to work with him to legally confront the Company. If he accepted his father's suggestion, his life would be of a fugitive in the forests of Gujarat. His girls could fall prey to outlaws if he took them with him and if he left them in Surat, Company officials would take them as hostages, besides all this, Sarfaraz would also be on the run. And so, after calming his father down he again urged him to pursue legal action in England.

Jafar insisted the girls continue to be stationed in Surat. This demonstration of the granddaughters of the last Nawab being anchored in their ancestral home would be a signal of strength. Sarfaraz would have to continue to stand guard over his granddaughters in

Surat and make lightening visits to Kamandiyah to demonstrate his presence and hopefully prevent the Company from building a case to annex Kamandiyah as a mismanaged principality by the local ruling chief; meanwhile he himself would go to England and build his case. Internal turmoil! Going to England did not guarantee success. It would test his father who while watching over the girls in Surat would make Kamandiyah vulnerable by his absence. Jafar gave himself up to nature.

Riding through pomegranate orchards then under lush neem trees that attracted singing birds like the koyal, he would gaze at fields which abounded with rabbits always alert to the deadly threat from the lone circling falcon. Then inevitably he would nudge his horse taking him deep into the jungles. Swaying past drooping branches he would make his way to Rojdi, the lost city. Sitting besides stones that went back millenniums, he would contemplate his future. Would his fate be the same as the ancient ruined city?

As the sun's downward trajectory began he would ride into the dried river bed. A faint call of a muezzin from a remote mosque and the flute played in a distant temple would soothe him. A turbaned, elaborately moustached shepherd who would be striding ahead of his flock would freeze on seeing his Prince's horse mounted silhouette against a setting sun. Was the shepherd looking at the sun setting on his Prince's once dazzling destiny? With eyes lowered the shepherd would offer a drink to the weary horse and bread to the troubled Prince. A humble word exchanged and bread broken the rider would sway the reins of his horse. Then darkness. The unrelenting sound of crickets would replace the singing birds. The black sky would magically unveil the beauty of the galaxy which it had hidden in its bosom. The beauty of the cosmos unravelled to the rider, would compel him to believe that he himself was part of that supreme creative force that had created the universe as he had known it in the mystical Sufi scriptures. He would ascend into a quiet trance, his horse gently moving in the dark night. If he was even a particle of that majestic force then he could create his own destiny. Which meant he could win. The horse jerked its neck, its eyes fearful. Fire from thrusting torches unnerved it. Jafar had let go of the reins and seeing their drifting Prince, some farmers rushed out of their huts to escort him back. These wandering days rooted a steely resolve to fight the Company. Everything would have to be put on the line in an epic quest for justice.

Returning to Surat, after months of deliberation, Sarfaraz and Jafar did the following: The fertile village of Waori (which Jafar had defended as a young teenager from the Makranis) was, along with a couple of other villages belonging to Sarfaraz mortgaged with immediate effect and hard cash raised against them. A part of Sarfaraz's house in Baroda was also leased out and cash raised. Three wealthy money lenders of Surat and Bombay who were already seeking their dues having helped Sarfaraz and Jafar raise money to manage Surat estates were handed over jewellery and convinced through clandestine lobbying to lend more to fund Jafar's fight in England. Father had now pledged virtually all to his son's cause to 'fight the good fight'. There was no more to give. The family had its back to the wall. And from here Jafar would have to fight and win. Jafar now wanted this fight so bad. This was a cause he had obsessed about. As a boy he had protected the rights of little fawns and new borns. Now the call to stand upto injustice against his own daughters rose with great force within him.

Nurturing the fire of dignity and pride that burnt within, in 1852, Jafar spurned the new offer from the Company of one half of the estates and £5,400 annual pension for the girls. For the girls and him, Jafar believed it was now – all or nothing. With cash in hand Jafar was determined to give the Company the legal fight of their lives. Having blockaded his legal options in Hindustan, the Company had cornered Jafar, but he had got what had long been his preferred battleground: England.

All this Sarfaraz had agreed to do for his son, but with one condition: a second marriage. It had to be done, the old man believed. He wanted a son to secure the line of succession to Kamandiyah. Initially reluctant, thinking the new responsibility would be a distraction from the cause, Jafar finally agreed. Basti, a petite young daughter of the Supreme Qazi, or head priest of Ahmedabad, was chosen as his bride and a simple ceremony performed in Surat in early 1853. Basti was delicate in frame with long light-brown hair, and she traced her origins to Iran. As stepmother to Ladli and Rahimun, Basti began her new role with enthusiasm. Jafar placed her in a house not too far from the Hushmut Mahal. From here she would regularly visit the girls and attend to their needs. The girls, however, resisted too much affection: they didn't want a stepmother. The relationship would never be warm, merely courteous, between Basti and the now 13-year-old Ladli and 11-year-old Rahimun.

While there would be physical intimacy between the new couple, Jafar showed little real feeling toward Basti. To her it seemed her husband was wedded to his cause, buried in paperwork, forever obsessing about his impending journey to England – and this only a few months after their marriage. As little as Basti liked it, she nonetheless put up with it. For Jafar life was all about getting to England as swiftly as possible. Over nine years he had maintained contact with Sir Richard Bethell, Sir Fitzroy Kelly and Sir Erskine Perry and now with his journey impending he let them into the scope of his plans.

The nine years since his previous journey had changed Jafar. He was now 35, and newly accomplished in the English language. This time, he believed, things would be different. Within, he had a raging fire to see this fight for justice through, whatever it took and however long. He knew that this time, besides the lobbying, he would have to engage professionals and learned lawyers to mount his legal resistance. He assembled a large team for the journey.

Lutfullah being dropped, his entourage would include a new

secretary, Ali Akbar Bahadur, who had a mastery of the English language. There was an additional interpreter, a dozen attendants. Five of whom were merry and curious fellows.[151] A valet and personal attendant named Dost Shah, a lead chef called Shaik who had a love for music and gambling. Shaikh personally supervised the packing of Hindustani spices and masalas he thought necessary to prepare the best Hindustani cuisine for his master. Then there was Noor, a short but energetic errand boy; an old doorkeeper named Mishameeram; and Raheem, a personal barber.[152] Last but not least, three musicians who played the sitar and *dhol* were included in the entourage for entertainment.

This time Jafar sent his large entourage before him with the objective of first gathering intelligence on the position of his English allies. His secretary and translators made arrangements for the long stay. A private office at 110 Gloucester Terrace was secured for Jafar and another larger residence near Chapel Street, close to Paddington, which would house the Prince and his team. Most of the entourage who had heard about the wonders of magnificent London from Lutfullah were anxiously awaiting their young master's arrival, hoping he would show them a fine time.

Jafar bade farewell to his family – an awkward good-bye to the young second wife and a warm embrace for his girls. As he lunged forward to get into his carriage, he paused briefly to look up at the window of his quarters. His eyes looked for his father from whom he hoped to draw courage. Sarfaraz looked back at his son. At this crucial juncture, both knew how grim the situation was. If Jafar failed in England the family would stand utterly destroyed. Sarfaraz had pledged virtually all he had towards his son's just cause. Failure in England meant the family would descend into an irrecoverable dark age. Creditors would mercilessly fall upon them, plunging the family into an abyss where only despair would become their unflinchingly loyal companion. But his father's eyes urged the son to struggle on. He whose name meant a river of abundance would now have to live up to the designation, face up to the prospect of ruination, and fight for the future dignity of his family.

For a second time Jafar's carriage sped out of Hushmut Mahal carrying within it the Prince who believed that justice lay oceans away and determined he was again to cross the waves in search of it. His Sufi spirit and will to reason for action welded in the fire of the battle-ravaged countryside had now shaped within him resolute qualities of unwavering confidence and fortitude. Emboldened, he was ready to clash with the fearsome cannon of Empire expansion – The East India Company. Jafar duly arrived in London a few months later having halted at Suez, then at Trieste on the Adriatic before progressing to Southampton.

—

His arrival in London was in December of 1853.[153] The city was bearing the onslaught of a fierce winter, and heavy snowfall greeted Jafar. Never having seen such a sight in his life, Jafar watched in amazement at the contrast between the seasonal scenic beauty of winter and the weather of his previous visit at the height of summer. Roof tops were covered with thick layers of snow, which also lay heavily on every pavement. Grey skies loomed and sharp chilling winds cut through Jafar's cashmere shawls as his carriage drove him to Chapel Street. The trees that in summer and autumn had displayed a magnificent mosaic of colourful leaves now looked stripped of life itself.

On reaching Chapel Street Jafar was shocked to see the state of his entourage. Some of the attendants had refused to leave the fireplace in their quarters since the time of their arrival. They feared freezing to death and were conducting all daily activities near the flames. Some had stopped eating, out of superstition, believing the devil himself might spring forth from European ingredients and consume their souls. The chefs were preparing measly meals and not venturing out. Mishameeram the doorman had been crying for days, dreading Jafar's arrival for fear that he would be made to stand out in the cold of the main entrance. Noor the short stocky attendant was obsessed with seeing his own breath in winter. Never having experienced anything of the sort he would stand outside the house breathing heavily trying to catch the smoke, while mocking the weeping Mishameeram.

Jafar's secretary Ali Akbar and the translators though were in reasonable spirit, thanks to the musicians who were keeping them entertained. Jafar immediately got an account from his secretaries of the current positions held by his English allies. Nine years had gone by. While Pulsford had retired from active politics and Scott, too, had settled into a quiet life in the country, Sir Richard Bethell, Sir Fitzroy Kelly and Sir Erskine Perry, the three leading lawmakers, were at the peak of their powers. Bethell had come to hold the position of Solicitor General to Queen Victoria; while Kelly who had held this position before Bethell, continued to be one of the most revered names in British law and enjoyed a formidable reputation as a 'special pleader'. More recently he had continued his electoral winning streak by being elected MP for Suffolk. Perry – a champion of women's property rights, blessed with an exceptional knowledge of Company affairs – was on his way to being elected as MP for Devonport. Having apprised himself of the position of his chief allies Jafar invited the three of them to his residence for a Hindustani dinner on 22 December 1853.

Unhappy with the Chapel Street house (which he found stifling) Jafar seized an opportunity to move immediately to 15 Warwick Avenue in Maida Vale, close to Paddington. This house he thought was befitting to his status. Having settled in he convened a meeting in the large living room. He issued orders to the chefs to go out shopping daily for fresh ingredients: Paddington markets would be most convenient. All attendants were to dress in Hindustani robes with the Surat state seals on their chests. They would each have individual beds in the servants' quarters. The task of ensuring the house had its fireplaces lit at all times would be rotated around all staff. Musicians were to play their harmoniums, sitars and dhols each evening to entertain Jafar and his secretaries.

Days had gone by since Jafar's invitations to dinner on 22 December, yet he had received no acknowledgement, and he was concerned. Maybe too much time had lapsed? Perhaps his old allies from nine years' previous were no longer so animated by his case? Each day that went by without a confirmation of attendance made Jafar more anxious. Still, he ordered the staff to prepare for an Asian dinner, and they swung into action. Shaikh the lead chef and Dost Shah the lead valet and attendant were given strict instructions regarding menu and protocol. Accordingly the two briefed their subordinates. It would be seekh kebabs and fish-fry for starters, followed by lamb biryani, chicken korma and yellow daal as main course. For pudding it would be kheer, a rich creamy dessert made of rice, milk and almonds. Shaikh and his two assistants draped themselves in woollen shawls and hurriedly made their way to Paddington market. Shaikh personally picked out a butcher and, having the English-speaking secretary translate, ensured the meat was fresh and straight off the shoulder. The butcher followed these strange instructions from what he considered to be strangely dressed Hindustani men.

Then Shaikh went about selecting snapper from the fishmongers and other ingredients such as rice, lentils, garlic and butter from which he intended to make ghee: all parts of his great culinary attempt to win the hearts of the powerful in Victorian England through the authentic taste of Hindustan. Dost Shah and Noor briefed the other servants – particularly Mishameeram the doorkeeper – on protocol and proper greetings. Each was to greet the visitors with a salaam and to stand in attendance behind the visitors with hands clasped in front. Mishameeram was given extra woollens and an especially warm turban since he would be standing outside the door waiting for the carriages to arrive.

The 22 December was a foggy day. Jafar paced up and down his rented living room. All preparations had been made but no word had arrived. Everything was ready but without a confirmation of attendance Jafar's hopes of remaking the acquaintance of Bethell, Kelly and Perry seemed to be receding. He did not admit as much, however, to his secretaries or attendants. Still he kept Mishameeram well cloaked and waiting outside the door. It was a bitterly cold night and fog from the day hadn't lifted but, rather, worsened. Mishameeram began to feel the cold cut through his cloak. Straining his eyes trying to look through the fog he was frequently distracted by the pesky Noor who teased the old man while repeatedly expelling draughts of materialised breath and grasping at the air before him.

Just as Jafar was preparing instructions to the staff to abandon the evening's plans, Mishameeram announced that he saw something. Squinting and hoisting up a lantern he made out the faint lamps of a carriage emerging from the fog. It was Sir Richard Bethell. Unknown to Jafar, all three men had sent confirmations to his previous Chapel Street residence.

At precisely 7 pm Bethell's carriage pulled in. Mishameeram greeted him and escorted him into Jafar's residence. Jafar and Bethell were meeting after a span of nine years, and they observed a certain formality. Within minutes the carriages of Kelly and Perry also arrived. The three Englishmen were dazzled by what they saw. Hindustani candles and lamps lit up the main living area. Thick beautiful Kashmiri carpets and rugs had been strewn about to keep the flooring warm. An elevated *diwan* had been placed on which Jafar sat, and around him were large cylindrical embroidered Hindustani cushions and pillows that completed the Oriental look of the living room. Soon the initial formal courteousness gave way to lighter conversation. Having established a certain sense of ease, Dost Shah entered and announced dinner. The guests tucked into the sumptuous mildly-spiced Hindustani dishes, appreciating the culinary skills of the chief chef Shaikh, who was summoned for a personal congratulation. Meanwhile the powerful politicians continued to marvel at their well-dressed surroundings.

As the evening progressed and the men moved back to the sitting area Jafar briefed them about all that had happened in the past nine years. Every detail was explained: particularly how the Company had precipitated the situation that left him with no choice but to fight them in England. Bethell, Kelly and Perry were outraged by the actions of the Company. According to them it was a clear violation of law, and immediate action needed to be taken before the estates were auctioned. Perry suggested recourse to the courts. But Bethell and Kelly thought otherwise. Both men believed that in order to stop the Company at the earliest the highest echelons of power had to be brought into play. They recommended the tabling and passing of a Bill in Parliament that would re-instate the pension and lift the sequestration of the estates in entirety. A victory in Parliament would ensure the Company would take no further unlawful action against the family. Bethell and Kelly's argument was formidable and persuasive to Jafar.

But such a course of action had never been personally followed by a Hindustani prince. What Bethell and Kelly were suggesting sounded brave and bold but would require immense amounts of patience and resolve from Jafar. As the conversation got more intense and detailed, attendants served chai to keep weary eyes open. Bethell and Kelly outlined the path to Parliament with typical astuteness. To get there Jafar's claim would have to be legitimised and in order to do so, Jafar would first have to appeal to the Judicial Committee of Her Majesty's Privy Council, with a supporting letter from Bethell favouring his claim. The Judicial Committee would not have the authority to pass judgement on the case but it could conceivably sanction a parliamentary intervention. Once such a recommendation was achieved, the doors to Parliament could be pushed open by Kelly and Perry. Once inside, both MPs would then press for the tabling of the Bill and work hard towards getting it passed. Having articulated this scheme to the young Prince, Bethell, Kelly and a now convinced Perry looked to Jafar for the final nod to proceed. For Jafar it meant hiring the services of both MPs, who were also the finest lawyers. But he didn't ponder for long. Just past midnight a flurry of vigorous handshakes signalled his approval to go ahead.

Over the next few months Jafar and his allies plunged into a series of intense meetings: some at their professional offices, others at Jafar's office at 110 Gloucester Terrace. Jafar's petition to the Judicial Committee of Her Majestys' Privy Council had to be a perfect document: one that captured every detail of the fall of the port, the Treaty of 1800, the subsequent violations of the Treaty and the current miserable state of affairs in Surat. For days the four men pored over the documents, comprehending nuances and framing arguments for the re-instatement of the pension and the lifting of the sequestration of estates. Bethell's supporting letter, too, would be crucial; and so scores of drafts were written and re-written.

As the cold winter days went by the presence in town of Jafar and his entourage captured the attention of many Londoners just as it had done before. But while Jafar was locked up for days writing and re-writing drafts with his allies, his attendants caught the eye of one Joseph Salter, a devoted missionary priest who worked for the London City Mission and whose primary focus was on Asians who had found themselves in Victorian London. Easy targets for Salter to convert to what he believed to be the true faith were the utterly poor and destitute Asian lascars who had arrived as sailors and menial labourers on European boats. Most of these lascars lived in East London, utterly impoverished and subject to diminished life expectancies. Salter's missionary work provided shelter for them and in turn they were ripe for efforts to convert them to Christianity. Having heard of Jafar's presence in London with a large number of attendants, Salter took it upon himself to enlighten these men to the true faith. He got a footing in Jafar's residence through a contact who had come to befriend Dost Shah, the chief valet, with a view to an interchange of language study. [154]

Salter soon made Jafar's kitchen his primary focus. He began frequenting it regularly under the guise of learning Hindustani from Dost Shah, but with the primary objective of what he saw as saving souls. While feasting on the delicious food he recited the Bible, its Gospels especially, desperate to enlighten the attendants. Salter noted:

> Two evenings a week in the Prince's kitchen were no mean opportunities. The smell of Indian ghee, garlic, sweet meats and jagree were all as novel as the language ... The Hindostanee Testament was the adopted reading-book, so that gospel truths were heard in that Mohamedan kitchen. The kitchen often became a place of revel after dinner with cards and tea placed on the table, the dhol or native drum would be brought forward and native songs sung. The Prince cared nothing for where his servants went or whom they brought home as long as they attended to all he wanted. The Prince himself was a tall and commanding person, a great specimen of Indian nobility, frank, open-hearted and liberal, constantly inviting English aristocracy to his house and sparing neither pains nor cost to entertain them.[155]

The kitchen soon became a melting pot of disparate visitors. Lascars who were Sikhs and Bengalis, also Muslim, heard about Salter's new watering hole and duly flocked to the kitchen, bringing all their life's woes and a desire to shrug off their misery by joining their countrymen in food and drink. Invariably an indulgence in gambling, dancing and singing would follow, and last until late evening. Shaikh the chef held centre stage when it came to after-dinner revelries. He – along with Noor and Raheem the barber – directed all kinds of gambling games in the smoky kitchen. The famous *teen patti*, or three-card game was popular and each time one of these attendants won or lost, a huge din was created. Raheem led the musical activities by bringing in the three special musicians who produced a rhythmic beat to which the entire kitchen danced.

Through it all, Salter continued to persevere with Dost Shah, who seemed to genuinely crave knowledge. As the two taught each other their native language, a friendship took root. Salter went about his business of preaching in an intelligent manner:

> I carefully avoided thrusting Christianity on the notice of these natives but it was my anxious solicitude to avail myself of suitable occasions and to let no opportunity pass that might be turned to a spiritual account. There were none in this suite that did not regularly hear from the Word of God, and from my own lips in English and Hindustani.[156]

Salter's efforts didn't, in the end, meet with much success. Mishameeram the doorkeeper's answer to Salter's visits was to fling himself into Mohamedan prayer and loud chanting. Every time Salter entered the kitchen, Mishameeram would purposely begin his prayers, leaving Salter initially bewildered but later as a curious observer of his praying rituals.[157] Noor, Raheem and Shaikh, meanwhile, paid little attention to Salter. Dost Shah was focused on improving his English but out of courtesy he gave Salter a patient hearing with regard to Christ and the Gospel.

One incident, though, finally broke Salter's resolve. The contact who had introduced him to Dost Shah was a lascar called Hamed from East London, who had heard many a sermon from Salter and had persuaded the latter that he had embraced Christianity. For a while, Hamed and Salter had not run into one another. When they did meet again at Regents Park on a cold but clear winter day, Hamed informed his tutor that he had got married, and in a manner that he assumed to be the Christian way. As Hamed described the nuptials, 'Beer and gin was brought, a fiddle and a broom. Then much was drunk and the bride and groom jumped over the broom, sang, played the fiddle and the marriage was done. All this in the Eastern

Prince's famed kitchen.'[158] Salter was livid to hear of such a profane travesty of the marriage sacrament and, believing that these Asians were beyond redemption, finally gave up.

—

Jafar's efforts in the meanwhile had been completely focused on paperwork and the impending correspondence. After months of drafting letters he and his allies were ready to send the documentation to the Judicial Committee of Her Majesty's Privy Council. Bethell's recommendatory letter was powerful and completely in favour of Jafar:

> It appears to me that the decision of Mr. Frere [to give only one half of the estates to the daughters] is erroneous and ought not to be submitted to and that Meer Jafur Alee would be entitled to appeal. The Legislative Council [that passed the Special Act of 1848 in Bombay preventing Meer Jafur Alee from challenging them and giving the Company immunity] has not, I conceive, the power to deprive anyone of the right to appeal. In my opinion the arrangement which was made on Meer Jafur Alee's marriage [of him succeeding the Nawab and managing the estates to be passed down to the daughters] ought to be sustained as a binding contract.[159]

This compelling letter, together with a detailed account of all that had befallen the family as prepared under Kelly's supervision, was sent to the Judicial Committee in March 1854. Jafar was now advised by his three English politician friends to wait for the formal response. It was hoped that they would recommend seeking parliamentary action. And so Jafar waited. It was during this period that he met someone who would capture his imagination completely.

The impressive Astley's Ampitheatre, famed for its large circus ring, was one of the most interesting venues in Victorian London. Its equestrian performances and circus activities were often frequented by English aristocracy. Recreations or dramatic representations of battles were popular acts. These extravaganzas could astonish with their live horse charges, booming gunfire, and spectacular stunts. Jafar had visited Astley's with the Russian Prince Soltikoff during his first visit in 1844. Knowing of his love for horses, Kelly now invited him to an evening show of the 'Battle of Waterloo' which would, ironically, feature the Duke of Wellington's victory over Napoleon. Having ensured he got use of his favoured light blue four-horse carriage, Jafar – with his chosen attendant Dost Shah and Noor standing behind the carriage – made his way to the theatre. Kelly had ensured the best front row seats from where he and his Hindustani friend could watch horses swishing right past their faces. The thrilling evening began with an ode sung in honour of those that had fallen at Waterloo. Standing in the front row, dressed in a white crinoline and singing with particular passion was one Mary Jane Flood: an aspiring actress trying to make her way in the English theatre scene. Of medium height, with blue eyes and light brown waist-length hair, she hailed from the town of Burnley, thirty miles north of Manchester. Unknown to her, she had captured Jafar's heart almost instantly.

No sooner had the event concluded that Jafar, never one to hold back, sent Noor and Dost Shah alongwith the English speaking Ali Akbar backstage to locate Mary Jane. Making their way through the departing English crowd, the three petitioned the doorkeeper of the large make-up rooms to let them see the lady. Ali Akbar carried a note from Jafar, written in English, requesting the pleasure of her company. Having located her and conveyed the note, they eagerly awaited a response. Mary Jane was struck by this rather bold overture, but charmed, too, as Ali Akbar pointed out Jafar amid the thinning crowd. An invitation to dinner at 15 Warwick Avenue was accepted.

Once again the attendants swung into action. For them this was great fun. The kitchen became the hub of gossip as they spoke about their master's weakness for English ladies, laughing and joking on the subject until late at night. Mary Jane arrived elegantly dressed in a light green crinoline, hair neatly tied back in a bun, slightly daunted yet excited to meet this man from the Orient. The conversation proved to be predictably formal as the two got to know each other. Jafar was struck most by Mary Jane's simplicity. She was of a mild and calm disposition, curious about her natural surroundings, and fond of gardening – or as much as she could engage in it at the rented house she shared with other acting colleagues in East London.

She was unaware of Hindustan, its customs or culture, and entirely ignorant about politics and the Company. She liked the simple things in life: walks in the woods, simple dresses and food, as well as her enjoyment of acting, though this was by no means a consuming passion. There was an ease about her that Jafar found utterly refreshing and uplifting at a time when he anxiously awaited a response from the Privy Council. For his part he told his guest about the forests of Kamandiyah, the wild life there and his rides in the fields. He did not speak about the grandiosity of his cause or of his illustrious ancestors. There was chemistry enough in the initial simplicity of their social intercourse. Charmed by the stories of the orient, Mary Jane looked forward to more. For the young actress – who had lost her parents at a young age, had no siblings and was yet to find her place in the world – Jafar's entry into her life was a noteworthy and pleasing occurrence.

Regular meetings followed, and the romance gathered momentum. Mary Jane would patiently listen to him as he opened up and, in time, told her all about his life – going so far as to speak of his second wife, Basti. Jafar's respect for Basti's status as his wife would not change, but that was the extent of his commitment. Compared to the lively Mary Jane, Basti hadn't stirred his heart. Surprisingly, Mary Jane raised no special objection to Jafar's marital status. He impressed her as forthright and candid: for her this was a sign of his character. While Jafar picked the simplicity trait in her quickly he also identified she carried a strong resolve for what she dedicated herself to. A character trait he himself had.

Jafar found Mary Jane's life fascinating. Here was a woman who had been orphaned at an early age and instead of capitulating under the weight of emotional and financial hardships, she had gone out into the world pursued her interest in acting and although she hadn't made quite a success of her career, Jafar found her spirit for life appealing. His first wife, Bakhtiar-un-nissa had been a princess brought up with all the luxuries possible, but also frail and sickly. Basti his current wife was given to religion being a theologian's daughter and there were no common interests the two shared. He himself, born a prince in a wild outlawed landscape had always chased adventure, lived life on the edge on many an occasion – be it fighting the Makranis at 16, or fighting the greatest colonising corporation in the world. And here in front of him was a woman prepared to do the same – seek adventure and take risks. Away from the pressures of Surat and Kamandiyah, Jafar had found love.

The preferred meeting place for Jafar and Mary Jane was the Regent's Canal area between Maida Vale and Paddington, which had come to be known as Little Venice thanks to the literary influence of Lord Byron. The gentle canal and waterways meandered through Maida Vale, overlooked by Victorian mansions. Jafar and Mary Jane spent most of the days leading up to the summer of 1854 on long walks with each other. By the time winter began its retreat and spring blossoms sprung everywhere, Mary Jane had lost her heart to the Hindustani Prince. She slowly pulled away from her acting interests and began spending most of her time in his company. Neither knew what the future might hold, but in love they undeniably were. If Jafar failed in his attempt at winning back the estates, he didn't know where life would take him next. Mary Jane feared he might go back to Hindustan and lead an armed rebellion against the Company. He had expressed that to her. The fear of losing the man she had come to love began to grip her, and having nothing of great value in England she urged him to take her with him wherever he went. He gave her his word he would do so secretly also admiring the brave decision of this woman to go with him regardless of whatever life threw at him.

The continued anxiety of awaiting a response from the Judicial Committee of Her Majesty's Privy Council often descended on Jafar and led him to seek solace in alcohol. On many an occasion, he would be seen by his attendants lying in Mary Jane's arms for hours, evidently filled with great anguish. But she had the power to comfort him. She even learned Hindustani cuisine. As Mary Jane spent more time at 15 Warwick Avenue, making it her home, the attendants marvelled at her fair looks. She had a pale but flawless complexion. If she wasn't the most stunning beauty, she was distinctive, and this was sufficient for the gossiping attendants to speculate on the possibility of her bestowing on Jafar a mixed-race white complexioned, blue-eyed boy prince. Dost Shah took it upon himself to drop subtle hints to her about how to impress Jafar yet further. He would smuggle kohl and dainty long earrings into the house and deliberately leave these around her lately stationed dressing table in the master bedroom. Picking up these hints Mary Jane gracefully adopted the accessories as provided.

Mishameeram the old doorkeeper did not, however, approve of the relationship. Considering it to be 'living in sin', he increased the frequency of his daily prayers in the hope of saving the house from any divinely-willed misfortune. Regularly reading certain verses and blowing them in all directions of the house, Mishameeram eventually came to the conclusion that Jafar, being a Muslim, was permitted four wives and so should marry Mary Jane at the earliest. Not daring to mention this to Jafar, he spoke about it only in hushed tones within the kitchen. But there, Mishameeram's talk was dismissed as nonsense. Noor, Raheem and Shaikh the jolly chef all enjoyed observing the course of Jafar's new romance and thought of their master as an Asian hero for winning the affections of an English maiden, thereby depriving some Englishman of the very same chance.

Summer had arrived and London warmed perceptibly. The beauty of the city was visible everywhere. There was a growing sense of anticipation in Jafar and a surge of new hope. It had been four months since he and his English allies had submitted the documents to the Judicial Committee. Jafar's anxious wait finally ended on 30 June 1854 when he received a reply. As expected by Bethell, Kelly and Perry, the Committee articulated its lack of authority to pass judgement in this case, but – most importantly and to the great delight of all – suggested action in Parliament. It further offered scathing observations and opinions with regard to the actions of the Company, especially the Governor and the Legislative Council in Bombay, stating that their actions were 'corrupt and tyrannical abuse of powers and that there must always be open to the claimant [Jafar] a right of complaint to the Parliament. Neither Parliament nor Crown being deaf to the voice of reason.'[160]

While this response was precisely what had been wished, it had come at a time when Parliament was no longer in session. But this gave Kelly and Perry some leeway to consider anew the strength of their arguments in the case. One aspect caught their attention anew: a point of great legal consequence that would require great and fertile legal minds to handle it. The Company in Hindustan had dealt with the family brutally – that much had been established. The path to Parliament seemed clear. However, the Company authorities in London had maintained throughout a diplomatic response to Jafar's claims. In the letters obtained during the 1844 visit, while they had completely ignored the question of the estates, they had mentioned that only a small portion of the £15,000 pension should be kept with the Company and the rest restored. The authorities in Hindustan, however, had not complied with this advice, and so Kelly and Perry feared that if they now pushed ahead into Parliament they could well come up against MPs inclined to counter Jafar's claims and compel him to seek justice once more with the Company authorities in London that had, after all, not completely rejected his demonstrations. For Jafar's case to be really compelling and strong, he would have to come across as one who had exhausted all his other options and was now seeking parliamentary intervention as a last and only hope.

The Company authorities in London remained completely unaware of Jafar's latest moves, and so Kelly and Perry fashioned a form of trap for them, asking Jafar to write to them one more time asserting his claims. If they rejected this, Jafar's case would be considerably strengthened, boosting his chances of winning in Parliament. But it required nerves of steel and great patience. Just when Jafar had thought he could approach Parliament, he was being counselled to wait longer. He had, moreover, grown so weary of dealing with the Company that he found it utterly painful and compromising to have to write to them again. But after much deliberation with Kelly and Perry, who prevailed upon him to act in the direction of the greater good, Jafar wrote to the Company Directors again in December 1854, a full year after his return to England.[161] Already frustrated at the slow progress, he would have to wait another excruciating six months for a response. But the Company Directors replied on 29 June 1855, stating that they considered his claims 'wholly inadmissable' and his case 'fully considered and finally decided.'[162]

Predictably obdurate, they had now walked straight into the trap set by Kelly and Perry. Now Jafar's case was robust, as the wronged Prince fighting against a brutal corporation, left with no choice but to approach Parliament. Bethell, Kelly and Perry had, ever since the first dinner meeting at 15 Warwick Avenue, reminded Jafar of the patience and resolve he would need. Now, eighteen months since his arrival back in England, they had guided the Hindustani Prince to the threshold of Parliament, where he would seek his showdown with the Company.

The good news and changed fortune that had entered his life Jafar attributed freely to the presence of Mary Jane. He was sure she brought him luck. The two celebrated by taking a slow and winding boat ride down Little Venice followed by a picnic in Regent's Park. Sitting under a large leafy oak as she drew her initials locked in with his (which happened to be the same) it was apparent to Mary Jane that Jafar was on the cusp of creating history. Jafar had spoken to her of Parliament as the final frontier, and victory there would mean everything to him. She now knew well the magnitude of his fight, and that no Hindustani had challenged England's own Company on their soil with such daring. She thought of what success would mean – but also what defeat might bring. If victorious, would Jafar keep his word and take her with him to live a peaceful life in exotic Hindustan? If defeated what would be the ramifications for their relationship – particularly if he went back and decided to defy the Company through armed resistance?

In the meantime Kelly and Perry began the process of accumulating all information, revising their study of the Treaty of 1800, going over more than one thousand pages of correspondence, and refining their arguments. The two powerful MPs prepared to go forth into Parliament, combining as the voice of the Hindustani Prince. In Kelly, Perry and Bethell, Jafar had deployed the biggest guns against the Company. The East India Company had underestimated Jafar's tenacity and endurance. He was about to descend upon them in their home country by spearheading and unleashing the greatest legal assault against them. A counterattack that would shatter reputations and have the colonising corporation pleading for respite.

7

Heat in Parliament

Over the following months Kelly and Perry worked tirelessly debating about the nature of the intended Bill. In Victorian England, Private Bills changed, altered or created new laws as they applied to specific individuals or even organisations, rather than the general people. Public Bills changed the law as applied to the general population. Both types of Bill, however, needed to be passed through both the House of Commons and then the House of Lords. For the Bill to become law it would need to be signed finally by the Crown. Both Bills also had to be brought to public awareness before and while they were going through Parliament, via regular interactions with the press.

In Jafar's case the fundaments were those of a Private Bill, but there were also angles that could have a political affect on the Company, that great colonising power in Hindustan. And while the argument in the Bill would be for the restoration of private property, Jafar's family pension was a political matter. The violation of the treaty of 1800 was a political violation, and so for the passing of the Bill it would have to be fought politically, too. If the Bill passed and Jafar won back the pension and the estates then it would be the first-ever political defeat for the Company in its own Parliament at the hands of a Hindustani. The two MPs then took the advice of the Speaker who recommended the Bill to be tabled as a Private one.[163] Kelly and Perry would do as the Speaker suggested while making the case with strong political arguments.

Kelly and Perry then identified certain MPs who had long wanted to see the Company brought to book for its unseemly conduct in Hindustan. A large number of these gave a patient hearing to the outline of Jafar's case and promised to support the Bill. Further, Kelly and Perry got more endorsements in favour of Jafar including G.L. Elliot who was Arbuthnot's predecessor as Agent in Surat. Elliot knew the family well and was happy to recount his memories of splendid dinners at the palaces in Surat.[164] Addressing Jafar with respect as 'His Highness', Elliot sent correspondence in Jafar's favour in no uncertain terms supporting his cause and stating 'You know my opinion of the case – I think you are entitled to all you claim'.[165] This was sound endorsement from the predecessor to Arbuthnot and having been Agent at Surat for six years.

Jafar briefed his secretary Ali Akbar to get the word out around London. A Private Bill meant the public had to be informed of its contents. This was a great opportunity to make the English public aware of the injustices wrought by its Company. Mary Jane and Ali Akbar went to work together, supervising the writing and publication of pamphlets that presented Jafar's case including letters and endorsements from Bethell as Solicitor General to the Queen and the plight of his daughters in bold headlines – these to be distributed all over London.[166] Ali Akbar then instructed Dost Shah and Noor to stand with these pamphlets in Regent's Park, Hyde Park Corner and other key thoroughfares. As people walked by them, this pair cut exotic figures. Dressed in Hindustani long flowing robes, they distributed the pamphlets with great eagerness. The public couldn't get enough, and the pamphlet quickly required a second print run, for which purpose Mary Jane and Ali Akbar went personally to the printers in East London. Shaikh, Raheem and Mishameeram and half a dozen of the attendants also got involved. Shaikh and Raheem stationed themselves in Paddington, distributing as many pamphlets as they could, creating a stir in the marketplace. The impact was extraordinary. Regular English people began thronging around 15 Warwick Avenue. Often they would be entertained in the now-renowned kitchen, the hospitality of which won over all comers. Being treated daily to kebabs and chicken korma, the grateful crowd was happy then to stand outside chanting, 'Justice for the Indian Prince!'

Seeing the nature of this unusual case, the Speaker advised Kelly and Perry to first present the Bill to a Select Committee appointed by him, who could give an opinion on the legality of the claim. The Select Committee unanimously ruled that it was just,[167] meaning that the Bill could be tabled in Parliament immediately. It was to be named the Nawab of Surat Treaty Bill.

By now, word had reached the Company about what they considered an audacious legal attack. Caught unawares, they hurriedly identified two MPs who might act as counters to the brilliant Kelly and Perry. These were Vernon Smith and James Weir Hogg. Smith, besides being MP for Northampton, was also the President of the Board of Control of the Company, having replaced Lord Ripon. Hogg, MP for Honiton, was also a Director in the Company. It fell to this duo to thwart Jafar's Bill in Parliament.

After months of painstaking correspondence Kelly and Perry extracted a date – 5 June 1856 – on which the Bill would be presented in Parliament. On the preceding day, however, Smith and Hogg were successful in a request to delay the reading, on the grounds that not all relevant materials had been submitted and that the evidence against the Company was insufficiently strong. That evening Kelly and Perry briefed Jafar about the determined resistance they could expect from MPs supportive of the Company. Kelly and Perry knew well of all the delaying tactics that could be used to thwart the tabling of the Bill, some of which they were already witnessing. What was of pressing concern, though, was that the Speaker had announced the last date for hearing all Private Bills in both Houses of Parliament would be 28 June 1856. If the matter was not in hand by then a delay of another year would be imposed. With only two weeks remaining with which to work, this was going to be a race against time. A new date was now issued for the reading – 11 June 1856. Jafar asked if he could drive with the MPs to Parliament on that day.

Kelly, though, had a yet more brilliant idea: he wanted Jafar to enter Parliament with him.

On the morning of 11 of June, after breakfasting with his steadfast MPs Jafar asked Kelly to give a call on the floor of the House to end British rule in Hindustan. Never had such a demand been heard in Parliament. The MP agreed. Tormented by injustice, Jafar's daring demand would soon echo in the Commons. Jafar entered his living room, followed by Kelly and Perry, to find all his attendants lined up and awaiting him. Knowing this was a critical day, each one of them reached out to him, bowed as he walked past, took his hand, kissed it and placed it on their eyes as a sign of reverence. Then the team of three climbed into Jafar's light blue carriage and drove to the Houses of Parliament.

As the horses galloped up the bridge across the Thames and approached the final destination, Jafar couldn't help feeling a sense of anxiety. What if the reading was thwarted again? On reaching Parliament Jafar witnessed the streaming passage of carriages belonging to other MPs. Disembarking along with Kelly and Perry, Jafar gazed long and hard at England's great bastion of law and justice. It was here that the fate of his daughters would be decided. Some MPs who were coming in and had heard of Jafar stopped to have a look at this man from distant Hindustan. Struck by his presence, a crowd soon gathered around him. Some wished him luck and even asked him to sign autographs. Others coldly stared and walked past. Paying such reactions no mind, Jafar walked past the main gate and examined the building with further interest. It wasn't large, and reasonable in beauty. He then turned and studied some work that was being done on a tower of considerable height – a clock tower that was to be known on completion as 'Big Ben'. Then, turning and shaking the hands of his allies, uttering a few encouraging words, Jafar placed himself between the two, ready to walk into Parliament.

Entering the Commons, Kelly and Perry, dressed in their fine suits and long curling white wigs, flanked Jafar, who wore a gold buttoned cream sherwani to his knees, contrasting with a ruby necklace and black turban also known as a *safaa*. The three took their seats in the second row. At the head of the chamber was the elevated chair of the Speaker, and before him a large mahogany table. From the ceiling hung a magnificent chandelier. On either side of the House were ascending rows of more than two hundred seated MPs. At both sides of the large hall were running balconies from which other members could observe proceedings. After other matters had been discussed the Speaker requested that Kelly commence the first reading. Almost immediately Vernon Smith, President of the Board of Control for the Company rose to oppose this, seeking a postponement for a further week, asserting that while the matter before the House had been entered as a Private Bill there were many aspects of it that were public in nature and required further clarifications.[168]

The Speaker this time would have none of it and requested Kelly to continue with his reading. It was apparent that Vernon Smith was just shouting at the wind. Kelly simply rose from his seat and began the reading. Commencing with the general courtesies, Kelly was soon into the stride of a passionate speech. He began with these words:

> Appealing to the honour and good faith of England this was a solemn appeal for justice and involved the character and good name of the nation.[169]

Vernon Smith did not interrupt. The Speaker and the whole House then listened as Kelly became expansive. In a scathing assault on the Company he informed the House of how the Company had first:

> more than fifty years ago [in 1800] on the strength of their large force "prevailed upon and forced the Nawab to reluctantly sign away his territory and army" in return for the annuity of £15,000 for perpetuity.[170]

He described the stopping of the pension for the little girls and the usurpation of the estates in 1842.[171] Then, he told his colleagues, with passion:

> I cannot understand after such language has been used [of providing the pension and ensuring the estates for generation to generation], this claim can be resisted.[172]

In a final controlled outburst he went on to recommend the most drastic action of bringing to an end Company rule in Hindustan:

> At all events, if contracts of this nature are to be evaded then I cannot help thinking that the sooner the British Government in the East [Hindustan] is brought to a termination the better.[173]

Kelly finished off leaving no scope for adjournment. The MPs around him were stunned by what they had just heard. He had spoken in all for nearly 10 minutes. His brilliant oratory skills, supported by the precise articulation of facts, had made a considerable impact. There was silence as he gazed around his fellow MPs and then took his seat. It required the passage of a few seconds before Hogg, the Company Director and MP from Honiton, decided to respond.

Hogg rose and shuffled through his papers. All eyes were on

him. He felt the pressure of Kelly's focused argument. On purpose he tried to deflect this by embarking on a long lecture concerning the fall of Surat and how Wellesley had taken over the city to provide better government.[174] It was apparent that most of the MPs weren't interested in such historical detail. They made it clear by creating a massive hubbub that compelled the Speaker to ask Hogg to turn his remarks directly toward the issues of the violation of the Treaty, the stopping of the pension and the sequestration of the estates. Feeling pressed and almost desperate Hogg expressed his anguish:

> I am sorry to trouble the House at so much length but … I am the more conscious that I have an up-hill case to deal with, as honourable members appear to have formed a pre-conceived notion upon the case…[175]

But the pressure on Hogg did not relent. Cornered, he shouted out a rejoinder to the charge of the stopping of the pension: 'No such thing. The claimant received £2,400 from the Liberal Government.'[176]

Hearing this, Kelly and Perry both rose in fury and led a heated onslaught upon Hogg. Pointing fingers at him vigorously they reminded him that the pension of £15,000 had to be restored in its entirety, with no measly compromise amount. The febrile atmosphere in the House was beginning to affect Hogg's thinking. Sensing humiliation, Hogg's face filled with anger. Having nothing more to say and finding himself completely exposed, he resorted to hurling a personal insult, looking at Jafar and describing the family of Surat and Jafar as 'low born.'[177]

Kelly and Perry had had enough. They again rose and, backed by an erupting House, roared their opposition to a now grimacing and snarling Hogg who decided to retake his seat. The personal slur on Jafar had seemed to exemplify the Company's frustration. Jafar was livid and urged Perry to press Hogg for an apology. But Perry calmed Jafar down. The noise was so loud and unrelenting that the Speaker had to intervene to maintain decorum.

Vernon Smith, the President of the Board of Control for the Company and MP for Northampton, now realised that there seemed to be mounting support for the Hindustani Prince and so he quickly amended his position, stating that he didn't seek the defeat of the Bill through delay but merely sought more time to read through the evidence.[178]

But by now the clear momentum was with Kelly and Perry. The Speaker then requested Perry to rise and respond to Hogg's and Smith's call for further adjournment. Perry was precise and articulate:

> Meer Jafur Ali has been for fourteen years endeavouring to bring this matter to an issue before a tribunal competent to try the question. The East India Company are bound to do him justice and it will not be consistent with justice that the discussion of this question be adjourned. Delay in a case between a powerful government and an individual implies defeat. The statements made by the member from Honiton [Hogg] I must say contain gross inaccuracies. I dissent from them from first to last. The petitioner declares the imputations casting a slur on his family and his origins to be grossly untrue and a proof of their untruth is contained in the documents.[179]

Perry having finished, the Speaker then invited other MPs to voice their opinions. MP after MP rose to speak in favour of Jafar, while Hogg and Smith watched in disbelief. Among the most prominent voices in favour of the Prince was J.G. Phillimore who called the Company's arguments 'miserable pettifogging' and hoped that the House would 'not allow the measure to be defeated by any argument.'[180] Mr Spooner, another prominent MP, said: 'The report is directly in favour of the claim and it is the duty as well as the policy of the House to support the claim as it has to do with property and I hope the House would not shrink from passing the Bill and that it is with great regret I see there is a proposal for postponement.'[181] John Macgregor considered this 'a question of great importance and that justice should be done in this case and Parliament would be guilty of dereliction of duty if it allowed the claim to be defeated.'[182] But the most scathing was Sir J. Fitzgerald, who thought it would be 'a denial of justice to allow any delay in granting redress in a case of the most flagrant tyranny on the part of the Bombay Government, the annuity being taken away by the East India Company on false pretences, the Company having been too long allowed to shirk this just claim. And it is the bounden duty of the House to interfere and stop the Company's course of injustice.'[183]

The support for the Hindustani Prince was rising like a tide. Jafar, sitting next to Kelly and Perry, sensed that the current was in his favour but kept a stoic expression and asked his allies to push for a vote right away. If the vote was taken swiftly, all three believed, the Bill would pass. Jafar felt the first tremors of excited anticipation rushing through him. It was that feeling that unabashedly bursts through any barriers of doubt: the exhilarating sense of impending triumph.

Then, to everyone's surprise, the Speaker abruptly endorsed Vernon Smith's call for more time to study the evidence, and announced a date – 18 June 1856 – for another reading of the Bill. The day's work was done. It had been a tense afternoon. For Jafar and his allies, making their way out of the Commons, there was an unavoidable feeling that they had been denied a certain victory.

That evening Jafar went with Mary Jane to the theatre: an outdoor performance in Regent's Park of Shakespeare's *Romeo and Juliet*. Jafar felt an avalanche of emotions within himself. For fourteen years he had been fighting the battle of his life. It was requiring him to exhibit nerves of steel and mental fortitude. Yet his Sufi heart had been captured by a woman's tender love. After the play Mary Jane insisted on the popular English culinary classic, fish and chips, at a food stall in the park. The long summer day in London drifted to a close with the two strolling down a pathway and Jafar recounting the day's affairs. There was a sniff of victory, the prospect for Mary Jane for a possible life in Hindustan. She wore a smile for the entire evening.

Over the following days the *Illustrated Times London* carried two related stories in its elaborate Parliament section, both of them demonstrating support for the Hindustani Prince. One was on the events of 11 June. The *Illustrated Times* described the debate in the House as a 'prolonged discussion of the Bill that had been designed to neutralise an act of injustice by the Company towards the heirs of the Nawab of Surat.'[184] But the second article published the same day in the paper was a much more detailed personal account of Jafar, his cause, and the precarious position in which the exposed Company currently found itself:

> Persons who are daily about London streets must have seen a light blue carriage of large dimension trimmed with silver and seated in the carriage Orientals robed and turbanded: The Nabobs. The East India Company signed a Treaty that the Nawab's heirs should forever receive an annuity of Rs. 150,000 (£15,000). The Company with a smartness savouring rather too much of Leadenhall Street refused to pay but not only that, seized the private estate of the deceased Nawab and turned the descendants upon the world without a shilling. Well, it is to remedy this wrong that Meer Jafur Ali has brought his affairs to Parliament. The Bill is now before the House and is understood will pass. When passed it will not only renew the payment of the annuity but also restore the arrears since 1842 and the private estate of which the family has been robbed. And so coming to the gentlemen riding in the light blue carriage and seen in the House is Meer Jafur Ali, the other, the attaché of this exalted personage. Meer Jafur Ali is a remarkably fine imposing man. No sooner do they appear in the lobby [of Parliament] they are surrounded by a whole levee of members. And if the bill will pass we should not be surprised if Meer

Jafur Ali Khan becomes famous in the country with whole columns given to his hospitality.[185]

In readiness for the second Commons session devoted to the Bill, Kelly spent an entire week writing what would become the most passionate speech he would give in his career. He had decided to unabashedly threaten the Company with the direct intervention of the Crown.

On the morning of 18 June, as the hearing was scheduled to begin, Kelly was entirely unsurprised when William Somerville, an MP supportive of the Company, sought a further postponement of the Bill.[186] The Speaker rejected this proposal and called upon Kelly to begin the reading. Thus Kelly began to deliver his carefully prepared speech:

> Sir, the question that is raised by this Bill is already before the House. With the territories of Surat in possession of The East India Company, I call upon them to perform their engagement and pay the promised annuity…[187]

Kelly proceeded to issue a challenge of remarkable importance:

> I will call upon the Minister of the Crown to bring forward the law officers of the Crown and let them declare what is the plain and simple meaning of a solemn engagement. On one side are the interests of a family and on the other the honour and fair fame of this country… I call upon the Government, unless they interpose to compel the East India Company to do justice, to bring forward the law advisors including the Attorney General, the Solicitor General and the Advocate to the Queen [Sir Richard Bethell], and let these eminent individuals say that a reasonable doubt in the claim can be

suggested ... I want to know what lawyer of reputation will come forward and hesitate to give judgement in favour of the claimant ... [188]

Then, powerfully illustrating the grave situation of Jafar's daughters, Kelly tugged at the heartstrings of MPs by delivering the next few sentences with immense passion:

The signature of the Nawab [in 1800] was procured to the treaty in which it secured the annuity to his descendants, to the infant children who now appeal for justice in this House. Now, having heard the plea of these children, what is the answer? The Company didn't just stop their pension but possessed itself of the private property of the Nawab and that of Meer Jafur Ali and having an officer of their own took upon themselves the disposition of that property which is a birth right (of the children).[189]

Pointing to various people involved in this affair he carried on:

All parties are assembled. Here is the claimant [Jafar]; here is the East India Company, here is the Crown and here are the people of this country. We are now all here assembled. I think that no lawyer will rise and no honourable gentleman will rise in this House and seek to put a different construction upon this treaty. We are before this House appealing for justice.[190]

The impact of Kelly's speech upon the House was spellbinding. As with his address during the previous reading, on this occasion, too, there was silence. The MPs favouring the Company knew very well that their argument was weak, and so they would have to resort to paper-thin conceits in order to delay or distract from the core issue.

Vernon Smith again rose and tried for the adjournment of the Bill but, seeing that he was going nowhere with such a ploy and that the Speaker was about to overrule him, he tried a distracting tactic: first trying anew to question the framing of a Private Bill instead of a Public one, then trying to make an issue of Jafar's political lobbying, which he described as unfair:

> Now Sir, of all the objectionable proceedings that could possibly take place upon the questions of this kind, any matter or private canvass is the worst. The Company is the governing power of India and if you are to allow that all persons who think themselves in any way aggrieved are to come over here and prosecute their claims by canvassing this country and introduce bills into Parliament, I think you will introduce one of the most objectionable principles. It is notorious that persons who do hold the situation of princes in India entertain a very strong notion that everything is conducted in this country by canvassing.[191]

Smith was referring to three important annexations in Hindustan, but he had only mentioned them in a way to suit his purpose. In 1848 Lord Dalhousie had annexed Satara, a large Maratha principality under the 'Doctrine of Lapse' policy. The Satara princes were descendants of Shivaji, the great seventeenth-century Maratha King. Having such a distinguished background did not prevent Dalhousie from forcibly annexing Satara when the Maharaja died leaving behind no male heir and outrightly rejecting the adopted son. The Satara family had desperately tried to get the attention of the Court of Directors and even Parliament through an agent they had sent to England. Bapojee, the agent, stationed himself in London and had lobbied hard for the noble Maratha family of Satara, but in the end, sadly, he didn't get his master's rights restored.[192]

More recently the Company had annexed two large principalities: Awadh [Oudh] and Sindh. Awadh was the most fertile of regions in northern Hindustan, and the Nawab had been deposed by the Company, which cited reasons to do with bad governance. Inclined to art, the ruler of Awadh was a cultural icon for his people, who loved him. The annexation of his principality would soon become a breaking point of patience for Hindustani princes who refused to give in to Company demands. Such would be the consequences of that annexation that, one year later, the Company would face an extraordinary armed uprising, sweeping across most of Hindustan, which it would label as 'the Mutiny of 1857.' Hindustanis, however, would speak of it as the First War of Independence.

Exiled in Calcutta Awadh's deposed ruler was a heartbroken man. But one of his wives, Hazrat Mahal, refused to give in to the Company. She had escaped with her son into the forests and was urging her troops and people to fight. The storm clouds of war were gathering in Hindustan. The mother of Awadh's ruler, though, had come to hear of Jafar's bold legal resistance in England, and had ventured to England to petition for her son's claims. She had sought out Jafar and asked for his advice on how to defeat the Company legally.[193] Their meetings were usually held at Jafar's residence, and he had willingly shared his knowledge of the British legal system with her, a set of lessons that she found invaluable.

The other annexed principality, Sindh, also contained within it the port of Karachi. The princes of Sindh, deposed by the Company and learning of Jafar's efforts in the British Parliament, had pitched up in England too and also sought Jafar's advice. Jafar had become the symbol of Hindustani resistance in England: the go-to man for other such aggrieved individuals. He encouraged these deposed royals of Sindh to stay and fight in England. One of the aspects of the legal pursuit Jafar had popularised was political lobbying – and it was this pursuit to which Vernon Smith referred in the House of Commons. Smith and other Company officials were terribly worried about the growing trend Jafar had begun, of challenging the Company in England. The dissension would have to be stopped.

Having pointed out the threat to the Company's reputation in England through 'canvassing', Vernon Smith continued his speech, choosing to focus on the difference between a Private and Public Bill, desperately trying to insist that Jafar's grievance fell into the latter category.[194] He seemed to be getting a certain degree of traction as Kelly and Perry watched some MPs nod their heads.

Smith then launched into an articulation of the 'office of the Nawab', mentioning that the Company was the authority that appointed the Nawab and that if it chose to appoint another individual then it could happily do so – an individual, moreover, who didn't necessary have to be from the family, and to whom the pension and estates would go. This was a weak argument because the Treaty was with the 'heirs and successors' and for over a hundred years there had been a hereditary line of heirs and succession. The assurance was for the 'family and descendants.' Nevertheless, Smith had set this argument to flight.[195] Kelly and Perry swiftly looked around to see if there were any nods: an indication that MPs were swayed by what they had heard. Smith had got a few nods with the Private versus Public Bill argument, and so Kelly and Perry looked out for any indication regarding the 'appointment of the Nawab' argument. To their relief there didn't seem to be any reaction. In fact, some MPs simply exuded uninterest at this line.

Seeing that he needed to spark some renewed attention to his argument Smith then spoke extensively about how the Company had, in his opinion, dealt liberally with the family. He referred to how the pension had been raised to £2,400 and then to £5,200.[196] Yet in the same breath he alluded to how the pension might lead to the creation of 'bad mock kings.'[197] Here, hinting clearly that Jafar might become one such, Smith was further floating the notion that that had Jafar continued to pursue his claims in Hindustan then he would have received another patient hearing. This was, again, a weak argument and much to Kelly and Perry's satisfaction MPs didn't seem interested. Some even interrupted Smith, trying to bring him back to the core issue of Treaty violation.

Smith quickly reassessed how his speech was going down

and, aware that the response was underwhelming, resorted to the one argument that had got him some traction: that concerning the classification of the Bill under discussion as Private rather than Public. Yet again a large number of MPs indicated a disinclination to follow where Smith wished to go. Then Smith did something most astonishing, which could only have been the product of desperation and a desire to save face for the Company, though it was not without guile. Smith turned to face Jafar where he sat in the second row with Kelly and Perry, and he directly offered to raise the pension to £7,500 (but only to the end of Jafar's and his daughters' lifetimes) and to return half of the estates.[198] This caught everyone by surprise.

Unknown to the House, the day before the current debate Smith as President of the Board of Control of the Company had called for an urgent meeting of the Court of Directors and other Board members. He had related the fact that on 11 June during the first reading of the Bill almost the entire House seemed to be in favour of the Hindustani Prince. Utter embarrassment and disgrace loomed for the Company. A decision was taken to try and sway the House away from reading the Bill as a Private one. But if that failed then Smith would be allowed the freedom to propose a compromise. What that might be would be decided by Smith in the moment.

And so, seeing the debate slipping from his hands, Smith took it upon himself as President of Board to make the offer he made. Smith believed that in doing this the Company would be seen as willing to compromise and to reach an understanding. If Jafar accepted, he would be made to feel that he was not returning empty-handed to Hindustan while the Company would retain half the pension and half the estates. If Jafar rejected the bargain he might yet be portrayed by the Company as a greedily inflexible man.

All eyes were now on Jafar. Seated in the second row he held his nerve. All that Smith was getting from him was a cold stare. Smith reiterated his offer, first looking at the Speaker and then directly at Jafar: 'I am willing the claimant should have an opportunity of considering this proposal – I mean the gentleman himself [Jafar].[199]

Smith was compelling Jafar to say yes; and in doing so he was trying to cut off Kelly and Perry. Looking at the two and then directly at Jafar, Smith continued:

I mean the gentleman himself [Jafar], because with due respect to my honourable friend [Kelly], I have seen the heat with which he has engaged in this cause and I know the energy and ability of this honourable friend [Kelly] behind me, but I think it should be considered by the claimant himself.[200]

Jafar kept calm, sensing this was a trap. If he said yes then it was all over. Seconds ticked by. There was silence in the House as everyone waited in anticipation. But still Smith received only a coldly unflinching stare. Kelly looked at Jafar. It was a clear sign of disapproval and an opportunity for Kelly to jump in: 'I wish I could accede to the suggestion that is proposed,' said Kelly, 'but it is impossible for me to do so.'[201]

The Company's emergency gambit had failed. With Jafar and Kelly having rejected the offer, another MP rose and spoke, this time in favour of Jafar, this Mr Napier looking at him all the while: 'My feeling about the Bill is that it is a claim of justice and the case embodied in the Bill is well founded in all its parts, never was there a just measure of Parliament.'[202]

The business was drawing to a close. Kelly kept looking at the clock. He wanted the vote to be called but Smith's argument, driven by the desire to forestall matters, had taken a great deal of time, while other MPs still needed to speak. Kelly was worried. It seemed Smith might have done just enough to push proceedings toward yet another reading. By offering half the pension and half the estates, he had bought time and some support. Another MP, by the name of Wigram, rose to speak of how liberal the Company was, and that the revenues of Hindustan should not be directed by a Private Bill to a private person.[203] The Speaker then indicated that the day was going to close and that the next reading would occur on 24 June 1856.

Just then an MP, Danby Seymour who felt tremendously for Jafar rose and pointing at the Hindustani Prince while looking directly at Hogg, said:

> I feel the highest esteem and respect for the gentleman [Jafar]. I am quite aware that he is of an ancient respectable family and that he only does what he believes to be the duty towards his children.[204]

Seymour couldn't help himself. He hadn't forgotten Hogg's insult to a father fighting for his daughters, an insult he had thought intolerable. The day ended. As Jafar and his allies made their way out, little was said. Seymour's last words for the afternoon had struck a poignant note and the heavy air in the House of Commons that had echoed with the cry for justice by Kelly laid heavy on all. Kelly and Perry would now have to close the Bill and push for a vote on 24 June itself. If the Company was successful in holding out with delaying tactics then the Bill would be considered defeated. The next six days would be exceptionally anxious ones for Jafar.

—

Intense discussions ensued between Jafar, Kelly and Perry. Jafar voiced the opinion in no uncertain terms that he hadn't sailed to England to return with only a half of the pension and half the estates. It was all or nothing. While Kelly and Perry lauded his passion, they knew that if the vote did not happen on the 24th then the cause would collapse. The Company could easily rescind the offer of half the pension and estates, and so Jafar would lose that, too. And so the major question was about how to play the day – how to manage each allotted hour of the session so as to ensure the vote happened. They knew time was of the essence. Kelly debated whether he should write and deliver another passionate speech that would push the collective sentiment over the line. But he abandoned that thought after much consideration. He did not want to take up too much time of the House. He believed he had made a strong impact on the conscience of the MPs and that the impact would last. Perry, too, would keep any arguments brief, allowing enough time for all MPs to have a say and ensure the vote happened.

On the morning of 24 June, Jafar and Mary Jane went for an early walk in Little Venice. It was a clear summer morning and as they strolled by the canal some passers-by recognised Jafar and approached him to wish him luck. Some denizens of Maida Vale who were now well acquainted with their famous Oriental neighbour waved and offered encouraging words from their balconies and windows. Mary Jane held her man's arm tight in admiration. He looked at her with love such as he had never felt for another. It was in the most testing time of life that Mary Jane was the woman he found standing by him.

As had been the norm set by Jafar, Kelly and Perry arrived at 15 Warwick Avenue to breakfast and ride to Parliament together. Kelly and Perry hoped to brief Jafar about how they planned to play the day. But Jafar wanted to relax everyone's nerves. On the most crucial morning of his life he elected to speak about matters closest to his heart. He talked about his girls: Ladli, who was now growing so fast, and the cheerful Rahimun. He told Kelly and Perry about how fascinated the girls were with the ways of the English: their customs, clothes and cuisine. He spoke to them passionately about the rural life in Kamandiyah; of the river Badar on the banks of which he was born, and how the canal at Little Venice reminded him of Badar's tributaries. He spoke about the crops his farmers grew – the watermelons in particular. He spoke of his love for horses and how he had been trained in riding and shooting by the proud Kathis. He longed to be back there. He wanted Kamandiyah to become the beautiful refuge for him and Mary Jane.

The two Englishmen listened and seemed to forget the

seriousness of the hours that lay ahead. Kelly and Perry also spoke of their own families, lightening the morning even further. Dressed in his lucky crimson robe, Jafar then made his way with Kelly and Perry to the light blue carriage that waited to carry them to Parliament. Pressure had given way to a feeling of serenity in all three men. Again they entered the House of Commons and took their seats. Kelly informed Jafar it was a full house of 241 MPs. Jafar looked around. Most eyes were on him. Kelly pointed out to Jafar the Deputy Chairman of the Company who had decided to make his presence felt on this day. Afraid of defeat, the Court of Directors hoped his presence might add some weight to their arguments. But what unfolded on this day was something Jafar and his allies had never anticipated.

On the announcement of the Speaker, Kelly rose and in a calm voice made a very brief statement, hoping that on this day justice would be served.[205] He didn't say more. It was now the turn of a man who had vehemently opposed the passing of the Bill: James Hogg. He had planned to make this his day. Hogg had earned the disapproval of several MPs for the personal insult he had hurled at Jafar, but this time he wanted to come back yet more strongly. Hogg had completely disapproved of the compromise proposed by Smith of half the pension and half the estates. He unleashed a speech that was steeped in anger and hatred.

Looking at Kelly he began: 'I will maintain my opinion to the last, unawed by majorities.'[206] Then, looking at his colleague Smith who had proposed the fudging halfway-house offer, he said:

> My honourable friend has adverted to a compromise. I do not care what opinion any honourable gentleman entertains who hears me. I say, whether it is an opinion favourable to this man [Jafar], or against him, whatever your opinion is, this compromise is discreditable, not to use a harsher term.[207]

Hogg seemed to be so riven with anger that he lost his train of thought. He then spent the next few minutes contradicting the stand of the Company, of which he himself was a Director. Then he suddenly issued a claim that neither he nor the Court of Directors had any objection to the private estates being restored.[208]

The Company was failing. Contradictions seemed to be issuing from its representatives. All in the House knew by now that Hogg's arguments were utterances that were completely unhinged and incoherent. Looking down at his papers and aware that Hogg was failing, Kelly couldn't suppress a smile, to which Hogg reacted frustratingly: 'I do not know why the right honourable gentleman [Kelly] should smile. I hope he would say it and rise and say what he means.'[209]

Kelly ignored Hogg and let him continue to engineer a debacle for the Company. For the next twenty minutes Hogg continued extolling Wellesley's annexation of Surat on the grounds that it brought better government. Smith and Hogg then contradicted each other on various aspects of the Treaty, and examples given to correlate the case with others.[210] But no one seemed interested in intra-Company bickering and Hogg's speech was interrupted by voices frequently trying to bring him back to Treaty violations. The next couple of hours saw the Company's representatives dramatically turn on each other and stoop to levels of ridiculous personal accusations.

Unable to take his colleagues' imprudence at dismissing the compromise he had suggested, an embarrassed Smith rose and said:

While I agree with many of my friends [Hogg's] opinions he has exaggerated them in a manner that can be hardly justified. My honourable friend [Hogg] is totally incompetent. That he is a most able advocate, I admit, if an advocate can be able who so overloads his statements as to weary the attention of his auditors and who states his case in such a manner as to array hostility against him, instead of the conciliate prejudices in his favour. I think I could prove to the House that the greater part of my embarrassment has risen from my resting upon the slippery support of the Court of Directors [Hogg being one].[211]

Jafar, Kelly and Perry looked on, holding back excitement as Company officials tore at one another. They were falling to pieces. Their reputation was crumbling on the floor of the Commons. Smith and Hogg who were supposed to be on the same side were engaging in the most unbelievable arguments against each other. It was destroying the Company's stand which they were supposed to guard: Smith continued lashing out at Hogg. Accusing him of being 'in a habit of assuming that Parliament attends to him as if he spoke on behalf of the entire Company,'[212] Smith then pointed at the Deputy Chairman, almost pleading for support on the compromise, saying: 'I speak in the presence of the Deputy Chairman. I believe we have perfectly agreed in this matter [the compromise].'[213] He then continued:

When my honourable friend [Hogg] taunts me will any man say I was not at liberty to form my own judgement? Does he mean to say that a body of men are always to maintain their position and stand like gods and have no permission ever to frame any other decision than their predecessors? I utterly abjure that doctrine. I am bound to tell the House since my honourable friend [Hogg] has talked of compromise that since this case first came to me it's about compromise. I feel mortified at what my honourable friend [Hogg] has been saying.[214]

Then looking at Jafar, Smith again offered something unexpected: an out of Parliament settlement on the condition that Jafar withdrew the Bill:

I believe whatever the compromises, they should be done in private. If this could be settled out of doors and the Bill withdrawn it would be an infinitely better conclusion. I stated that with the sanction of the Court of Directors I was prepared to do so.[215]

Not only was the Company in complete disarray and totally divided in opinion: they were now desperately – under Smith, the President of the Board – looking for a way to get out of Parliament. The ground was fast shifting under the Company's feet. Smith was almost pleading with Jafar for an outside settlement and hoping that Jafar might get Kelly and Perry to step in and withdraw the Bill in favour of the private arrangement. Smith waited nervously hoping to hear something in his favour from the second bench where Jafar, Kelly and Perry sat. He looked at Jafar.

Fourteen years of struggle came alive in Jafar's mind. He thought of how as a 17 year old his destiny found its way as the custodian of the House of Surat. For years the Company had hounded him in Hindustan. For years they had blocked every road to justice for him. They had brought him, his father and his girls to the brink of ruin. They had robbed his girls of their birthright. Now in their own Parliament, he had with Kelly and Perry led the most daring legal counterattack. The Company was on the ropes, looking desperately towards him for a settlement, hoping he would give a sign to withdraw the Bill. How the tables had turned! The hunters were now the hunted. The House watched in silence again and all eyes were on Jafar. There wasn't a sign of emotion on his face. Smith had his answer. Jafar's cold stare signalled no compromise. He was going to take the Bill to a vote.

Smith was experiencing a sensation of imminent defeat. When he next spoke, there was a resignation in his voice:

As far as my vote is concerned, I shall vote against it [The Bill], but as regards any opposition in this House, it is hopeless. I still think this Bill should be altered. The opinion out of the doors [outside Parliament] is "Here is a poor fellow robbed by a great Company and it is a duty to take up his cause against those who are so treating him." I shall not trespass further upon the time of the House. I have acted with the parties [Jafar, Kelly and Perry] by offering them a compromise with the utmost frankness and I hope cordiality.[216]

This was the time to bring matters swiftly to a close. Kelly then played his trump card to put any doubts to rest. Before the Speaker could ask for a vote, Kelly wanted one last strong closing statement in favour of Jafar. But it wouldn't be him who would deliver it. He signalled by a nod of his head to his right: it was a gesture to get Bethell, Solicitor General to the Queen, to rise. Kelly had brought in Bethell as a counter to the Deputy Chairman of the Company, who had just witnessed Smith and Hogg presiding over the death of any hope the Company had of salvaging their situation. Kelly now wanted Bethell to deliver the killer blow. Bethell rose to speak:

The East India Company entered into a contract with the representative of an ancient dignity by which he surrendered his fortunes and his perogatives [In 1800], and they undertook to make a provision for himself and his family; but the manner in which they carried their subsequent proceedings into effect was a plain violation of all natural justice. They believe they should be the sole judges. They proceeded to another act of mockery of justice, which was to delegate to their own officer the power of pronouncing the final decision. I think the House will have discharged a great duty by passing this Bill. This Private Bill will have a merit which I fear very few Public Bills will have.[217]

Kelly now looked at the clock. The Speaker rose and gave his consent to the Private Bill. Then came the signal to vote: ayes in favour of passing the Bill, noes against. This was what Jafar had been waiting for so long. He gripped the side of his seat, looked around and shut his eyes. An enormous cry went up. It was a thunderous roar. Jafar's senses told him he was hearing right. The sound was continuous and reverberating. So strong was it that it compelled Jafar to open his eyes. He looked around all the benches in front first, then he turned to the right and left, and then finally straining back he looked upwards behind. All he could see was a sea of MPs, all of whom had risen screaming with their hands raised: *Aye! Aye! Aye!* This was the moment that none in Hindustan could have seen, but Jafar's eyes did see it. England had risen in support for the young Hindustani Prince and against its own Company.

For nearly five minutes the shouting of *Aye!* went on. Those five minutes seemed hours to Jafar. Not waiting for the Speaker to count, a large swarm of MPs rushed to Jafar. He was soon surrounded. Some reached out to his shoulders from behind, shaking them in approval, still yelling *Aye!* Some held him by the arm and a few put their arms around him. Kelly and Perry were surrounded, too. Such was the noise that the Speaker had to repeatedly call for calm. Some MPs who had supported Jafar but had never spoken with him rushed now to introduce themselves. Jafar was completely surrounded. The House had never seen an outpouring such as this. Finally the Speaker managed to get some order and calm the House. The count had to be done.

The MPs refused to leave Jafar's side, most wanting to be seen standing next to the oriental. The count began. With each passing second it became even clearer. Out of the 241 votes, the final count was 213 Ayes to 28 noes.[218] The Bill had passed with an overwhelming majority.[219] The Company's arguments had been destroyed in what was its first political defeat in the House of Commons at the hands of a Hindustani. When the result was announced another massive roar went up. Completely surrounded in his seat Jafar heard a new chant arise. *Bravo! Bravo!* This state of affairs continued for nearly half an hour as each of the 213 MPs who had voted in his favour tried to make their way to Jafar and congratulate him. Kelly and Perry, amid this chaos, congratulated each other and then Jafar. But

Jafar didn't just want a handshake. Finally being able to rise from his seat he reached out to his two great allies and gave each of them a warm embrace, for both had done so much to orchestrate this most dazzling victory.

Kelly and Perry then began asking MPs to make way so that the two could leave the House. It took them another half an hour before they could exit, for MPs reached out to shake their hands as they walked past. Jafar, though, requested some extra time and sat back in his seat. The House began emptying. Jafar looked around, took a few deep breaths, and savoured the moment of triumph in solitude. Sitting now almost alone in the House, he felt his nerves relax. This was the bastion of British law and justice. This is where he had defeated the most powerful corporation in the world. This is where he had exposed the colonising power of his homeland. At the peak of its powers the Company stood humiliated, its reputation torn asunder. After ten minutes of quiet, Jafar made his way out. As he walked out of the corridor that opened into the main ground he saw Kelly, Perry and Bethell standing waiting for him. Behind them were nearly all the 213 MPs that had voted for him. They had waited for him to come out. Kelly reached out and lifted Jafar's right arm, Perry and Bethell got hold of his left and together they lifted Jafar's arms aloft in the air. All 213 MPs roared *Bravo! Bravo!* Then Kelly gave the call of 'Three Cheers for His Asiatic Highness', the title with which the *Times* had addressed Jafar. All 213 MPs then burst into *Hip Hip Hurray! Hip Hip Hurray! Hip Hip Hurray!* As Jafar walked towards his light blue carriage the cheering then took the form of 'For he's a jolly good fellow.' Jafar was cheered all the way until he climbed into his carriage, whereupon he waved to his supporters.[220] His faith in British judiciary seemed vindicated.

At 15 Warwick Avenue Mary Jane and his attendants waited in great anticipation. Seeing his carriage approach, Mary Jane rushed down from the first floor and threw open the front door. Mishameeram the doorkeeper had darted out already to open the carriage door. Shaikh, Raheem and Noor now hastened out of the kitchen. Dost Shah, who had been cleaning a portrait of Jafar's two girls, finished it quickly with two swipes, and ran to the door. Ali Akbar the secretary, plus the musicians and other half a dozen attendants who crowded the main living room were hoping very much, too, to hear the outcome.

Kelly, Perry and Bethell disembarked first; then Jafar, who wore a smile. With a nod of his head and a clenched fist, he signalled victory to Mary Jane. She ran and flung herself in his arms. The attendants went crazy. Mishameeram fell to the floor, bowing low and kissing Jafar's hand. Dost Shah burst into tears and ran back to see the portrait of the girls. Sobbing profusely with joy he brought out the portrait and stood at the main door holding it high in the air. Each attendant then rushed out, bowing low. Some kissed Jafar's hand. Some fell to his feet. Jafar walked up the stairs to the main entrance gazing at the portrait of his girls that Dost Shah still held up in the air, tears rolling down his cheeks. Dost Shah lowered the portrait as Jafar gently kissed it and entered the house.

That evening it wasn't just Jafar's entourage who had waited in anticipation for the result. Not far away in London, the Queen Mother of Awadh who had come to England hearing of Jafar's brave charge, and also the Prince of Sindh, both awaited the news. Jafar instructed Noor to go right away and invite them both for a celebratory dinner party. The attendants swung into action. It would be a fabulous evening over lamb biryani, shami kebabs, lamb korma, vegetarian pulao and the most delicious Indian desserts including the shahi tukda made of almonds and milk. Bethell, Kelly and Perry joined the party and lingered to the early hours, savouring the food, wine and music.

Over the next few days Kelly and Perry went about the task of passing on the baton to the Earl of Albermale and the Marquess of Clanricarde to champion Jafar's cause in the House of Lords.[221] As a special case, a specific date of 7 July was given with instructions that only an hour would be allocated for this Bill. Since there were many other pending matters and all Private Bills had to be addressed in finality on that date, just an hour would be given to the Nawab of Surat Treaty Bill. This meant the Earl of Albermale and the Marquess of Clanricarde would have to close the debate on that day itself. Although the Earl of Albermale and the Marquess pushed hard, the House – pressured by the Duke of Argyll who backed the Company – declared a lack of proper time to debate the Public versus Private angle; and so the Bill remained in abeyance with a chance to reopen it again after some months.[222] In the eyes of the Company this could have meant defeat of the Bill. Although Kelly assured Jafar that the House of Lords was a reflecting body and would not thwart the Bill, the Duke of Argyll had made a passionate plea in favour of the Company.

For Jafar, the delaying tactics meant justice denied. In order to prevent any mischief from the Company Jafar acted swiftly and wrote directly to the Crown seeking intervention.[223] Bethell who had regularly kept Victoria and Albert abreast about Jafar's case, sought a meeting with them to discuss the issue. Word reached the Company about this. The Company knew well they could now be on the verge of witnessing direct Crown intervention in Jafar's case. Besides, their reputation had taken a pounding in Albert's eyes after Jafar's victory in the House of Commons.

The Company officials in London dealing with Jafar's case were by now a beleaguered lot. Jaded and tired they were. But equally weary was Jafar. Presently, this epic struggle had left him holding onto the last strands of hope. It was true that Jafar had won a spectacular victory in the House of Commons, but what was also evident was that the House of Lords had stalled the Bill. The question now was who would blink first? The tiring Company or the unrelenting Hindustani Prince who was searching deep into his last reserves of willpower? Finally, on 20 November 1856 the Company made the formal offer to Jafar that he had so longed for.[224] The deal would see the restoration of the entire pension of £15,000 out of which £10,000 would be for the girls and £5,000 to be divided between the last Nawab's two widows. Besides this, being pressed hard by Kelly and Perry for damages, the Company agreed to pay Jafar another £20,000. This would be accounted for as a face-saving 'gift for the girls' marriages alongwith the arrears since 1842.'[225] With regards the estates Jafar had to appeal to the Privy Council again, which he would in time. The result would again be in Jafar's favour: The Privy Council gave the order to lift the illegal sequestration for a year. Jafar would have to assess the estates and take them under his charge.[226] Arbuthnot's recommendation for public auction of the estates now stood crushed.

It took nearly eleven months after the victory in the House of Commons to get all the paperwork in place, minute details agreed and finally signed. These were moments of much reflection. The one person Jafar reflected upon most was his ageing father. Jafar had come such a long way in his pursuit of justice. The boy prince of Kamandiyah who rode carefree in his father's lands had, upon his marriage to the princess of Surat as a 17-year-old, signed up to a challenge to safeguard the family. This challenge had come to define his life and he had risen to meet it brilliantly. But his efforts to fight the Company would not have been possible without the support of his father who had put all he had on the line, almost bringing him to financial ruin. Jafar would acknowledge this, hailing his father's position in his final correspondences with the Company.[227]

But now, Jafar felt a certain sense of emotional release. Kelly realised as much. He wanted Jafar to begin enjoying England again. Kelly invited him for celebratory events, particularly shooting. On one such occasion at a Captain Jay's estate the *Standard* which, like many papers, had come to enjoy reporting on Jafar, observed his Oriental presence closely and reported on his reputation of being an excellent shot with a rifle.[228] He had scored heavily that afternoon, enjoying the sport immensely and ensuring he came out a winner in a shooting event which was followed by a *dejeuner* with Mary Jane by his side. The exotic couple were generating curiosity.

On another occasion he was invited to the London Tavern as part of the anniversary festivities of the City Orthopaedic Hospital. It was an ironic meeting with the current Duke of Wellington.[229] As Jafar entered, the press, in particular the *Morning Post* announced his entry as 'His Highness of Surat'.[230] The Duke's entry was announced with all necessary titles, too. The current Duke took his place and stood at a distance. He had followed the Hindustani Prince's case closely, knowing of the Treaty of 1800. After speeches and much ceremony during which Jafar voluntarily contributed financially to the hospital, the two came face to face. Jafar had Mary Jane by his side. Awed by the presence of the Duke, Mary Jane curtsied. Jafar gave no salutation. Not a word was said between the two men – all that passed was a courteous nod acknowledging each other's presence. That would be the last encounter between the custodian of the House of Surat and the House of Wellington.

London's society seemed to be relishing this cross-pollinated couple. Jafar's light blue carriage carrying him dressed in Hindustani robes and Mary Jane became a much sought out object.

At a ball and dinner hosted by Sir Richard Bethell the couple entered later than others. Jafar, timing their entry for impact. He was dressed in a black sherwani and a Mughal dagger neatly buried in a dark green cummerbund. Mary Jane wearing kohl in her eyes, carried herself with grace, her arm lodged in Jafar's. Bethell rose at their entrance and as they made their way in and seeing the Solicitor General to the Queen rise, all rose to welcome the couple. Hesitating to dance, Jafar held back. He was utterly unaccomplished in Western dance. Mary Jane politely turned down requests standing by Jafar and watching the spectacle. Made to sit at the head of the table Jafar with Mary Jane not too far away held conversation that ranged from

Hindustan to shooting in the English countryside and from politics to Ascot.

In the meanwhile much word had begun coming from Hindustan. The country had erupted in flames. Many a deposed prince had raised the banner of revolt. The northern and central plains of Hindustan were now flowing with Hindustani and English blood. The first war of independence was at its peak. Jafar consulted Kelly and Perry, who assured him that whatever the consequences in Hindustan the signing of the legal documents in England bound the Company now in totality. Jafar's thoughts were on a different plane, however. What if the Company lost the war? He would surely have to then rule independently in Surat and Kamandiyah. It was vital that he got back as soon as possible.

Would he take Mary Jane to a land that was now baying for English blood? What would their life be there? Besides, Jafar's wife Basti and his two daughters were also waiting for him.

8

Taking Leave

It was an overcast day in September 1857. *The Royal Cornwall Gazette* reported on the end of the Parliamentary sessions. It lamented the lack of glamour and attributed it to the absence of two personalities: 'This splendour (of the closing session) was nowhere to be seen. No Queen, and even the Nawab of Surat, who generally haunts the Houses of Parliament was not present.'

He was at the docks of Southahmpton on his way back to Hindustan. Kelly, Bethell and Perry stood and watched as Jafar approached them, Dost Shah walking behind him, ceremoniously carrying a covered tray. The English trio were keeping their promise to bid a proper farewell to the Prince for his journey home.

Jafar's luggage had been loaded onto the ship and his entourage had boarded. Jafar had waited to board, wanting to see his English allies – much as he had waited for them upon his return to London in December 1853. He had spent almost four years on this visit, and those years had been stunningly eventful. Patience and tenacity had won him all that he had wished for. But his victory wouldn't have been possible were it not for the trio of brilliant English politicians.

Jafar offered thanks to them, and then Dost Shah unveiled the tray. For each man, there was a gift of a cashmere shawl and an ornamental Hindustani dagger. Embracing each of them in turn, Jafar extended an invitation to visit Hindustan. The three had been charmed by all that they had learned from him of the ancient land. They did not hesitate in accepting the offer. Jafar then climbed the gangway to the main deck. As the ship pulled away he waved.

Kelly yelled: 'Until we meet again, Your Asiatic Highness…in Hindustan!'

Jafar signalled with a smile and a wave.

In the event, none of the three would ever make it to Hindustan. This was to be the last they saw of each other.

Behind the three men was a gathering of English ladies waving frantically. Jafar smiled. They weren't waving at him. Mary Jane had now emerged on deck, and she took Jafar's arm. The ladies were some of her acting colleagues. Jafar had kept his word to take her with him to Hindustan, and she was taking a leap of faith. At the height of the first Indian war of independence this brave young English woman had decided to put her life in danger in accompanying the man she loved and hopefully build a life with him in Hindustan. This act of courage from Mary Jane made Jafar fall even more deeply in love. It reminded him of his voyage to England for a cause that he chose to pursue against all odds. She looked forward to her new life under the sun. But there were many things in which Mary Jane would have to be trained. There was the issue of what would be her relationship with Basti, as well as those with Jafar's daughters, and his parents.

Onboard the ship, with over a month in hand, Jafar went over all the necessary protocol. Sometimes the detail was overwhelming for Mary Jane. Dost Shah, who had supplied her with cosmetics and jewellery in the early days of the romance, now comforted her in her moments of anguish, reassuring her that the people in the Prince's land would be just as enamoured by her blue eyes as she would be with their customs and ways.

But beyond the protocol Jafar's deeper concern was the war of independence. If the Company won, would he then be allowed to marry Mary Jane? He had come to love her deeply. Hindustanis were not permitted, however, to marry Englishwomen. If the Company was defeated then Jafar was resolved to take two great steps – he would declare independent rule in Surat and marry Mary Jane immediately.

Jafar had written to his father with the news of his triumph; and an enormous reception greeted him in Bombay, with an even bigger one in Surat. But as his carriage made its way into Hushmut Mahal, Mary Jane sitting beside him, Jafar felt anxiety. The first to come out and greet them was Sarfaraz. The old leopard hunter still stood up straight and proud at the age of 87. He kissed his son's forehead and took him inside. Jafar kept Mary Jane close. She curtsied then performed a bow and salaam as she had been schooled. Sarfaraz gently touched her head as a mark of acceptance. In the small living room were the now 17-year-old Ladli and 15-year-old Rahimun, and in fair distance Jafar's mother Raja Begum. Jafar rushed forward to embrace his daughters. The girls had waited so long for their father to return, and he had come home having ensured their rights were restored. The girls acknowledged Mary Jane coolly. They had resisted Basti and it would be the same with Mary Jane. For them it was just one parent – Jafar and they only craved his love. Jafar's mother was now old and frail but she recognised him vaguely caressing his face with quivering hands. It was she who had encouraged his spiritual education under the tutelage of the Sufi master Hasan Shah Pir of Kamandiyah.

After a few days came the meeting Mary Jane dreaded most. Jafar took her to the house in which Basti lived. From behind a *chilman,* a long veil suspended from the ceiling Mary Jane saw first a shapely silhouette. Jafar introduced the two women. Word had already reached Basti of her husband's English love interest. Given to God, prayer and etiquette, Basti parted the *chilman* and looked at Mary Jane. She could not help but find this woman interesting – in her English dress, the way she did her hair in a bun, and her different mannerisms. In a gesture that stunned Mary Jane, Basti daintily extended her hand, signalling friendship. But how long would it last?

Jafar immediately ordered a cottage to be built for Mary Jane not too far from Basti's house. Meanwhile he kept a close watch on the war of independence. Things were dramatically turning in favour of the Company, and this was not a good sign for his plans to marry Mary Jane.

In short order Jafar also began inspection of the estates. Sequestration had been lifted which meant he had to carry out all necessary checks and take the estates back under his control. But he was faced with some horrific sights. Under the neglect of Company officials, virtually every property stood destroyed. The Mehmudi Bagh, renowned for their poppies, built by Tegh, were barren and dusty. The majestic Dariya Mahal (also built by Tegh) which had shimmered in the Tapti was now close to collapsing in entirety. The Aena Mahal, built by Hafiz-ud-deen was in the most dilapidated state, threatening to fall completely at any minute. All the gardens built by Afzal-ud-deen – including the Dilfiza Bagh, renowned for its white lilies, the Nagheena Bagh, and the Afzal Bagh – were utterly destroyed. Deprived of proper irrigation and care, every garden was a picture of misery. Worse, some of the land had been encroached upon by bribing Company officials. The whole picture was shocking.

Jafar swiftly summoned those encroachers and paid them off, assuming full custody of the lands and gardens and placing them in his daughters' names.[231] He knew well that the crumbling buildings were now too far gone. But the vast acres of land on which they stood were still a great prize. And it would be from here that his girls, helped by the large pension their father had secured for them, would over time build new homes and a new life.

Jafar spent much time setting up a management team, surveying and securing the lands with walls, gates and fences, also re-taking full custody of Hushmut Mahal, which was to become known as the 'Old Palace'. He extended the property and began construction of new wings. While he went about this work, Mary Jane explored the city. The huge population of bustling Surat initially overwhelmed her. Travelling in a carriage most of the time, or else on foot with armed guards to prevent any violence against what the locals now called a *firangee*, Mary Jane developed an interest in the textiles and fabrics for which Surat was renowned. She visited the brilliant Hindu and Jain temples immersing herself in local culture.

The Company soon crushed the Indian uprising: Jafar's hopes of marrying Mary Jane were dashed. Both felt utterly disappointed. Jafar wrote to Company officials requesting a special permission to marry, but this was refused.

While people in Surat and the general public of Gujarat began resigning themselves to the fact that the war had been lost and Hindustan would still remain a colony, the Company was facing a real predicament back in its homeland. There was mounting disapproval of the Company's treatment of Hindustanis, and pressure was mounting for a transfer of power from Company to Crown. Jafar's fight in Parliament, the growing visits to England by deposed princes seeking justice, and the bloody war of independence had combined to expose the various injustices and malpractices of Company officials. Victoria's heart was known to have melted hearing Duleep Singh's story. This Sikh Prince of Punjab had as a boy witnessed the brutality with which the Company had annexed his kingdom. Punjab had been decimated and Duleep had been sent into exile in England by the Company. Victoria in time had taken him under her wings and showered motherly love on him, in time even becoming the godmother to his children. Victoria had had enough of the Company. Months after the war of independence was crushed, in 1858, Hindustan was placed under direct Crown rule.

Jafar in the meanwhile turned his attention to the lands closest to his heart, in Kamandiyah. It is here that he would now channel most of his energy. At 87 Sarfaraz was too old to administer and within a few months of Jafar's return his mother died. Both father and son grieved her immensely. Having lost his wife, Sarfaraz wanted to return to Kamandiyah and Baroda. He had done his duty as a grandfather to the girls and watched over them while their father fought for them in England. But now with Jafar returned he craved retirement. It would be in this tiny rustic principality that Mary Jane would live and love Hindustan. Kamandiyah was more intimate. It was the opening of a new phase in life for Jafar: the former boy prince now returned to his true home.

Together with Mary Jane and Basti, Jafar began settling in Kamandiyah. Villagers in their white turbans flocked from surrounding areas, not least to look at Mary Jane. Some climbed trees, others came on foot, yet more brought out their specially decorated bullock carts to show these off to the Englishwoman. The large compound of the stone Darbargadh filled with villagers daily, all wishing to see the blue eyed, golden haired *firangee*. Mary Jane responded with flair and calm. She visited peoples' homes, whether these were made of bricks or mud. Under thatched roofs she took sugary sweet tea with them. Village ladies came out of doors covering their faces with their saree veils but dropped them just to get a glimpse of Mary Jane. Some took her hair in their hand. Others pushed their faces right in front of hers just to more closely inspect the colour of her eyes.

The Sufis called each day in Kamandiyah. Sitting by the shrine of Jafar's master, Hasan Shah Pir, the mystics that came each day in reverence whirled in devotion to the departed soul. Under the shade of a neem tree the Sufis dressed in deep blue cloaks and read beads, their intense eyes lost in trance swirled in ecstacy, their tresses caressing their face as musicians beat drums into a frenzied mode. Mary Jane was overcome by this exhibition of unabashed love and desire for the unknown. Holding Jafar's hand tight, she immersed herself in the drum beats. She felt herself letting go. As the music reached its crescendo she could be seen swaying in rhythm, eyes shut with Jafar beside her. On other occasions the bells of the Ram temple would call her. Walking barefoot with Jafar into this temple, both would be welcomed by the Brahmin priests. Once in the temple she would sit for hours next to Jafar listening to the *bhajans*.

A unique relationship seemed to take root between Basti and Mary Jane in Kamandiyah, each coming to understand the other's position. In this country setting, with its large open fields, the two ladies shared work experiences. Mary Jane rolled up her sleeves and flung herself headlong into helping farmers choose key areas where wells could be dug in order to better manage water supply. She helped in channelling canal systems for irrigation and drainage. While she had no local knowledge of this, she learnt on the job, working shoulder to shoulder with locals. This voluntary exhibition of interest and practical work, although initially inspected curiously by village folk, soon earned her a widespread respect. It was apparent she loved the outdoors. Local fairs and bazaars were held in Kamandiyah that attracted farmers from nearby villages. In these markets Mary Jane put on singing concerts, and taught the little girls English songs and carols. The local singers taught her native songs in turn. Her most passionate pursuit was to work closely with Jafar in building a library.

Basti was more reserved, conscious of her legal status. She devoted her efforts to beautifying the Darbargadh, adding swings and local fauna. Mary Jane took to regional flowers and planted the divinely fragrant jasmine and the brilliant bougan-villa which vigorously crept up the facade of the Darbargadh. Basti ensured the women folk of the villages were granted a say in local justice. Most evenings Mary Jane and Basti would sit in the courtyard and share their experiences amidst the lingering fragrance of jasmine. At times Jafar would instruct the erection of tents on the banks of the river where over dinner the day's events would be discussed. These tranquil times, however, were not to last long.

Gossip was never far away. The village folk questioned the legality of Mary Jane's position with regard to Jafar. She was naturally keen to be married. Jafar once again wrote to the British authorities seeking permission, but again this was denied. It was from one of the tents by the river that much speculation arose one late evening when a Christian priest and a Muslim mullah were secretly ushered in and sent away during the dark of night. Some believed that a surreptitious marriage ceremony had taken place in the tent. Others thought it was merely an evening dedicated to Sufi discussion on matters of faith. There was no confirmation on the matter from either Jafar or Mary Jane. But where previously there had been friendship between the two ladies, this was now ended. Jealousy took root.

Mary Jane believed that were she to fall pregnant then this would surely force the British authorities to agree to legalise any unauthorised union that might have taken place in the tent. An Englishwoman with a child, she imagined, would compel the authorities to that extent. But it was wishful thinking. The village folk, too, were gossiping on the point of which one of the two women would bear Jafar a child. A sort of race had begun and the two women ceased speaking to each other, both contesting for Jafar's attention. No female friendship could survive in such a scenario.

It was Basti who would first announce her pregnancy, and eventually give birth to a son in 1859. For Jafar and his father in particular, this was the brightest news. Tormented for years with the fear of not having guaranteed succession to Kamandiyah, Sarfaraz and Jafar's anguish finally ended. The child was named Zulfikar, this name chosen by his grandfather. Typical of the old man, it meant 'a flashing sword'. It was almost as if Sarfaraz had defied time and mortality in order to see the birth of a grandson. The following year, 1860, he died at the age of 90, having been such a stalwart support to his son. Jafar mourned the loss deeply.

A few good years of monsoon alongwith a new network of wells and canals ensured that agricultural yield was robust in Kamandiyah and Jafar paid off the mortgages his father had raised against some of the lands and other villages including Waori, so bringing them back into his fold. Jafar's defense of Waori from the marauding

Makrani hordes when he was just a boy of 16 was an act that had not been forgotten. His precision shooting back then had prevented the sacking of the village. During one of his regular visits to Waori, this time in April 1863 he entered the village carrying little Zulfikar, now a boy of 4, in his arms. A massive crowd had gathered to see him and the new boy prince. Fierce faces wore smiles for a change, most of them genuine. Both father and son, with Basti and Mary Jane by their side, were repeatedly garlanded. Three men then rushed forward with flowers. One of these prostrated himself at Jafar's feet and begged to be taken into Jafar's personal service. He pledged lifelong loyalty. His name was Abdul. Jafar agreed. Village elders now surrounded Jafar, for they didn't approve of his decision. The man was young and had just entered the village recently, though when it came to cutting wheat he wielded a sharp sickle with exceptional skill. No one knew his origins, however. Jafar looked at the young man. He had given his word; and so, with a signal from Jafar to his other attendants, the strapping youth was taken into the entourage.

Surat soon began to require demandingly regular attention and personal supervision from Jafar. These long schedules meant that Mary Jane, Basti and little Zulfikar also began spending more time in the city. Five years after his return to Hindustan Jafar had begun to make good progress in Surat. Some of the creditors were close to being paid off. Others were still very much around and while there was slow progress in paying all of them, there was a system set up to clear their dues. Most of the old buildings had fallen and the land was cleared for measured new construction to commence. Hushmut Mahal seemed to be rising like a phoenix from the ashes. Horses were bought, stables re-established. Servants and stable boys were now being paid. Jafar had also set up a textile mill, the first in Surat: it would bear his name and provide another source of income for his girls. A couple of gardens too, particularly *Dad-e-ilahi*, were beginning a slow recovery. Good monsoons always helped gardens, and rains lashed Surat in 1863.

All of July, it poured. Sheets of rain swept past the façade of Hushmut Mahal one evening. Visibility was utterly diminished. Jafar stood with Mary Jane on the balcony. He reflected upon his success in laying the foundations for a legacy that his girls could take forward in Surat; and how in Kamandiyah he could look forward to spending time with his son teaching him how to hunt man-eaters. He was a happy man as far as his children were concerned.

But the women in his life were not satisfied, and he had only himself to blame. Basti had felt near-completely ignored by her husband throughout their marriage, and this filled him with guilt. He had given her a separate house, since his daughters weren't particularly affectionate towards her, and he had hoped that this would afford Basti her own identity; but it had led only to loneliness for her. Mary Jane's presence in his life, while initially accepted by Basti, had become intolerable to her. But the troubled state of Jafar's conscience, his unease at the looks of despair Basti sent in his direction, only made him withdraw even further from her. He had stopped going to her. The future division of his estates was clear, at least. His daughters would inherit in Surat, his son in Kamandiyah and other villages, and therefore Basti, too, stood secured. It was Mary Jane's lack of security that weighed on Jafar. He hadn't given Basti love but he had secured her future. To Mary Jane he had given love but no comparable prospects.

Dost Shah announced supper. Jafar and Mary Jane went inside to partake of it. The candle lights flickered as draughts of wind gusted their way into the space. The loud downpour and the sound of thunder made conversation between Jafar and Mary Jane almost impossible. Jafar ate his first morsel and then immediately looked about him, uneasy. Within seconds he was grasping for the collar of his round-necked shirt, tearing at it. He couldn't breath. Blood began to issue from his nose and mouth at an alarming pace. Suffocating, and falling to the floor, Jafar dragged the crockery down to the ground with him. Mary Jane rushed to him and yelled at Dost Shah to fetch water. Dost Shah turned, frantic, but emerging from the shadows was the young sickle swinger from Waori, bearing an earthen cup filled with water. Dost Shah grabbed it and gave it to Mary Jane, who was nursing Jafar's head in her lap. He was in excruciating pain and visibly struggling with blood now flowing profusely through his lips. He couldn't sip the water and with a wave of his hand he dropped the earthen cup to the floor where it shattered. But in breaking, it revealed itself. At the bottom was written 'Makrani'. Dost Shah and Mary Jane saw as much. Within seconds the sickle swinger had unsheathed the blade he used to cut wheat – a weapon he very evidently intended now to use on Jafar. He came down with one swift blow but Mary Jane thrust out an arm to deflect the sickle blow and got deeply slashed instead of Jafar. Yelling in anguish, she shoved at the traitor's thighs as he readied himself to strike another blow. But Dost Shah, slipping in Jafar's and Mary Jane's blood, removed the dagger from his master's waist and, with one swinging motion, turned and buried the blade in the sickle swinger's belly. There was blood everywhere. As the traitor vanished into the darkness of death he wore a smile on his face. Jafar had suffered the slow but lethal poisoning by mixed-cyanide. His murderer had avenged the Makrani defeat at Waori.

Jafar suffered for two days, surrounded by *hakeems*, Basti, Mary Jane, his two daughters and his infant son. In his fast-fading final moments he did two important things. He summoned Sir Theodore Hope, Collector of Surat, the highest civil administrative post of a region at that time. Now, sitting by Jafar's bedside, he listened to the Prince's last words.

Jafar's first instruction sent a chill down Basti's spine. Making Hope his son's legal guardian, he instructed him to make arrangements to send 4-year-old Zulfikar to England without delay. Jafar wanted Zulfikar to have a modern education and to acquire the fine tastes and manners of a Victorian English gentleman.[232] Besides, he feared for the young boy's life. The Makranis were known for their vengeful tempers that could wipe out entire generations. Then, looking at Mary Jane, Jafar made his second crucial instruction, telling Hope to make a provision of £75 per month for her, advising also that when Zulfikar came of age he would have to do the same and fulfil that responsibility.[233] Then the weakening strength of his eyes desperately searched for his daughters, summoning them to draw near, Jafar held their hands tightly. His last look was only for them. He was dead at 46. His daughters, Ladli now 22 and Rahimun 20 broke down instantly. Their father had come to mean everything to them. His battle against the Company had become legendary in Surat. They believed they owed everything to the man that now lay lifeless in front of them. It was he who had stood between them and utter destruction. They had hardly known their mother. Their father had devoted his life to a struggle overseas and within six years of his return was dead. Their grandfather who had watched over them was dead too. There was an emptiness that crept in.

The city of Surat closed down in mourning. The Nawab risala reversed their arms and led a parade by the funeral procession. Ladli chose the *Dad-e-ilahi* garden as her father's burial place. It was a garden that Jafar was reviving with new mango trees. In time, his grave would become a mausoleum for followers of his story. Ladli and Rahimun married men of stature. Ladli's husband, a Prince of Belha in the Deccan. Aided by the restored pension and the saved lands the two built a new large home for themselves in Surat; as did Rahimun and her husband.

Hope, almost immediately after the burial, took Zulfikar to Kamandiyah and carried out the formal investiture of the boy prince with the title of Darbar of Kamandiyah. Basti, however, fought hard against Jafar's instruction that the boy be sent to England. Hope tried everything to prevail upon her the benefits of what Jafar had willed, but she would have none of it. She felt undone by Jafar even in his last moments. She feared loneliness immensely and the boy's departure would mean a rudderless existence for her.

Mary Jane was devastated. She locked herself in her cottage for days, grieving over the man she had loved so dearly. For her it seemed the world had come crashing down. The romance had lasted 9 years but for her it had seemed a lifetime. She had given Jafar all her love. Now she felt emotionally barren. In an alien country that she loved nonetheless, she simply didn't know what her future would be. Emerging after days of mourning she was met by British officials who insisted she return to England, where she could begin a new life. Mary Jane rejected any such suggestions, and immediately requested to be taken to Kamandiyah. There in the Darbargadh, with the consent of Basti (who had been prevailed upon by Hope to allow her that visit), Mary Jane spent an entire month. She looked after Jafar's library, cleaning every book, arranging others by title and drawing up lists with serial numbers. She spent time with the farmers and the little girls to whom she had taught carols. In Jafar's memory she had a tent erected on the banks of the river and there she slept at night and wandered the banks in solitude, reliving those moments when she walked with her man by the canal in Little Venice, Maida Vale.

Hope met with her after a month. Basti was angry and she wanted Mary Jane out. Hope insisted that a meeting between the two ladies had to happen in Surat to mend ways. There, with Hope as mediator, an angry Basti rounded on Mary Jane, declaring that if she didn't return to England then she wouldn't receive her monthly allowance. Hope prevailed upon Mary Jane to return. And so she conceded.

Back in England Mary Jane spent some time in London trying to get work in theatre but good roles weren't available to her. Aged 45, she had past her prime. She retired to her hometown of Burnley to lead a quiet life. Every month her allowance reached her. In her later years, most Sundays at 11 am she would receive a knock on her door. She would be expecting this visitor. A handsome young Hindustani Prince – dressed in a fine English suit, groomed with long sideburns and a slightly twirled moustache – would make his way from Hastings in Sussex to visit Mary Jane in Burnley every week. Unfailingly he would arrive at her door with seasonal English flowers. He spent time with her listening to her stories, particularly those that concerned a man whom he had never known. He took care of her. She cooked roast chicken most times he visited, and cooked it well done to ensure his Hindustani palate didn't find it raw. Just as his father had liked it.

On 4 January 1876 the *Manchester Courier* reported: 'Amongst the arrivals from Europe were his Grace d'Ayeres d'Orneilas de Vasconeiles, Colonel Nasan Lees and Meer Zulfikar Ali son of the late Nawab of Surat'. Hope had succeeded in impressing Jafar's final wish upon Basti. After being held onto by his mother for years after his father's death, the teenage Zulfikar was sent to England for a modern education. He stayed for many years, learning the ways of an English aristocrat. His visits to Mary Jane were most cherished. He came to love her like a second mother and she reciprocated as the only son she had known. One incident, however, would bring him back to his roots. Zulfikar's baptism in England didn't go unnoticed by English aristocracy and the news also found its way to Basti's ear in Hindustan.[234] Utterly distraught that her son had been converted to Christianity, she proceeded to make Hope's life miserable, insisting on her son's return. After several years in England, Zulfikar would return to take charge of Kamandiyah.

Today, as a sleepy little town, Kamandiyah still wakes to the wonderful chiming of bells in the Ram and Shiva temples. The villagers still call onto the spiritual powers of Hasan Shah Pir, Jafar's Sufi master. The master lies there in his quiet shrine under a neem tree unknown to the world how his teachings of Ghazalis 'inspired intuition' had inspired his young pupil to take on the might of an Empire.

Surat as a port had met a ruthless and miserable end under the English East India Company. It never rose again as a prominent maritime city: Bombay overtook it in every respect. But in time Surat would find its own identity. Driven by the brilliant entrepreneurial spirit of its people and the ingenuity of its merchants, Surat would rise again. Inspired by the vision of Jafar in setting up the textile mill, many an entrepreneur would follow suit. This time Surat would re-emerge with meteoric pace as the textile capital of an independent nation. It soon came to be known as the 'Silk city of India'. What defines Surat today, however, is its astonishing position as the world's epicentre of diamond cutting and polishing. In a sensational revival of the city's economic fortune and power, the imaginative jewellers and diamond merchants work tirelessly to provide the best service available globally. Close to 80 per cent of the world's diamonds are cut and polished in Surat and then sent to their commercial destinations. Under a liberalised Indian economy, modern Surat is the fourth fastest growing city in the world.

Jafar's grave in Surat lies within the old city. The 'Dad-e-ilahi garden' is a garden no more, surrounded by shops and small businesses. On Jafar's grave is a plaque written in Urdu: in English it reads 'Syed Meer Jafar Ali Khan Bahadur of Surat, belonging to the family of the revered Hazrat Modud Chishti' – a distinct mention of his Sufi lineage. His unique legacy, as a Hindustani Prince who defeated the East India Company in the House of Commons, remains unmatched.

The Times 26 August 1863 reported: "He was not like the great part of princes passing their time in indolence but spent the greater portion of his life ministering to the wants of his people." His accomplishment was captured brilliantly by the greatest Persian and Urdu poet, Ghalib, who upon his death wrote: 'The oak has fallen. The star from the Orient that sparkled in England shines no more.' Every July the summer's stranglehold of the Gujarat plains begins to ease and the baking stones on the parched Badar river bed cool with the monsoon breeze as it sweeps and then soars westwards. It carries with it a hushed whisper. A whisper as fresh as the first drop of rain. One that can be heard in the rustling neem trees on the river banks and in the jasmine that Mary Jane had planted. In anticipation the bougan-villa then turn deep pink and crisp white. Just then the Badar river bursts through and flows with great might.

Notes

1. *The Moslem Noble – His land and his People* by Marianne Young, pgs 4, 5
2. *Surat in the Seventeenth Century* by Gokhale, pg. 149
3. *Surat Port of the Mughal Empire* by Ruby Maloni, pg. 162
4. Gazetter of Bombay Presidency II, pgs. 116–117
5. Ibid., pg. 116
6. Ibid., pg. 116
7. *History of Gujarat* by M.S. Commissariat Volume III, pg. 539
8. Ibid., pg. 558
9. Ibid., pg. 558
10. bid., pg. 558
11. *The Gaikwads of Baroda* by James H. Gense, pg. 13
12. Ibid., pg. 14
13. Ibid., pg. 17
14. *History of Gujarat* by M.S. Commissariat Vol III, pg. 691
15. The Gazetter of the Bombay Presidency Surat & Broach Volume II
16. *History of Gujarat* by M.S. Commissariat Vol III, pg. 592.
17. Ibid., pg. 595
18. *The Gaikwads of Baroda* by James H. Gense, pg. 62
19. Ibid., pg. 120
20. Ibid., Jonathan Duncan's Minutes page xx
21. Ibid., pg. 55
22. Ibid., pg. 60

23. Ibid., pg. 62

24. Ibid., pg. 65

25. Ibid., pg. 74

26. Ibid., pg. 75

27. Ibid., pg. 76

28. Ibid., pg. 86

29. Ibid., pg. 85

30. Ibid., pg. 88

31. Ibid., pg. 88

32. Ibid., pg. xxi

33. The Gazetteer of the Bombay Presidency, Gujarat, Surat and Broach, Volume II, printed at the Government Central press 1877.

34. The Gazetter of the Bombay Presidency, Gujarat, Surat and Broach Volume II

35. Ibid.,

36. *The Gaikwads of Baroda* by James H. Gense pg. 135

37. Ibid., pg. xxii

38. Minutes of Evidence taken before the Select Committee on the Nawab of Surat Treaty Bill, Ordered by the House of Commons to be printed 9 June 1856 Bill 0, pgs. 16, 17

39. Surat 1 April 1771, Nabob Afecodin Amedcan India Office Records Misc Letters Received 1771 E/1/55

40. Papers regarding the treaty with Nasiruddin and the Company IOR/F/PARL/2/133, pg. 3

41. Ibid., pg. 84

42. Ibid., pg. 84

43. Ibid., pg. 65

44. Minutes of Evidence taken before the Select Committee on the Nawab of Surat Treaty Bill, Ordered by the House of Commons to be printed 9 June 1856 Bill, pg. 38

45. Ibid., pg. 38

46. 'British Conquest and Dominion of India' by Sir Penderal Moon, Part One 1747–1857 pg. 296

47. *A Comprehensive History of India, Civil, Military and Social*, publ. by Blackie and Son Vol 2 by Henry Beveridge pg. 717

48. Exhibit of Meer Sarfaraz Ali's lineage presented as part of the Nawab Surat Treaty Bill 1856 in the House of Commons

49. *The Ruling Chiefs, Nobles and Zamindars of India* by A. Vadivelu, pg. 547

50. The Bombay Gazetteer-Kathiawar Agency 1914, pgs. 12–13

51. *Memoir of the British Army in India during the Mahratta war* 1817 & 1819 Vol I by Lieut. Colonel Valentine Blacker, pg. 371

52. Testimonials and recommendatory notes to Mir Sarfaraz Ali Saheb-Letter by Sir John Malcolm to Meer Sarfaraz Ali. Printed at The Diamond Jubilee Printing Press, Ahmedabad 1900

53. Khaziutaul Insab by Syed Abdula Ahmad Afsoos Sehaswani publ 1959, pg. 126

54. Kathiawar Directory – General information and statistics relating to the province of Kathiawar and the various native states comprised within it by Hormazji Kadaka 1886, pg. 277

55. History of Kathiawar, Chapter xiv

56. Minutes of Evidence taken before the Select Committee on the Nawab of Surat Treaty Bill, Ordered by the House of Commons to be printed 9 June 1856 part 2, pg. 9

57. Ibid., pg. 28

58. *Seamless Boundaries, Lutfullah's Narrative*, edited by Mushirul Hasan, Oxford University Press, pgs. 132, 186.

59. Minutes of Evidence taken before the Select Committee on the Nawab of Surat Treaty Bill, Ordered by the House of Commons to be printed 9 June 1856. R.K. Arthunbot late Agent for the Honourable the Government Surat to J.P. Willoughby, Chief Secretary to Government of Bombay 3 November 1845, pg. 20

60. Minutes of Evidence taken before the Select Committee on the Nawab of Surat Treaty Bill, Ordered by the House of Commons to be printed 9 June 1856 Nawab of Surat Treaty Bill Part 1, pgs. 33–34

61. Minutes of Evidence taken before the Select Committee on the Nawab of Surat Treaty Bill, Ordered, by the House of Commons to be printed 9 June 1856 Part 2, pg. 9

62. Letter produced in the Privy Council, Petition to Her Majesty in Council from Meer Jafur Alee and his two daughters and Ameeroo-nissa Begum and papers connected therewith, pg. 20

63. Ibid, pg. 21
64. Ibid, pg. 22
65. *Seamless Boundaries, Lutfullah's Narrative*, edited by Mushirul Hasan, Oxford University Press, pg. 186
66. Complaints preferred against the Nawab of Surat Afzal-ud-din Khan of having seized and ill-treated two police peons – Bombay government sent letter of remonstrance to the Nawab IOR/F/4/1626/65102, April–November 1835
67. Dispute between the Nawab of Surat Afzal-ud-din Khan and the Bombay Government regarding a consignment of mangoes seized by customs office IOR/F/4/1816/74897, 1838
68. Papers regarding the dispute between the Nawab of Surat Afzal-ud-din Khan and Mirza Abdulla Beg Khan-Adbulla Beg is handed over to the Nawab by the British Authorities and subsequently commits suicide IOR/F/4/1866/79226, January 1815–August 1840
69. *Seamless Boundaries, Lutfullah's Narrative*, edited by Mushirul Hasan, Oxford University Press, pg. 193
70. Death of Nawab of Surat, Boards Collections 89496 to 89514, 1842–1843, Vol 2005, F4, 2005, Records Department
71. Tracts on Personal Affairs 1793–1855 The Case of Meer Jafur Alee Khan Bahadoor of Surat, pg. 5 and 6
72. *The Tears of the Rajas* by Ferdinand Mount, pg. 345
73. Minutes of Evidence taken before the Select Committee on the Nawab of Surat Treaty Bill, Ordered by the House of Commons to be printed 9th June 1856, Nawab of Surat Treaty Bill Part 2, pg. 15
74. Ibid., letter dated 28th August 1842, pgs. 4, 5
75. Ibid., pg. 22
76. *Times of India*, 28 February 1844
77. Minutes of Evidence taken before the Select Committee on the Nawab of Surat Treaty Bill, Ordered by the House of Commons to be printed 9 June 1856 Part 1, pg. 28
78. Ibid., pg. 29
79. Ibid., pgs. 33–34
80. Ibid., pg. 29
81. Minutes of Evidence taken before the Select Committee on the Nawab

of Surat Treaty Bill, Ordered, by the House of Commons to be printed 9 June 1856 part 0, pg. 85

82. Ibid., pg. 85

83. Ibid., pg. 85

84. Minutes of Evidence taken before the Select Committee on the Nawab of Surat Treaty Bill, Ordered, by the House of Commons to be printed 9th June 1856 part 2, pg. 60

85. Ibid., pg. 85

86. Ibid., pg. 60

87. Ibid., pg. 60

88. Ibid., pgs. 62, 63

89. Ibid., pg. 61

90. Ibid., pg. 49

91. Ibid., pgs. 4 and 5

92. *Seamless Boundaries, Lutfullah's Narrative,* edited by Mushirul Hasan, Oxford University Press, pg. 198

93. Ibid., pg. 199

94. Ibid., pg. 202

95. Ibid., pg. 203

96.   93.   Ibid., pg. 204

97. Ibid., pg. 205

98. Ibid., pg. 207

99. Ibid., pg. 209

100. Ibid., pg. 210

101. Ibid., pg. 211

102. Ibid., pg. 211

103. Ibid., pg. 212

104. Ibid., pg. 212

105. Ibid., pg. 213

106. Ibid., pg. 214

107. Ibid., pg. 214

108. Ibid., pg. 214

109. Ibid., pg. 214

110. Case of Meer Jaffur Alee Khan Bahadoor of Surat, pg.. 6

111. Ibid., pg. 6

112. *Seamless Boundaries, Lutfullah's Narrative*, edited by Mushirul Hasan, Oxford University Press, pg. 214

113. Ibid., pg. 215

114. *Counterflows to Colonialism* by Michael H. Fisher, pg. 394

115. Ibid., pg. 394

116. Ibid., pg. 394

117. *Seamless Boundaries, Lutfullah's Narrative*, edited by Mushirul Hasan, Oxford University Press, pg. 216

118. Ibid., pg. 216

119. Ibid., pg. 216

120. *The Morning Chronicle,* 11 June 1844

121. Ibid.

122. *The Morning Post*, 11 June 1844

123. *Seamless Boundaries, Lutfullah's Narrative*, edited by Mushirul Hasan, Oxford University Press, pg. 218

124. Ibid., pg. 220

125. Ibid., pg. 220

126. Ibid., pg. 222

127. Ibid., pg. 218

128. Ibid., pg. 218

129. Ibid., pg. 223

130. Minutes of Evidence taken before the Select Committee on the Nawab of Surat Treaty Bill, Ordered by the House of Commons to be printed 9 June 1856 part 0, pgs. 67, 68

131. Ibid., pg. 12

132. Ibid., pg. 86

133. Case of Meer Jaffur Alee Khan Bahadoor of Surat, pg. 6

134. *Seamless Boundaries, Lutfullah's Narrative*, edited by Mushirul Hasan, Oxford University Press, pg. 223

135. Case of Meer Jaffur Alee Khan Bahadoor of Surat, pg. 6

136. Minutes of Evidence taken before the Select Committee on the Nawab of Surat Treaty Bill, Ordered by the House of Commons to be printed 9 June 1856 part 0, pg. 85

137. Ibid., pg. 85

138. Ibid., pg. 85

139. Ibid., pg. 85

140. Ibid., pg. 86

141. Ibid., 86

142. Ibid., pg. 86

143. Ibid., pg. 86

144. Ibid., pg. 86

145. Ibid., pgs. 66–70

146. Ibid., 13

147. Case of Meer Jaffur Alee Khan Bahadoor of Surat pg.8

148. Ibid., pg. 9

149. Ibid., pg. 11

150. Ibid., pg. 12

151. *The Asiatic in England* by Joseph Salter, pgs. 40–50

152. Ibid., pgs. 40–50

153. Case of Meer Jaffur Alee Khan Bahadoor of Surat, pg. 12

154. *The Asiatic in England* by Joseph Salter, pgs. 40–50

155. Ibid., pgs. 40–50

156. Ibid., pgs. 40–50

157. Ibid., pgs. 40–50

158. Ibid., pgs. 40–50

159. Case of Meer Jaffur Alee Khan Bahadoor of Surat, pgs. 38, 39

160. Ibid., pg. 13

161. Ibid., pg. 14

162. Ibid., pg. 15

163. Debate of The Nawab of Surat Treaty Bill 1856, pg. 4

164. Case of Meer Jafar Alee Khan. Appendix C. Elliot's letter to HH Mir Jafar Ali Khan

165. Ibid.

166. *Coutnterflows to Colonialism* by Michael H. Fisher, pg. 402

167. Debate of the Nawab of Surat Treaty Bill 1856, pg. 4

168. Hansard Nawab of Surat Treaty Bill 11th June 1856 Vol 142

169. Ibid.

170. Ibid.

171. Ibid.

172. Debate of the Nawab of Surat Treaty Bill 1856 , pg. 5

173. Ibid., pgs. 5, 6

174. Ibid., pg. 10

175. Ibid., pg. 13
176. Ibid., pgs. 15-16
177. Ibid., pg. 19
178. Ibid., pgs. 24, 25
179. Ibid., pg. 25
180. Ibid., pgs. 30, 31
181. Ibid., pgs. 31, 32
182. Ibid., pg. 32, 33
183. Ibid., pg. 31
184. *The Illustrated Times,* 14 June 1856
185. Ibid.
186. Debate of the Nawab of Surat Treaty Bill 1856, pg. 35
187. Ibid., pgs. 35, 36
188. Ibid., pgs. 37, 38
189. Ibid., pg. 39
190. Ibid., pg. 40
191. Ibid., pg. 50
192. *Counterflows to Colonialism* by Michael H. Fisher, pg. 289
193. Ibid., pg. 421
194. Debate of the Nawab of Surat Treaty Bill 1856, pg. 51
195. Ibid., pgs. 52-54
196. Ibid., pg. 57
197. Ibid., pg. 60
198. Ibid., pgs. 60, 61
199. Ibid., pgs. 60, 61
200. Ibid., pgs. 60, 61
201. Ibid., pg. 63
202. Ibid., pg. 93
203. Ibid., pg. 104
204. Ibid., pg. 106
205. Ibid., pgs. 107, 108
206. Ibid., pgs. 108-171
207. Ibid., pgs. 108-171
208. Ibid., pgs. 108-171
209. Ibid., pgs. 108-171
210. Ibid., pgs. 108-171

211. Ibid., pgs. 108-171
212. Ibid., pgs. 108-171
213. Ibid., pgs. 108-171
214. Ibid., pgs. 108-171
215. Ibid., pgs. 108-171
216. Ibid., pgs. 108-171
217. Ibid., pgs. 183-185
218. Ibid., pg. 194
219. Ibid., pg. 194
220. RETURN to two orders of the House of Commons. 16 March to 14 May 1857. Correspondence between Mir Jafar Ali Khan and the Court of Directors of The East India Company. Letter by Mir Jafar Ali Khan dated 15 July 1856
221. Hansard Parliament archives, 7 July 1856
222. Ibid.
223. *Counterflows to Colonialism* by Michael H. Fisher, pg. 404
224. RETURN to two orders of the House of Commons. 16 March to 14 May 1857. Correspondence between Mir Jafar Ali Khan and the Court of Directors of The East India Company. Letter to Mir Jafar Ali Khan dated 20 November 1856.
225. Ibid.
226. *Counterflows to Colonialism* by Michael H. Fisher, pgs. 404–405
227. Letter by Meer Jafar Ali Khan to East India Company hailing Sarfaraz's position. RETURN to two orders of the House of Commons 16 March to 14 May 1857. Correspondence between Mir Jafar Ali Khan and the Court of Directors of the East India Company
228. *The Standard,* 17 October 1856
229. *The Morning Post,* 2 May 1857
230. *The Morning Post,* 2 May 1857
231. *Counterflows to Colonialism* by Michael H. Fisher, pg. 405
232. Letter by Sir T.C. Hope regarding Mir Zulfikar Ali's guardianship and education in England
233. Contract with Mary Jane Flood
234. Autobiography of Meer Zulfikar Ali, published by Harker & Hodges House 1919

Glossary

Aarti: worship

Ahimsa: non-violence

Angarkhas: coats

Bazu-bands: arm-bands; armlet

Bhajans: songs sung in praise of Lord Ram

Chai: tea

Chilman: a long Indian veil suspended from the ceiling

Culgee: feather of the Bird of Paradise set in a golden locket

Darbar: court; also a title for certain ruling princes in Kathiawar, Gujarat.

Darwaza: gate

Dhol: Hindustani drums

Diwan: raised seating which can be ornately carved; laid out with cushions

Firangee: foreigner

Firman: order

Hakeems: local Hindustani doctors

Hamams: large baths

Howdas: golden seats

Jharokas: balconies

Khanqaah: retreat

Machan: a wooden plank lodged high up in tree-tops

Mahouts: elephant riders

Munshis: clerks of powerful merchants

Mutasadi: governor or one who resides and holds court and manages city administration in the heart of the city

Nautch: dance

Nawab risala: personal guards

Nazranas: tributes

Neem: a local herbal tree

Nikaah: Muslim marriage ceremony

Purdah: veil

Qawwals: Sufi singers given to ecstacy

Qilledar: controller of castle and fleet

Shahi Qila: emperor's fort

Sherwani: Hindustani long coat

Silsilas: school of thoughts

Qazi: priest

Tabla: Indian drums played by hand

Tankha: subsidy

Teen patti: a three-card game

Tehzeeb: culture

Urs: a celebration of the merging of a Sufi soul with the creator

Vazier: prime minister

Zenana: ladies chambers

Select Bibliography

Young, Marianne, *The Moslem Nobel: His land and his people*. London: Saunders and Otley, 1857.

Gokhale, B.G., *Surat in the Seventeenth Century*. London: Curzon Press, 1979.

Maloni, Ruby, *Surat Port of the Mughal Empire*. Mumbai: Himalaya Publication Press, 2003.

Commissariat, M.S., *History of Gujarat, the Maratha period, Volume III: (1758-1818)*. Longmans, Green & Company, Limited, 1980.

Gense, James H., *The Gaikwads of Baroda, Volume X*. D.B. Taraporevala Sons & Co, 1942.

Vadivelu, A., *The Ruling Chiefs, Nobles and Zamindars of India*. Madras: G.C. Loganadham, 1915.

Haasan, Mashirul (ed.), *Seamless Boundaries: Lutfullah's Narrative beyond East and West*. Delhi: Oxford University Press, 2007.

Mount, Ferdinand, *The Tears of the Rajas: Mutiny, Money and Marriage in India 1805-1905*. United Kingdom: Simon and Schuster, 2016.

Fisher, Michael. H., *Counterflows to Colonialism: Indian Travelers and Settlers in Britain, 1600-1857*. Delhi: Permanent Black, 2004.

Salter, Joseph, *The Asiatic in England: Sketches of sixteen years' work among Orientals*. Seelay, Jackson, and Halliday, 1873.

Autobiography of Meer Zulfikar Ali. United Kingdom: Harker & Hodges House, 1919.

Arbuthnot, R.K., *Observations on the case of Meer Jaffur Ali Khan: The Case of Meer Jaffur Alee, Khan Bahadoor of Surat*, London: 1855.

Index

Photo Credits